ASPECTS OF WISDOM

IN

JUDAISM AND EARLY CHRISTIANITY

UNIVERSITY OF NOTRE DAME
CENTER FOR THE STUDY OF
JUDAISM AND CHRISTIANITY
IN ANTIQUITY

Number 1

Aspects of Wisdom
in Judaism
and Early Christianity

ROBERT L. WILKEN
editor

UNIVERSITY OF NOTRE DAME PRESS
NOTRE DAME   LONDON

Copyright © 1975 by
University of Notre Dame Press
Notre Dame, Indiana 46556

Library of Congress Cataloging in Publication Data
Main entry under title:

Aspects of wisdom in Judaism and early Christianity.

Bibliography: p.
Includes index.
1. Wisdom literature—Criticism, interpretation, etc.
—Addresses, essays, lectures. 2. Bible. N. T.—Relation
on Old Testament—Addresses, essays, lectures. 3. Midrash—History and criticism. 4. Philo Judaeus.
5. Christianity—Early church, ca. 30–600—Addresses,
essays, lectures. I. Wilken, Robert Louis, 1936–
BS1455.A8   231'.6   74–27888
ISBN 0–268–00577–X

Manufactured in the United States of America

Contents

v

7. Jewish Wisdom and the Formation of the
   Christian Ascetic   169
   William R. Schoedel

Acknowledgments

THE ESSAYS INCLUDED IN THIS VOLUME WERE ORIGINALLY presented at a seminar on wisdom in late antiquity sponsored by the Department of Theology of the University of Notre Dame. I wish particularly to thank the directors of the Rosenstiel fund for providing the funds to make the seminar possible. The seminar itself was planned and organized by my colleagues Professors Joseph Blenkinsopp and Elisabeth Schüssler Fiorenza, who have continued to assist in the publication. I wish also to thank several other scholars whose essays contributed to the work of the seminar: Professor Josephine Ford, also of Notre Dame; Professor Glenn Chesnut of Indiana University South Bend, Professor Robert Coughenour of Hope College, and Professor Jonathan Z. Smith of the University of Chicago. Finally I am grateful to the Rev. Harry Culkin who originally prepared the bibliography for the seminar, Mr. William Johnston and Ms. Theresa Silio who assisted in the editing of the volume, and Mr. John Ehmann and Ms. Ann Rice of Notre Dame Press for their interest and assistance.

Robert L. Wilken

Contributors

HENRY A. FISCHEL
Professor of Near Eastern Languages and Literature
Indiana University at Bloomington

ELISABETH SCHÜSSLER FIORENZA
Associate Professor of New Testament
University of Notre Dame

JEAN LAPORTE
Associate Professor of Patristics
University of Notre Dame

BIRGER A. PEARSON
Professor of Religious Studies
University of California at Santa Barbara

JAMES M. ROBINSON
Professor of Religion
Director of the Institute for Antiquity and Christianity
Claremont Graduate School

WILLIAM R. SCHOEDEL
Professor of Classics and Director of Religious Studies
University of Illinois at Champaign-Urbana

ROBERT L. WILKEN
Associate Professor of the History of Christianity
University of Notre Dame

Abbreviations

AB	Analecta Biblica
AdRN	*Ab(h)oth de R. Nathan*
ANANT	Abhandlungen zur Theologie des Alten und Neuen Testaments
BASOR	*Bulletin of the American Schools of Oriental Research*
Bib	*Biblica*
BHTh	Beiträge zur historischen Theologie
BJRL	*Bulletin of the John Rylands Library*
BVCbr	*Bible et vie chrétienne*
BZAW	Beihefte zur Zeitschrift für die altestamentliche Wissenschaft
BZNW	Beihefte zur Zeitschrift für die neutestamentliche Wissenschaft
BT	Babylonian Talmud
DBS	*Dictionnaire de la Bible, Supplement*
EncJ	*Encyclopaedia Judaica*
ET	*Evangelische Theologie*
FRL	Forschungen zur Religion und Literatur des Alten und Neuen Testaments
HTR	*Harvard Theological Review*
HUCA	*Hebrew Union College Annual*
Interpr	*Interpretation*
JAAR	*Journal of the American Academy of Religion*
JAOS	*Journal of the American Oriental Society*
JBL	*Journal of Biblical Literature*
JEnc	*Jewish Encyclopedia*
JHS	*Journal of Hellenic Studies*

JQR	*Jewish Quarterly Review*
JT	Jerusalem Talmud
NT	*Novum Testamentum*
NTS	*New Testament Studies*
NTSupp	*Supplement to Novum Testamentum*
PA	*Pirke Ab(b)oth*
R	Rabba, e.g., Lev[iticus] Rabba
RAC	Reallexikon für Antike und Christentum
RB	*Revue Biblique*
REJ	*Revue des Études Juives*
RGG	*Die Religion in Geschichte und Gegenwart*, 3rd ed.
SBL	Society of Biblical Literature
SBT	Studies in Biblical Theology
SGKA	Studien zur Geschichte und Kultur des Altertums
SNTS	Society for New Testament Studies
StANT	Studien zum Alten und Neuen Testament
SUNT	Studien zur Umwelt des Neuen Testament
SVF	*Stoicorum Veterum Fragmenta*, ed. von Arnim
TDNT	*Theological Dictionary of the New Testament*
TTZ	*Trier Theologische Zeitschrift*
TU	Texte und Untersuchungen
TZ	*Theologische Zeitschrift*
UJEnc	*Universal Jewish Encyclopedia*
WMANT	Wissenschaftliche Monographien zum Alten und Neuen Testament
ZAW	*Zeitschrift für die alttestamentliche Wissenschaft*
ZKG	*Zeitschrift für Kirchengeschichte*
ZNW	*Zeitschrift für die neutestamentliche Wissenschaft und die Kunde der älteren Kirche*

Abbreviations of Philo of Alexandria

Abr.	*De Abrahamo*
Aet.	*De Aeternitate Mundi*

Agr.	*De Agricultura*
Cher.	*De Cherubim*
Conf.	*De Confusione Linguarum*
Congr.	*De Congressu Eruditionis gratia*
Cont.	*De Vita Contemplativa*
Dec.	*De Decalogo*
Det.	*Quod Deterius Potiori insidiari soleat*
Deus	*Quod Deus sit Immutabilis*
Ebr.	*De Ebrietate*
Exs.	*De Exsecrationibus*
Flacc.	*In Flaccum*
Fug.	*De Fuga et Inventione*
Gig.	*De Gigantibus*
Her.	*Quis rerum divinarum heres sit*
Jos.	*De Josepho*
Leg. Al.	*Legum Allegoriarum*
Legat.	*Legatio ad Gaium*
Migr.	*De Migratione Abrahami*
Mos.	*De Vita Mosis*
Mut.	*De Mutatione Nominum*
Op.	*De Opificio Mundi*
Plant.	*De Plantatione*
Post.	*De Posteritate Caini*
Praem.	*De Praemiis et Poenis*
Prob.	*Quod omnis probus liber*
Q.E.	*Quaestiones in Exodum*
Q.G.	*Quaestiones in Genesin*
Sacr.	*De Sacrificiis Abelis et Caini*
Sobr.	*De Sobrietate*
Som.	*De Somniis*
Spec. Leg.	*De Specialibus Legibus*
Virt.	*De Virtutibus*

Introduction

THE SIGNIFICANCE OF WISDOM FOR THE RELIGIOUS HIStory of late antiquity has emerged slowly. It was not too many years ago that the study of ancient wisdom was confined primarily to some of the later books of the Hebrew Bible, e.g., Proverbs, or to certain aspects of Judaism during the period of the Second Commonwealth. And even here the wisdom literature has long been a stepchild neglected in favor of the Pentateuch, the Psalms, or the prophets. Wisdom was, in the phrase of R.B.Y. Scott, a "foreign body" within the Hebrew Bible, and among the wisdom books only Job, and that perhaps because of its preoccupation with theodicy, has received extensive consideration in scholarly circles.

How limited our view of wisdom has been can be seen, for example, in the article on "Weisheit" in the third edition of the standard reference work *Die Religion in Geschichte und Gegenwart,* that bellwether of changes in theological and religious scholarship (cf. for example the articles on Gnosticism in the three editions, 1st, 1909–13, 2nd, 1928–32, 3rd, 1957–62). In the volume published in 1962 there are two articles on wisdom, one dealing with wisdom in the ancient Near East and in the Hebrew Bible and the other on "wisdom poetry," also confined to the ancient Near East and the Hebrew Bible. Neither article discusses, except in passing, wisdom in Judaism, in the Greco-Roman world, or in Christianity. No doubt when the fourth edition appears at some future time the articles on wisdom will take a somewhat different form and embrace a much wider range of material.

The neglect of wisdom is difficult to understand. From

the time of Ben Sira through the tannaitic and amoraic
periods the figure of the sage is well known and plays a
central role in the life of the Jewish communities. The
sages formed a distinct class during the first centuries of
the Common Era, distinguished, according to *Sifre Deuteronomy* (343), "by its walk, by its speech, and by its dress
in the street." Combining both practical wisdom and common sense with the study of the Bible and Mishnah these
sages dominated the intellectual life of Judaism for centuries.[1] Equally important during the same period was the
wise man of the philosophical schools, particularly in Stoicism. The sophos embodied moral and religious values
with practical good sense and was able to instruct his
fellows in the art of living.[2]

And even though Christianity did not invest as much in
the sage as did Judaism or the philosophical and religious
movements of the Greco-Roman world, the place of wisdom in the development of early Christianity is more
important than has hitherto been recognized. Recent studies in the New Testament have begun to uncover the
importance of wisdom for the understanding of early
Christianity, but its significance goes far beyond the first
few generations.[3] Clement of Alexandria, for example,
cites Proverbs and Sirach (Ecclus.) extensively in the *Instructor* and the first two books of the *Stromateis*. Clement's use of the Jewish wisdom books, citing actual texts
some two hundred times, reflects an extraordinary preoccupation with wisdom literature, unprecedented in Christian writers before him, suggesting that Clement wrote
these sections of his work with the wisdom books open
before him.[4] Prior to Clement most citations of wisdom
literature occur in the context of moral exhortation, as for
example Rom. 12:17–21, James 4:6, 1 Pet. 5:5, 1 Clem.
30:1–2. And in the *Instructor* where Clement cites wisdom
sayings on conversation, laughter, eating and drinking,
sleep, cosmetics, clothes, and so forth his concern is moral.
But in the *Stromateis* wisdom texts are used to develop an
understanding of the relation between philosophy and

theology and to provide a rationale for his theological enterprise. "It is a good thing, I reckon, to leave to posterity good children. This is the case with children of our bodies. But words are the progeny of the soul. Hence we call those who have instructed us, fathers. Wisdom is a communicative and philanthrophic thing. Accordingly, Solomon says, 'My son, if you receive the saying of my commandment, and hide it with you, your ear shall hear wisdom.' He points out that the word that is sown is hidden in the soul of the learner, as in the earth, and this is spiritual planting, 'And you shall apply your heart to understanding, and apply it for the admonition of your son.' For I think that soul joined with soul, and spirit with spirit, in the sowing of the word, will make that which is sown grow and germinate."[5]

Origen, writing in the generation after Clement in Alexandria, singles out "wisdom" as the most appropriate title for Jesus. After discussing a number of the titles which appear in the gospels Origen concludes that wisdom is the most ancient and the most proper to him.

> Thus if we collect the titles of Jesus, the question arises which of them were conferred on him late, and would never have assumed such importance if the saints had begun and had also persevered in blessedness. Perhaps Wisdom would be the only remaining one, or perhaps the Word would remain too, or perhaps the Life, or perhaps the Truth, not the others, which he took for our sake. And happy indeed are those who in their need for the Son of God have yet become such persons as not to need him in his character as physician healing the sick, nor in that of a shepherd, nor in that of redemption, but only in his character as wisdom, as the word and righteousness, or if there be any other title suitable for those who are so perfect as to receive him in his fairest character.[6]

Two other relatively unexplored areas of ancient Christian wisdom are the commentaries from the patristic period on wisdom books and the monastic collections of wisdom sayings. Origen, Hippolytus, Didymus, Evagrius, and Chrysostom wrote commentaries on Proverbs, and in some cases extensive fragments are preserved in the catenae. Bede the ecclesiastical historian also wrote a commentary on Proverbs. Gregory the Wonderworker (third century) wrote a paraphrase on Ecclesiastes, as did Dionysius of Alexandria, Athanasius, Gregory of Nyssa, Apollinaris of Laodicea, Theodore of Mopsuestia, and others. We know of commentaries on Job by Origen, Didymus, Ephraim, Chrysostom, Evagrius, Hesychius, Theodore of Mopsuestia, Augustine, Julian of Eclanum, and Gregory the Great. Monastic writers also prepared collections of sayings which seem in part to be modeled on the wisdom books. And there seems to be some relation between interest in the wisdom books and these collections of sentences. Evagrius, for example, who wrote commentaries on Proverbs and Job, wrote a book entitled *Monachikos* comprising one hundred sayings for those who lived as anchorites and fifty other sayings for more zealous and studious monks. He also wrote a book modeled on Proverbs called *Mirror for Monks and Nuns.* Antony, Macarius, Athanasius, and Basil also prepared sayings for monks.[7]

If we consider who wrote commentaries on the wisdom books and prepared collections of wisdom sayings it seems that the wisdom tradition was more congenial to some groups of Christians than to others. In the persons mentioned above there is an unusually high number of figures who come from Alexandria or who were directly influenced by Alexandrian teachers or who shared a similar intellectual outlook. It is perhaps not insignificant that the Wisdom of Solomon was written in Alexandria and that Sirach was translated there. It appears that wisdom literature was most attractive to those writers who were the most hellenized, yet it eventually finds a home in monasticism.

It is time, as Jack Suggs remarked in his recent book on wisdom in the Gospel of Matthew, to move wisdom from the footnotes to the title page. "For too long," wrote Suggs, "the traces of wisdom speculation present in Matthew have been treated as tangential or eccentric traditions foreign to the purpose and theology of the evangelist. They constitute, in my opinion, certain proof that one aspect of Matthew's thought has been unfortunately neglected. The description 'A Footnote to Matthean Christology' cannot be used, because it is the express aim of this report to lift the wisdom motif out of the footnotes of scholarly discussion, where it can be too quickly written off as an unexplained outburst of Johannine ideology."[8] Suggs is speaking only of Matthew, but his remarks reflect what is happening in the study of the Christian gospels as well as the larger history of Christianity and Judaism. No doubt some may brush off the new fascination with wisdom as only the latest fad in theological scholarship; theological scholarship is peculiarly susceptible to the allure of fads. Yet the new interest in wisdom may be more, and it is the conviction of the contributors to this volume that it is more than a momentary seduction.

This volume of essays arose out of a seminar held at the University of Notre Dame in 1973. This seminar on wisdom in late antiquity was composed of students and faculty from Notre Dame as well as a number of visiting scholars who graciously joined the work of the seminar for several two-day working sessions. The seminar was purposely designed to be exploratory. We wished to inquire whether wisdom was as significant a factor in the religious history of late antiquity as some were claiming. We invited a number of scholars from other universities and from Notre Dame to discuss aspects of wisdom that seemed important in their respective fields of specialization. Some of the participants specialized in the Hebrew Scriptures, others in the philosophy of the Greco-Roman world, others in the religious history of the ancient Near East, others in the New Testament, in Gnosticism, in Judaism, in the history of early Christianity. The seminar hoped to locate those areas

where wisdom played an important role and to suggest
new directions research and scholarship might take in the
future. It was, as it were, a seminar in search of a question.
We wished to discover how one might profitably approach
the study of wisdom in the many contexts in which it
appears and how one might best mine the material which is
available.

In the course of the seminar we learned that wisdom, in
contrast for example to apocalyptic, is an extraordinary
cross-cultural phenomenon and could be found in different
forms in all the religious currents of late antiquity. In his
study of wisdom in the rabbinic tradition Professor Fischel
shows in remarkable detail how deep was the interpenetra-
tion of Jewish and Hellenistic culture via the medium of
wisdom. In his conclusion he observes that what happened
in Judaism may in fact be characteristic of wisdom in
other cultural settings. "Wisdom literature seems always to
have been an accepted intercultural and interethnic coinage, appropriated as religiously neutral or non-committal."

From a somewhat different perspective several of the
other essays in the volume show how wisdom was a common coinage of interacting religious currents within the
Greco-Roman world. William Schoedel's analysis of the
unpublished document from Nag Hammadi, *The Teaching
of Silvanus,* indicates that not only ideas but also the
forms of Hebrew wisdom, as transmitted through the Sep-
tuagint, provided a unique vehicle for Silvanus to express
his understanding of Christianity. My own essay suggests in
a tentative way that some Christians in the second century
were as interested in "sayings" which had come down in
the Greek philosophical tradition as they were in the
sayings of Jesus. Many of these sayings express similar
ideas to those of Jesus or the wisdom books of Judaism,
suggesting perhaps that whoever put together the Christian
collection entitled the *Sentences of Sextus* drew on both
Hebrew and Greek wisdom tradition. Elisabeth Fiorenza's
essay on wisdom in the early Christian hymns shows that

within the context of early Christian missionary activity wisdom tradition provided a vehicle by which early Christian missionary efforts could meet the religious problem of fate or necessity.

These are only a few indications of how, as a result of the seminar, our conception of the role of wisdom in late antiquity was extended beyond the more familiar wisdom books of the Hebrew Bible. The essays in this volume are offered in the hope that they will encourage others to explore some of the questions we have only raised. At this point in the history of scholarship we are not in a position to assess how important wisdom will be in understanding Christianity and Judaism. That it is important, however, we are confident. One suggestion comes at the conclusion of Schoedel's essay. He observes that the study of wisdom tradition may help us to understand "why the 'delay of the Parousia' was overcome with relative ease—from the beginning possibilities other than apocalyptic were alive in Christianity; and it may also help us to see why Alexandrian Christianity developed so distinctive a theology—it relied perhaps on a special tradition of Hellenistic Jewish and Christian wisdom."

This volume includes a selection of the papers delivered at the seminar. Because of the nature of the seminar (scholars in widely different fields speaking out of different traditions of scholarship) I thought it wise not to include all the papers in one volume. Too many collections of essays seem to be the result of accident or circumstances. I have tried to avoid this difficulty by including only those papers which fall within a fairly fixed chronological period and which treat Christianity and Judaism. The volume includes essays on Christianity and Judaism during the first two centuries of the common era. We hope that the essays will serve as a research tool for students and scholars who wish to work further in the field.

Robert L. Wilken

NOTES

1. See the articles on "sage" in *EncJ* 14, 636–655.

2. See, for example, the material collected in H. von Arnim, *SVF* III, 146–171.

3. See Robinson, " 'Logoi Sophon': On the *Gattung* of Q," in Robinson and Koester, *Trajectories through Early Christianity* (Philadelphia, 1971), pp. 71–113, and works by Suggs, Beardslee, Perrin in the Bibliography.

4. W. Völker, "Die Verwertung der Weisheits-Literatur bei den christlichen Alexandrinern," *ZKG* 64 (1952–53), 1–33. See André Mehat, *Étude sur les 'Stromates' de Clement d'Alexandrie* (Paris, 1966), p. 53, for a graph of the use of Proverbs and Ecclesiasticus in Clement. The actual number of citations is, for Proverbs: *Exhortation:* 5; *Instructor* 1: 10, 2: 16, 3: 22; *Stromateis* 1: 46, 2: 48, 3: 10. For Ecclesiasticus: *Instructor* 1: 13, 2: 20, 3: 10; *Stromateis* 1: 6, 2: 5.

5. *Stromateis* 1.1 (Staehlin, p. 3).

6. Origen, *Commentary on John* 1.109–124.

7. See in this connection H. Gressmann, *Nonenspiegel und Mönschsspiegel des Euagrios Pontikos zum ersten Mal in der Urschrift herausgegeben*, TU, no. 39 (Leipzig, 1913).

8. M. Jack Suggs, *Wisdom, Christology, and Law in Matthew's Gospel* (Cambridge, Mass., 1970).

1: Jesus as Sophos and Sophia: Wisdom Tradition and the Gospels

James M. Robinson

A NUMBER OF SAYINGS OF JESUS IN THE GOSPELS CAN BE classified form-critically within forms familiar from wisdom literature.[1] The present essay takes this for granted rather than analyzing these forms anew. In a previous essay I have argued that the form of Q as a whole is that of wisdom literature, i.e., collections of sayings of the sages.[2] Again I shall presuppose this rather than argue the point here. I propose instead to investigate the relation between Jesus and personified wisdom, Sophia, in these sayings.

God's wisdom can be personified, as if she herself were a person functioning as a street preacher to call people to their senses, e.g., in Proverbs 8:

1   Does not wisdom call,
      does not understanding raise her voice?
2   On the heights beside the way,
      in the paths she takes her stand;
3   beside the gates in front of the town,
      at the entrance of the portals she cries aloud:
4   "To you, O men, I call,
      and my cry is to the sons of men.
5   O simple ones, learn prudence;
      O foolish men, pay attention.
6   Hear, for I will speak noble things,
      and from my lips will come what is right; . . ."

1

One may assume that this street scene was suggested not by an encounter with a disembodied Sophia, but rather by the more common encounter with a sophos, a sage, a wisdom teacher. Much like Jesus and the Rabbinic schools, he would collect about him his pupils, through whom the sapiential tradition would be handed down from generation to generation. It was not the name of the individual sage that was decisive—Solomon as the sage *par excellence* was the ideal pseudonym—but rather the truth, the wisdom taught by the sage. Many affirmed his wisdom to be true for many had found it to be true. The truth was by and large construed more as day-by-day prudence verifiable in experience, and less as revelation through the mighty acts of God to a given person upon whose authority its validity in part depended. However within the context of Judaism the two kinds of truth merge. In wisdom literature this took the form of extending the line of sages back through holy history. The great recipients of God's successive revelations in history are standardized into a sequence of emissaries through whom Sophia spoke.

The Wisdom of Solomon serves as a good instance of this trend, for it presents the stage in the development of wisdom literature typical of the period just prior to Christianity. Composed about the middle of the first century B.C.E., it documents the convergence of Jewish wisdom literature with apocalypticism and Hellenistic philosophy as well as with Israelite *Heilsgeschichte*. Notice the way Sophia is superimposed on *Heilsgeschichte* in chapter 10:

1   [Wisdom] protected the first-formed father of
        the world,
    when he alone had been created;
    she delivered him from his transgression,
2   and gave him strength to rule all things.
3   But when an unrighteous man departed from her
        in his anger,
    he perished because in rage he slew his brother.
4   When the earth was flooded because of him,
        wisdom again saved it,

steering the righteous man by a paltry piece of wood.

5 [Wisdom] also, when the nations in wicked agreement had been confounded,
recognized the righteous man and preserved him blameless before God,
and kept him strong in the face of his compassion for his child.

6 [Wisdom] rescued a righteous man when the ungodly were perishing;
he escaped the fire that descended on the Five Cities. . . .

9 [Wisdom] rescued from troubles those who served her.

10 When a righteous man fled from his brother's wrath,
she guided him on straight paths;
she showed him the kingdom of God, . . .

13 When a righteous man was sold, [wisdom] did not desert him,
but delivered him from sin.
She descended with him into the dungeon,

14 and when he was in prison she did not leave him,
until she brought him the scepter of a kingdom
and authority over his masters.
Those who accused him she showed to be false,
and she gave him everlasting honor.

15 A holy people and blameless race [wisdom] delivered from a nation of oppressors.

16 She entered the soul of a servant of the Lord,
and withstood dread kings with wonders and signs. . . .

11:1 [Wisdom] prospered their works by the hand of a holy prophet. . . .

One finds a similar understanding of *Heilsgeschichte* in one of the Q passages most closely related to the wisdom tradition (Luke 11:49–51; 13:34a/Matt. 23:34-37a):

Therefore also the Wisdom of God said, "I will send them prophets and apostles, some of whom they will kill and persecute," that the blood of all the prophets,

shed from the foundation of the world, may be required
of this generation, from the blood of Abel to the blood
of Zechariah, who perished between the altar and the
sanctuary. Yes, I tell you, it shall be required of this
generation. . . . O Jerusalem, Jerusalem, killing the
prophets and stoning those who are sent to you!

This concept of Sophia speaking through the Old Testament prophets[3] continued into the Christian gnosticism of
the second century C.E. (Irenaeus, *Adversus Haereses*
1.30.11 on the Ophites):

> They distribute the prophets thus: to Ialdabaoth be-
> longed Moses, Joshua son of Nun, Amos, and Habak-
> kuk; to Iao, Samuel, Nathan, Jonah, and Micah; to
> Saboath, Elijah, Joel, and Zechariah; to Adonai, Isaiah,
> Ezekiel, Jeremiah, and Daniel; to Eloi, Tobias and Hag-
> gai; to Oreus, Micah and Nahum; to Astapheus, Ezra and
> Zephaniah. Each one of these extolled his father and
> god. But Sophia herself also uttered many things
> through them concerning the First Man, the Imperish-
> able Aeon, and about that Christ, who according to
> them is above, and she forewarned and reminded men of
> the imperishable light, and the First Man, and the de-
> scent of Christ. At this the rulers were terrified, and
> amazed at the novelty of the things which were being
> proclaimed by the prophets.[4]

This way of unifying the history of religions into a series
of prophets all spokesmen for the heavenly Sophia was
characteristic of Near Eastern religions that emerged from
the biblical tradition. The Manicheans for example used
this pattern to appropriate the religious history prior to
their founder, whom they honored as *primus inter pares* in
a long line of prophets.[5] Rather than claiming exclusivity
for their founder, they only claimed for him a climactic
and final position, which of course functionally achieved
for him (and them) a preeminent position.

The christology of Q has more affinity with this broad
tradition than is usually realized. It is difficult to free
ourselves from the christocentric context in which we have

come to know Q, namely as a sermon in the life of Jesus as interpreted by Matthew and Luke. Seen in its own terms, Q presents a culminating chapter in a long sapiential *Heilsgeschichte* embracing as earlier chapters the whole Old Testament from Abel to Zechariah.[6] Jesus functions as such a *primus inter pares* in a further sapiential passage of Q (Luke 11:31—32/Matt. 12:42.41):

> The queen of the South will arise at the judgment with the men of this generation and condemn them; for she came from the ends of the earth to hear the wisdom of Solomon, and behold, something greater than Solomon is here. The men of Nineveh will arise at the judgment with this generation and condemn it; for they repented at the preaching of Jonah, and behold, something greater than Jonah is here.

What is even more striking than the prehistory provided by the Old Testament to the culmination of Sophia's activity is the fact that two figures share this culminative role in Q, John the Baptist and Jesus. Only Q of all the gospels accords to the preaching of the Baptist such importance, as addressing authoritative proclamation valid in its own right directly to the hearer rather than serving primarily to refer him to Jesus (Luke 3:7—9/Matt. 3:7—10). It is precisely in relation to Sophia that John and Jesus stand parallel (Luke 7:33—35/Matt. 11:18—19):

> For John the Baptist has come eating no bread and drinking no wine; and you say, "He has a demon." The Son of man has come eating and drinking; and you say, "Behold, a glutton and a drunkard, a friend of tax collectors and sinners!" Yet wisdom is justified by [all] her children.

Here Sophia's children vindicate her by affirming both John and Jesus. Of course that is not to ignore a superiority over John accorded to Jesus as Son of man through the apocalyptic tradition. This differentiation in status derived from apocalypticism is so familiar to us that we are more likely to ignore the parallel into which the use of the

wisdom conceptualization tends to bring them. Furthermore there is, in spite of the culminating role they share, a
continuation of their role in the disciples. Not only does
the mission of the disciples in Q (Luke 10:2–12/Matt.
9:37–38; 10:7–16) continue Jesus' message of the kingdom. There is also the difficult saying that blasphemy
against the Son of man is pardonable, whereas that against
the Holy Spirit is not—which may mean rejection of Jesus
during his ministry is pardonable but rejection of the
congregation's current ministry is not.[7] (The term Holy
Spirit is feminine in Semitic languages and at times is
interchangeable with Sophia.) Hence Q displays in its wisdom sections a tendency to relativize the uniqueness of
Jesus by imbedding his preeminent message within a long
chain of wisdom's spokesmen throughout the Old Testament and, though culminating in John and Jesus, continuing in the Church.

The preeminence of Jesus in the Q tradition is derived
conceptually from the identification of Jesus with the
coming Son of man who will determine mankind's fate at
the last judgment. In the later layers of Q, to which the
main wisdom sayings belong,[8] this futuristic christology is
read back into the public ministry of Jesus. He was already
Son of man. Once the public ministry is defined as that of
one already Son of man, then some conceptualization is
needed for carrying through this new positive christological assessment of the public ministry. It was the wisdom
conceptualization which provided such a category. The
wisdom concept weakened somewhat the exclusive claim
inherent in the Son of man concept, and conversely the
Son of man concept tended to attribute to Jesus a more
exclusive role than the wisdom alone would have per-
mitted.

The very fact that John is associated with Jesus as
messenger of the heavenly Sophia indicates that one cannot yet speak of a Sophia christology in the sense of the
incarnation. One may wonder how Q would have con-

ceived the coming of Sophia into contact with (John and) Jesus. The Wisdom of Solomon 7:27 suggests an unreflected indwelling:

> Though she is but one, she can do all things, and while remaining in herself, she renews all things; in every generation she passes into holy souls and makes them friends of God, and prophets.

The gnostic conceptuality would be much more complex. The Ophite passage already cited as a gnostic instance of the series of prophets sent by Sophia describes the coming of Sophia to Jesus as follows (Ireneaus 1.30.12–13):

> When the Sophia who is below knew that her brother [Christ] was coming down to her, she . . . prepared a baptism of repentance, and prepared in advance Jesus, so that when he came down Christ would find a clean vessel, . . . As Christ descended into this world, he first put on his sister Sophia. . . . And Jesus, being born from a virgin by the activity of a god, was wiser and purer and more just than all men. Bound up with Sophia, Christ descended, and so Jesus Christ came to be. Many of his disciples, they say, did not know the descent of Christ upon him, but when Christ descended on him, then he began to perform acts of power, to heal, and to proclaim the unknown Father, and to confess himself openly as son of the First Man. At this the rulers and the father became angry with Jesus and arranged for him to be killed. While he was being led to it, Christ himself and Sophia went off, they say, to the Imperishable Aeon, but Jesus was crucified.[9]

It is clear that in this gnostic conception the divine pair Christ and Sophia simply inhabit Jesus temporarily, without establishing any essential relation to him. The fact that he is wiser than all men, though sensed as fitting, is ultimately irrelevant, in that he and his human wisdom die but Sophia lives on forever. Actually, the Ophite view is the adoptionistic misunderstanding of the coming of the Spirit at baptism in Mark and would probably also be a

misunderstanding of Q, if Q too had a baptism narrative
(which is somewhat obscured, due to the overlay of Mark).
But some such transfer of Sophia from person to person
must be assumed down through history, and the adoptionistic entrance and exit from a person may be the way Q
would have conceived of the shift of Sophia from John to
Jesus at John's death. It would not apply so simply at
Jesus' death because of his role—not derived from the
wisdom tradition, but from apocalypticism—as the coming
Son of man.

Recent research on Q has recognized the most distinc-
tively wisdom sayings of Q to belong to a later layer in the
tradition, as the Q tradition moved out of its Palestinian
milieu into the wider Hellenistic Jewish Christian environment where the final redaction itself took place. In fact,
since the editor-author cast the material into a literary
genre derived from wisdom literature, one can conceive of
the author himself as part of this wisdom trend that
surfaced in the late stages of the Q tradition.[10]

The passage that has often been designated the latest in
Q is the thanksgiving,[11] which in itself has two layers, in
that the concluding verse functions as an interpretation of
the preceding thanksgiving. The thanksgiving itself runs
(Luke 10:21/Matt. 11:25–26):

> In that same hour he (rejoiced in the Holy Spirit and)
> said, "I thank thee, Father, Lord of heaven and earth,
> that thou hast hidden these things from the wise and
> understanding and revealed them to babes; yea, Father,
> for such was thy gracious will."

This falls within the wisdom group of sayings in Q, here
with a polemic directed at the officially wise, the Jewish
establishment, e.g. the scribes and rabbis. To this thanksgiving is then appended[12] the following interpretation
(Luke 10:22/Matt. 11:27):

> All things have been delivered to me by my Father; and
> no one knows who the Son is except the Father, or who

the Father is except the Son and any one to whom the Son chooses to reveal him.

If the first line can be explained on the apocalyptic background, the last three lines, the exclusive reciprocal knowledge of Father and Son, can best be explained on the basis of the wisdom tradition. But what is most significant for our purposes is that here, even if at the very latest stage in the Q tradition, Jesus is not simply cast in the role of one of Sophia's spokesmen, even the culminating one, but rather is described with predications that are reserved for Sophia herself. In the past several years there has been a trend away from the claims made especially by Ulrich Wilckens for an early Sophia christology in Corinth and Q;[13] scholars today prefer to locate the full identification of Jesus as Sophia incarnate as taking place first in Matthew.[14] However, the most recent treatment of Q, by Siegfried Schulz, while sharing this trend, cannot avoid at this point conceding *de facto* that such an identification takes place in this passage. One need merely read his interpretation of the three lines in question about the exclusive reciprocal relation of Father and Son to reach the conclusion that Jesus is here understood as Sophia:

> Here as [in the wisdom tradition of Late Judaism] the "Son" has the same function as the heavenly Sophia, in that he speaks as sole revealer and redeemer. Only the Father knows the Son, as in the wisdom tradition God knows wisdom: It is for all men in principle hidden and unattainable [Job 28; Proverbs 30:1ff.; Baruch 3:9; 4:4]. Only God knows [wisdom] and finds its path; only when [wisdom] reveals itself is it recognized. It is this reciprocal knowledge, which has parallels in Hellenistic mysticism, that can be adequately explained only in terms of the inner relationship between God and the heavenly Sophia. Like the heavenly Sophia, the Son is the sole mediator of revelation of God, and the content of this heavenly revealed knowledge is in both cases wisdom [Wisdom of Solomon 6:12—9:18] or the

Son himself. The exclusivity of the mediation of salvation is apparent in both cases.[15]
It is precisely this exclusivity which had been lacking in
the wisdom sections of Q up to this point: Jesus had
shared the role as Sophia's spokesman with John the
Baptist, but also with the prophets of the Old Testament
and the Church. This had been the main reason one should
not speak of a Sophia christology in Q—Jesus, rather than
being identified with the exclusive Sophia, has been identified as the *primus inter pares,* the most important, of her
many spokesmen. But at least in the last stage of the Q
tradition this no longer prevails. The exclusivity of Sophia
is attributed to the Son, who is identified with Jesus.
Although one may concede the inappropriateness of speaking of a Sophia christology in Q by and large, if by that one
would mean Jesus is identified as the preexistent Sophia
incarnate (in analogy to the Johannine prologue), it seems
appropriate that one acknowledge at least at the last stage
of Q that the shift to a Sophia christology has been made.
    This Sophia christology that emerges at the end of the Q
tradition comes to fruition in Matthew, which in general
seems to carry forward the Q trajectory more than does
Luke. Matthew's Sophia christology becomes apparent in
its redaction of the wisdom sayings of Q.[16] In Matt.
11:19b the Q saying "Wisdom is justified by her children"
is reformulated "Wisdom is justified by her deeds." This
shift is to be interpreted in terms of Matthew's redaction
throughout this section. In 11:2 he opens the section on
John and Jesus with reference to John in prison having
heard about "the deeds of the Christ," which Jesus itemizes
in response to John's emissaries. These "deeds" are then kept
in view in verses 20–24 as the "mighty works" Jesus
performed in towns that rejected him. The thanksgiving
that in Q culminated in the identification of Jesus with
Sophia follows immediately in Matthew, who appends
further wisdom material which, like the culmination of
that Q section, is applicable to Jesus only because he is
Sophia incarnate (11:28–30):

Come to me, all who labor and are heavy-laden, and I will give you rest. Take my yoke upon you, and learn from me; for I am gentle and lowly in heart, and you will find rest for your souls. For my yoke is easy, and my burden is light.

These concepts, familiar in wisdom literature, are also applied to the Torah, and hence point to another trait of Matthew's Sophia christology. Judaism had already identified Sophia with the Torah, by affirming that Sophia, so often rejected by men and having no permanent abode on earth, had come to reside in the Torah (Ecclus. 24).[17] It would fit well with Matthean theology in general to see in the Jewish concept of the "incarnation" of Sophia in the Torah an analogy for carrying through the identification of Sophia with Jesus.

Matthew's Sophia christology is also apparent in his editing of a second wisdom section of Q.[18] The Q saying that began (Luke 11:49): "Therefore also the Wisdom of God said, 'I will send them prophets and apostles,' " is edited by Matthew (23:34): "Therefore I send you prophets and wise men and scribes" It is not enough to say Matthew simply eliminates the reference to Sophia. Rather one must recognize that he identifies Sophia with Jesus, by attributing to Jesus not only a saying previously attributed to Sophia, but by attributing to Jesus the content of the saying, namely Sophia's role as the heavenly personage who throughout history has sent the prophets and other spokesmen. It is to himself as preexistent Sophia that he refers in saying a few verses later (Matt. 23:37): "How often would I have gathered your children together as a hen gathers her brood under her wings."

The Gospel of Thomas reports Matthew's stance rather well. In the equivalent to the Caesarea Philippi scene of Peter's confession in the canonical gospels the Gospel of Thomas in saying 13 reports Matthew's confession: "You are a wise philosopher."

The apocryphal Gospel of the Hebrews has much the same Sophia christology as emerged in Matthew, namely that Sophia finally found her resting place in Jesus. The standard Sophia *topos* is unmistakable, even though the passage, describing Jesus' baptism, uses the equivalent term Spirit, since this is the term the tradition used for what came on Jesus at baptism (Jerome, *Isaiah Commentary* on Isa. 11:2):

> But it came to pass when the Lord had come up out of the water the whole font of the Holy Spirit descended upon him and rested on him and said to him: My Son, in all the prophets I was waiting for you that you should come and I might rest in you. For you are my rest. You are my first-begotten Son that reigns forever.[19]

By this time, i.e. the first half of the second century C.E., the identification of Jesus as Sophia had become widespread. In Justin (*Dialogue* 100.4) one reads that Jesus "is also called Sophia . . . in the words of the prophets."

The trajectory of wisdom traditions which we have sketched in terms of christology may also help to clarify the position of Q in another important respect, namely its lack of a passion narrative. This will emerge if we trace one other strand of the wisdom tradition that we have thus far neglected. This is the theme that wisdom is so regularly rejected on earth she finally returns to heaven. The *locus classicus* is Enoch 42:1–2.

> Wisdom found no place where she might dwell;
> Then a dwelling-place was assigned her in the heavens.
> Wisdom went forth to make her dwelling among the children of men,
> And found no dwelling-place:
> Wisdom returned to her place,
> And took her seat among the angels.[20]

This motif of wisdom's withdrawal is current in Jewish apocalypticism as characteristic of the last times. The *topos* that is particularly relevant to us here goes back to Prov. 1:28. Sophia the street preacher says that because she has called and they have not hearkened: "Then they will call upon me, but I will not answer; they will seek me diligently but will not find me." But it recurs in apocalyptic literature (4 Ezra 5:10): "Then shall intelligence hide itself, and wisdom withdraw to its chamber—by many shall be sought and not found."[21] This is echoed in a wisdom saying of Q: After Sophia so often sought to win Jerusalem only to be rejected, judgment is pronounced (Luke 13:35/Matt. 23:38–39): "Behold, your house is forsaken. And I tell you, you will not see me until you say, 'Blessed is he who comes in the name of the Lord!' " Here the withdrawal of Sophia is put into the apocalyptic context of the future judgment by Jesus the Son of man at his parousia. The judgmental apocalyptic context has appropriated the Deuteronomistic view of history as consisting of repeated rejection of the prophets until in the end Israel is itself rejected.[22] The whole section of Q is dominated by the concept of the suffering prophet: "I will send them prophets . . . , that the blood of all the prophets . . . may be required of this generation. . . . O Jerusalem, Jerusalem, killing the prophets. . ." (Luke 11:49–50; 13:34/Matt. 23:34–37). John and Jesus and the Christians are in the line of these prophets, much as in 1 Thess. 2:14–15, ". . . the Jews who killed both the Lord Jesus and the prophets, and drove us out. . . ." Both in this Deuteronomistic tradition and in the sapiential tradition all the slain prophets and sages are on much the same level. Attention is actually not on the rejected spokesmen but on the rejected Israel. In such a context the death of Jesus has neither unique nor saving significance. Jesus himself has unique saving significance, because of the apocalyptic christology of the older Q tradition that identified Jesus with the coming Son of man. But his death was given theological interpretation first in the later stratum of Q where it is not interpreted on the basis of sacrificial traditions, but within the traditions that saw in his death only the culminating instance of the rejection of God's spokesmen by Israel.

One may use this latest sapiential layer on Q as one's point of departure for understanding the author of Q. This is confirmed by the fact that he chose a literary genre typical of wisdom literature.[23] The Gospel of Thomas shares this sapiential genre with Q, and it may be no coincidence that it reflects the same sapiential tradition of the withdrawal of Sophia (Logion 38):

> Jesus said: Many times have you desired to hear these words which I say to you, and you have no other from whom to hear them. There will be days when you will seek Me and you will not find Me.[24]

This sapiential context would also help to explain why Q and Thomas omitted a theology of the cross and a passion narrative. One of the major ideological objections to the existence of Q has been the inability to conceive of anyone in primitive Christianity who would write a gospel without including a passion narrative. This is because primitive Christianity has been too monolithically conceived in terms of the sole kerygma of cross and resurrection, from which the gospel form of Mark and John is in part derived.[25] The Deuteronomistic and sapiential concepts of the rejection and death of the divine emissary as documented in Q would well explain how a primitive Christian in good standing, namely standing in that tradition, would have recorded the Jesus traditions important to him as a collection of sayings without a passion narrative.

We have sketched a trajectory of wisdom tradition beginning late in the Old Testament and moving, via participation in Jewish and primitive Christian apocalypticism, into a prominent role in the late stages of the Q tradition. By this time the identification of the apocalyptic Son of man with Jesus applied not only to the future but already to his public ministry. This called for some theological category for comprehending his public ministry as a positive category in its own right. The final emissary of Sophia becomes this category. If it did not give Jesus an exclusive or unique role, it did give his public ministry a positive and even preeminent role that it had not previously had, at least on a conceptual level, in that particular tradition. The association of this final emissary of Sophia with the unique apocalyptic Son of man made it easy to heighten the

christology in the wisdom sayings of Q by according to the
Son Sophia's unique relation to the Father, in effect iden-
tifying Jesus with Sophia herself. This Sophia christology
was then further developed in Matthew, and in the first
half of the second century became common, in the Gospel
of the Hebrews, the Gospel of Thomas, Justin Martyr, and
so on, and thus became a permanent if minor ingredient in
all subsequent christology.

NOTES

1. Rudolf Bultmann, *The History of the Synoptic Tradition*
(New York, 1963), esp. "Logia (Jesus as the Teacher of Wisdom),"
pp. 69–108; William A. Beardslee, "The Wisdom Tradition and the
Synoptic Gospels," *JAAR* 35 (1967), 231–240; *Literary Criticism of
the New Testament* (Philadelphia, 1970), esp. chap. 3, "The Proverb," pp. 30–41.
2. Robinson and Koester, *Trajectories through Early Christianity*
(Philadelphia, 1971), esp. chap. 2: " 'Logoi Sophon': On the *Gattung* of Q," pp. 71–113.
3. O. H. Steck, *Israel und das gewaltsame Geschick der Propheten: Untersuchungen zur Uberlieferung des deuteronomistichen Geschichtsbildes im Alten Testament, Spätjudentum und Urchristentum*, WMANT 23 (Neukirchen-Vluyn, 1967).
4. *Gnosis: A Selection of Gnostic Texts*, ed. Werner Foerster,
trans. R. McL. Wilson (Oxford, 1972), I, 91–92.
5. New documentation for this motif is found in the Cologne
Mani Codex. See A. Henrichs and L. Loenen, "Ein griechischer
Mani-Codex (P. Colon, inv. nr. 4780)," *Zeitschrift für Papyrologie
und Epigraphik* 5 (1970), 139–140, 158–159; A. Henrichs, "Mani
and the Babylonian Baptists: A Historical Confrontation," *Harvard
Studies in Classical Philology* 77 (1973) 54–55.
6. See my essay "Basic Shifts in German Theology," *Interpr* 16
(1962), 82–85.
7. Siegfried Schulz, *Q: Die Spruchquelle der Evangelisten* (Zürich, 1972), pp. 249–250.
8. Dieter Lührmann, *Die Redaktion der Logienquelle*, WMANT
33 (Neukirchen-Vluyn, 1969), p. 97.
9. *Gnosis*, ed. Foerster, I, 92.

10. Lührmann, *Redaktion*, pp. 97–98.

11. Ernst Haenchen, *Die Apostelgeschichte*, Meyer-Kommentar (Göttingen, 1961), p. 32, note 1.

12. With regard to the relation of the appended verse to the thanksgiving formula see my essay "Die Hodayot-Formel in Gebet und Hymnus des Frühchristentums," *Apophoreta: Festschrift für Ernst Haenchen*, BZNW 30 (Berlin, 1964), pp. 194–235, esp pp. 226–228.

13. E.g. in his article on "Sophia" in *TDNT* VII, 515–517, 519.

14. M. Jack Suggs, *Wisdom, Christology, and Law in Matthew's Gospel* (Cambridge, Mass., 1970), pp. 19, 28; Lührmann, *Redaktion*, p. 99.

15. Schulz, *Q.*, pp. 224–225.

16. Suggs, *Wisdom*, pp. 55–58.

17. Hans Conzelmann, "The Mother of Wisdom," in *The Future of Our Religious Past*, ed. J. M. Robinson (New York, 1971), pp. 230–243.

18. Suggs, *Wisdom*, pp. 58–61.

19. Edgar Hennecke and Wilhelm Schneemelcher, *Apocryphal New Testament*, trans. R. McL. Wilson (Philadelphia, 1959), I, 163–164.

20. R. H. Charles, ed., *The Apocrypha and Pseudepigrapha of the Old Testament* (Oxford, 1913), II, 213. See Rudolf Bultmann, "Der religionsgeschichtliche Hintergrund des Prologs zum Johannesevangelium," *Exegetica* (Tübingen, 1967), pp. 10–35.

21. Charles, ed., *Apocrypha and Pseudepigrapha*, II, 570.

22. Steck, *Geschick*, pp. 232ff.

23. This is worked out in my essay "Logoi Sophon" in Robinson and Koester, *Trajectories*, pp. 71–113.

24. *The Gospel According to Thomas*, ed. A. Guillaumont, H.-Ch. Puech, G. Quispel, W. Till, and Yassah 'Abd al Masih (Leiden, 1959), pp. 23, 25.

25. Helmut Koester, in Robinson and Koester, *Trajectories*, pp. 161–162.

2:Wisdom Mythology and the Christological Hymns of the New Testament

Elisabeth Schüssler Fiorenza

WISDOM SPECULATIONS AND WISDOM TRADITIONS HAVE decisively influenced early Christianity. Recent studies have convincingly demonstrated the influence of Jewish-Hellenistic wisdom speculation upon the theology of Paul and his opponents at Corinth as well as upon the Gospel tradition. The earliest stage of the Q tradition understands Jesus as the final emissary of Wisdom. The latest stage identifies him with Wisdom herself insofar as the relationship between son and father is conceived in terms of the relation between the heavenly Sophia and God (Luke 10:21f/Matt. 11:26f). Matthew's christology develops further this identification of Jesus and the figure of Wisdom.

Wisdom speculation and wisdom theology are also postulated as background for the different christological hymns of the New Testament. A discussion of these hymns encounters a vast amount of scholarly research, an enormous diversity of hypotheses, and a large variety of methodological and theological questions.[1] In a first section the main form-critical and *religionsgeschichtlich* discussions of the christological hymns and their methodological presuppositions will be reviewed. Rather than survey all the possible options, I shall mainly analyze two significant positions of recent research which in my opinion paradigmatically reveal the methodological difficulties of any

investigation of these hymns. The critique of these positions will seek to demonstrate that neither the distinction
between Jewish and Hellenistic nor the assumption of a
"basic myth" or that of a trajectory of a "developing
myth" is adequate to define the place of the New Testament christological hymns within the theological history
of early Christianity or to specify the religious milieu in
which they originated.

In a second section I shall argue that recent research on
wisdom and gnostic literature has abandoned the conception of a basic myth underlying the different articulations
of it in the various accounts of Jewish-Hellenistic wisdom
speculation and gnostic theology. Instead of a trajectory of
a "developing myth," a trajectory of "reflective mythology" is suggested. This "reflective mythology" uses mythical materials as thought categories for its own theological
reflection and conception.

In a final section the methodological insights developed
within wisdom research will be applied to a discussion of
the New Testament christological hymns.

The Methodological Presuppositions of Form-Critical and *Religionsgeschichtlich* Approaches

What are the theological and the historical problems
posed by these hymns? The theological question is: Why
do these hymns use the language of myth to speak of Jesus
of Nazareth who was not a mythic figure but a concrete
historical person? Why and how did these hymns begin to
portray Jesus Christ as a preexistent heavenly being, who
was involved in the creation of the world, descended from
heaven and was manifested in the flesh, and who was
exalted and enthroned over all earthly and heavenly
powers? This description of Jesus Christ in the language of
myth is even more astonishing when one keeps in mind
that the New Testament christological hymns do not

belong to a later stage of christological development but are among the earliest christological statements found in the New Testament.

Scholars have attempted to answer these theological questions mainly by form-critical and *religionsgeschichtlich* analyses. They have *first* been concerned in the reconstruction and the form-critical definition of the hymns and their *Sitz im Leben* in the early Christian communities and *second* in locating these hymns within the religious contexts in which these hymns originated. By such analysis they have hoped to provide an answer to the theological question of why the Jesus of Nazareth was understood in mythological language.

Form-Critical Approach

Because no direct record of early Christian hymns such as psalm-, hymn-, or prayerbook exists, hymnic units have to be reconstructed by form-critical studies. The New Testament hymns under consideration are consequently secondary productions of scholarly reconstruction and not primary texts. As long as the original of the hymns is lacking, their reconstruction will remain an exegetical task that can never find a definitive solution. The specific literary delineation, the formal classification, and the extent of secondary or redactional additions to the original hymns can be ascertained or known only to the extent that the hymnic style (*Stilempfinden*) of Judaic or Greco-Roman literature is known and only to the extent that the vocabulary and theological motifs of the individual New Testament authors who incorporated the hymn in question are understood. Although scholars still discuss the extent and form of the hymns, they basically agree on which texts should be considered as New Testament christological hymns. The general consensus is that Phil. 2:6–11; 1 Tim. 3:16; Col. 1:15–20; Eph. 2:14–16; Heb. 1:3; 1 Pet.

1:20; 3:18, 22, and the prologue of John's Gospel represent such early christological hymns.[2] Moreover, agreement exists that the poetic units in question are hymns and have their *Sitz im Leben* in the worship of the early Christian community. However, it no longer appears possible to give a more precise definition of this liturgical *Sitz im Leben* as for instance the celebration of baptism or of the eucharist.

Although Deichgräber[3] maintains that one can define the place of the christological hymns in the theological history of Christianity without analyzing their theological motives and without discussing their history of religious background, K. Wengst[4] does not believe this to be possible. Wengst is less concerned with a theological analysis of the hymns than he is with their classification and *religionsgeschichtlich* milieu. Wengst identifies the milieu with terms such as "Jewish Christian," "hellenistic Jewish Christian," or "Gentile Christian," yet in the first century such distinctions between what was Jewish and what was Hellenistic are no longer adequate.

Wengst establishes four different *Gattungen* of hymns or songs as he calls them, each consisting of two distinct parts: *first:* the *Weglied* or Song of Journey (Phil. 2:6–11; 1 Tim. 3:16; 1 Pet. 1:20; 3:18, 22); *second:* the *Schöpfungsmittler-Inthronisationslied* or Song about the Mediator in creation and his enthronement (Heb. 1:3; Col. 1:15–20); *third:* the *Versöhnungslied* or Song of Reconciliation (Eph. 2:14–16; Col. 2:13–15); and *fourth:* the *Inkarnationslied* or Song of Incarnation (Ignatius, Ephesians 19:2f and John 1:1–5, 11, 14–16). Whereas the first *Gattung* is patterned after the gnostic way of the redeemer from heaven to earth and back to heaven the other three *Gattungen* are influenced by Jewish wisdom speculation. The second part of the first three *Gattungen* is similar insofar as it stresses the exaltation of Jesus Christ, whereas the last *Gattung* reflects in its second part the incarnation.

Neither Wengst's classification of the hymns nor his

location of their *Sitz im Leben* is based upon an analysis
of the formal elements and theological motifs of the
different hymns but depends upon and is correlative
to his delineation of the historical religious influences
upon the hymns. For example, Wengst attributes the
Schöpfungsmittler-Inthronisationslied and the *Inkarnationslied* to the Jewish-Hellenistic communities because of
the presence of wisdom influence.[5] He suggests that, de-
spite the traces of Jewish-Hellenistic wisdom influences in
the first part, the *Weglied* belongs to a gentile Christian
community because it is patterned after the way of the
gnostic redeemer.[6] Wengst's treatment is in my opinion
inadequate because it lacks appropriate categories for the
delineation of the religious milieu that constitutes the
matrix of the early Christian hymns.

Another reservation pertains to his failure to reflect
adequately the relationship between this matrix and the
early Christian community. The terms wisdom or redeemer
myth or religious background are avoided. Instead Wengst
refers to religious parallels without defining their relation
to the early Christian communities in which the hymns
originated. Although the adage that a parallel consists of
two lines that never meet may be true, the precise question
to be raised for the hymns is when do the parallels meet.
In other words, Wengst does not address the question:
How is the *Sitz im Leben* of the hymns related to the
religious milieu in which the Christian community is
living? The form-critical question cannot be adequately
answered unless the *religionsgeschichtlich* milieu is care-
fully defined and delineated. Is this milieu "influenced" by
Jewish Wisdom speculation? Do the writings of Philo of
Alexandria or the later gnostic writings represent this
milieu? Is a single myth the "background" to the New
Testament hymns (be it a Jewish-Hellenistic Wisdom myth
or a gnostic redeemer myth) or are different and distinct
concepts employed here? If such a single myth stands
behind the New Testament christological hymns, the ques-

tion should be asked: Which function did this myth have within the Jewish-Hellenistic Wisdom circles or the gnostic groups and their respective theologies?

Religionsgeschichtlich *Discussion*

The question of the historical religious "background" of the New Testament hymns has been explicitly addressed by J. Sanders in an exemplary manner.[7] He assumes that all hymns have as their basis the same myth and he maintains that this myth has its origin in the same pre-Christian religious circles. Sanders reconstructs one basic pattern which is in many ways similar to Deichgräber's reconstruction. In his opinion the hymnic passages "seem to present the same myth of the redeemer, involving his participation in creation, his descent and ascent to and from the world, and his work of redemption."[8] The pattern of this redeemer myth consists of eight elements. These elements, however, are not found together in one hymn. Here Sanders is apparently employing the same method as Bultmann and Wilckens since they have also sought to reconstruct one basic original myth out of the different expressions and various forms of the Wisdom myth. Eight elements make up this redeemer myth in which the redeemer is: (1) the possessor of unity or equality with God (Phil. 2:6; Col. 1:15, 17; Heb. 1:3; John 1:1); (2) the mediator or agent of creation (Col. 1:16; John 1:3); (3) a part of or sustainer of creation (Col. 1:15, 17f.; Heb. 1:3; John 1:4); (4) descended from the heavenly to the earthly realm (Phil. 2:7; John 1:5,9); (5) one who dies (Phil. 2:8; Col. 1:18; 1 Tim. 3:16; 1 Pet. 3:18); (6) and is made alive again (Col. 1:18; 1 Tim. 3:16; 1 Pet. 3:18); (7) one who effects reconciliation (Col. 1:18, 19f.; Eph. 2:14–16; 1 Tim. 3:16; 1 Pet. 3:19; Heb. 1:3); exalted and enthroned and to whom the cosmic powers become subject (Phil. 2:9–11; 1 Tim. 3:16; 1 Pet. 3:22; Heb. 1:3).[9]

This reconstructed hymn represents a mythical divine

drama of cosmic dimensions. It consists of two parts and has its origin and preparation "in the general (or in some particular) religious milieu of Early Christianity." [10] Sanders proceeds to define this milieu and the genesis of the hymn. In reviewing the research on the religious background of the hymn, he favors the progressive hypostatization concept of Dürr and Ringgren over that of the redaction of a highly developed gnostic revealer myth which has been developed by Bultmann with respect to the prologue in John. Sanders, however, combines this concept of progressive hypostatization under the influence of and addition of mythological ideas from other religions with the concept of a "developing myth" as proposed by D. Georgi[11] in reference to Phil. 2:6–11. The root and direction of this developing myth can, according to Georgi, already be seen in the Wisdom of Solomon. This myth belongs with the dualistic understanding of the world to "the essential components of this new thinking that one calls gnostic."[12] As a result of the progress of this developing myth the various divine figures (e.g. Sophia, Logos, and primal man) already began in Sander's opinion to converge and to take on similar redemptive aspects in pre-Christian Judaism. The Christ figure in the New Testament hymns represents another stage in the process of this developing mythical understanding. Moreover, the religious milieu, in which the New Testament christological hymns have their origin, is described not only with the help of such concepts as progressive hypostatization and emerging mythical configuration and development, but also with reference to cosmic dualism. But no reason exists for presupposing gnostic influence, since such a cosmic dualism is already present in some segments of pre-Christian Judaism, as the Qumran writings demonstrate. This religious milieu is claimed as the matrix for the concepts found in the hymn incorporated into the prologue of John's Gospel (i.e., for John 1:1–11) and in the *first part* of the other hymns under discussion with the exception of Eph. 2:14–16.

The religious background to the *second part* of the New

Testament christological hymns is more problematical. This part speaks of the cosmic reconciliation, of exaltation, and of enthronement. The closest parallels to this myth, which is contained in the second part of the hymns, are to be found in later gnostic literature. This evidence, however, would speak either for a dependency of this literature upon the New Testament hymns or for a dependency of the New Testament hymns upon this gnostic literature. A third possibility would be that the myth of cosmic reconciliation in the second part of the hymns was already connected with that of the first part in pre-Christian Judaism.

Sanders attempts to establish this third possibility and to demonstrate that both parts of the New Testament christological hymns were already connected in pre-Christian Judaism. Therefore, he analyzes first the Odes of Solomon, whose Jewish origin appears evident to him, then two writings of Nag Hammadi of pre-Christian origin, and finally, the thanksgiving psalms of the wisdom schools. The Odes of Solomon illustrate that Judaism under the influence of another religion, namely, the cult of Adonis, could conceive of redemption similar to that of the New Testament hymns. Sanders finds in the Odes that all the decisive elements of the New Testament hymns are already present, e.g. "hypostatization of divine qualities in a developing myth, redemption involving reunification of the disparate elements and cosmic reconciliation. . . ."[13] However, Sanders grants that there are only allusions to the concept of "cosmic reconciliation" and that the odist had only a slight interest in the cosmic aspect of redemption. The only traces of "cosmic reconciliation" found in the Odes have to do with the incorporation of the redeemed in the redeemer (e.g. Odes of Solomon 22.2: "He who gathers the things that are betwixt").

The thesis that Judaism under the influence of other religions can bring forth a myth of redemption receives further corroboration from the Gospel of Truth and the Apocalypse of Adam. Sanders concludes "that the three groups—NT Christological hymns, Nag Hammadi texts (especially the Apocalypse of Adam), and the Odes of Solomon—represent a more or less parallel development of concepts infiltrating the various religions of the eastern Mediterranean world around the beginning of the Christian era."[14] The formal matrix from which some of the Odes and the New Testament hymns originated is the Jewish wisdom schools. From these schools come not only the thanksgiving psalms but also the New Testament hymns. Sanders therefore assumes that the New Testament hymns were originally thanksgiving hymns even though the standard thanksgiving formula is not used in connection with the hymns. The only evidence for this assumption is Col. 1:12–14 which is considered by Sanders as an introductory thanksgiving to the hymn Col. 1:15–20. But it is questionable if Col. 1:12–15 and 1:15–20 originally belonged together or if they represent two different pieces of tradition.[15] It is surprising that Sanders insists on the thanksgiving character of the hymns and thus on their liturgical *Sitz im Leben* of the early Christian community, since he himself proposes as the matrix of the developing myth the Jewish wisdom schools which displayed a "learned, non-cultic psalmography." The psalms or hymns of these schools were according to S. Mowinckel[16] chiefly instructive and approximated the didactic poem.

However, a more serious methodological question pertains to Sanders's concepts of "progressive hypostatization" and "developing myth." He maintains: ". . . what is virtually the same myth, from the same religious milieu, from the same linguistic (liturgical) context occuring at various times and places as a particular instance of articulation, receives a variety of interpretations and applications from the several New Testament writers."[17] According to Sanders, the christological hymns of the New Testament in their different articulations thus reflect one stage of this developing myth. The trajectory of this myth has its starting point in the Jewish wisdom schools, and the gnostic Nag Hammadi texts reveal a considerably more advanced stage of this trajectory than the New Testament christological hymns do. The hypothesis of a "developing myth" which receives a variety of interpretations appears to be based upon the philosophical understanding that we can reconstruct the "essence" of this myth which unifies all the differences and particularities of its various expressions. Linguistic philosophy has uncovered as mistaken such a craving for unity. Wittgenstein[18] has shown that this desire for unity, the craving for essences, leads us into confusion. Whereas philosophers have traditionally looked for sameness and unity, Wittgenstein looks for differences and multiplicity. Following this linguistic lead it would be appropriate to abandon the conception of "one single myth" or one "developing myth" as the root and basis of all christological hymns, which are only particular articulations of such a basic hymn.

This review of two methodological approaches to the early Christian hymns indicates that the question of the place of these hymns in the development of early Christian christology as well as their relationship to the religious milieu of the time—be it Jewish-Hellenistic wisdom speculation or (Jewish) gnostic theology—still remains open. Neither the category of "progressive hypostatization," nor that of a "basic myth" or a "developing myth," nor that of "religionsgeschictlich parallel" or "background" is adequate to define the theology and milieu of the christological hymns found in the New Testament. A growing consensus, however, appears to be developing that the matrix of these hymns is the Jewish-Hellenistic wisdom speculation. It might therefore prove helpful to analyze recent approaches to the Jewish-Hellenistic wisdom speculation and to gnostic literature in order to gain different categories for a discussion of the christological hymns in the New Testament.

Wisdom Myth and Reflective Mythology

Jewish-Hellenistic wisdom speculation conceives of Wisdom as a heavenly figure. She is preexistent, participates in creation, lives in close union with God, and seeks to dwell among men. Especially striking is the variety of sexual images applied to Wisdom. She is mother, wife, lover and beloved, virgin and bride. As such a heavenly figure Wisdom is described for the first time in Job 20 or Prov. 1–9. The preexistence of Wisdom and her participation in the creation of the world and of man is clearly expressed in the Wisdom songs in Prov. 8:22–31; Job 28:25–27; Ethiopian Enoch 42:1–3; Ecclus. 24:1–12; Wisd. of Sol. 7:21–26. The present hiddenness and inaccessibility of Wisdom for man (Job 28:13) is seen in some works as a consequence of the rejection of Wisdom by man (Ecclus. 1:20–32; Eth. En. 42:1–3; 84:3). This hiddenness is however in the apocalyptic texts projected to the end-time (4 Ezra 419; Syriac Baruch 48:36). But not all Wisdom texts maintain that wisdom is completely withdrawn. According to Ecclus. 24:7ff. and Bar. 3:9; 4:2 (LXX), Wisdom found her "resting place" (*anapausis*) in Israel and Jerusalem; whereas according to Wisd. of Sol. 7:24–27f. (cf. also Ecclus. 6:20–22; 1:10.15) Wisdom dwells with those who seek for her and belong to the righteous and elect ones. The guiding principle of the works of Wisdom is soteriological and is oriented toward creation and men. This concept of Wisdom as a heavenly, preexistent figure is at first glance something strange and enigmatic in Judaism and it cannot be quite harmonized with Jewish theology and thought.

Two major hypotheses have been suggested to explain the concept of Wisdom as a preexistent heavenly figure within Jewish theology: Wisdom as a poetic personification of a divine function or wisdom as a myth in its own right. The first suggests that the notion of personal Wisdom developed as a poetic personification or hypostatization of a divine function.[19] Its parallel developments within Israelite theology would be the progressive hypostatization of the Word, of Truth, or of steadfast Love. Yet Wisdom appears less to be a hypostatization of an abstract concept than a real personal being. Since most of the characterizations and descriptions of Wisdom use the language of myth, Wisdom cannot be explained merely as a metaphorical personification of certain attributes of Yahweh. The recognition of the employment of mythic language has led historians of religion to reject the hypothesis of personification and to suggest that the figure of Wisdom has its explanation in reference to a foreign mythical goddess,[20] e.g., Isthar, Maat, Isis, Aphrodite, Psyche, Demeter, and Kore.

Since a single myth or goddess could not be named as standing behind the Wisdom figure in Jewish writings, a second hypothesis was suggested. It sought to reconstruct an older single myth of Wisdom behind the partial expressions and fragments of the myth which are found in the diverse Wisdom writings. Attempting a reconstruction, Rudolf Bultmann[21] describes the myth of Wisdom as follows: Wisdom is preexistent, was a companion of God before creation, and actively participated in the creation of the world. She seeks a dwelling on earth among men but does this in vain since her message is rejected. She comes to her own possession but men do not receive her. She returns therefore to heaven and remains hidden there. God alone knows the way to her. The hiddenness of Wisdom, however, is not absolute. She reveals herself to the elect, to the friends of God, and to the prophets. This basic wisdom myth can be most clearly seen in the section of Eth. En. 42 where we find a direct reference to the futile descent of heavenly Wisdom and her return to heaven.

The linguistic criticism levelled against Sanders's reconstruction of a basic developing myth applies, in my opinion, also to this attempt to distill a basic wisdom myth from the partial accounts of the figure of Wisdom found in diverse Jewish—Hellenistic and gnostic literature.

In sum, we are faced with two hypotheses concerning the mythical character of Wisdom. Either Wisdom is seen as having her own myth and this myth stands in the background of both Jewish and gnostic speculations about wisdom, or the figure of Wisdom is understood as derived from some authentic mythic deity. In the face of this situation, the methodological distinction between genuine myth and the usage of myth or theological reflection has been suggested. If progress is to be made in this question, then it is necessary to "distinguish more sharply than is customary between mythical material and reflective mythology as a current form of theology."[22] "Reflective mythology" is not a living myth but is rather a form of theology appropriating mythical language, material, and patterns from different myths, and it uses these patterns, motifs, and configurations for its own theological concerns. Such a theology is not interested in reproducing the myth itself or the mythic materials as they stand, but rather in taking up and adapting the various mythical elements to its own theological goal and theoretical concerns.

This methodological distinction has been applied with advantage to wisdom literature, Philo, and gnostic literature. In my opinion it also can and should be applied to the New Testament christological hymns. A glance at how this distinction has been applied to these other bodies of literature can provide insights for an interpretation of the christological hymns.

An analysis of Ecclus. 24:3ff. reveals that the "mixing of motifs" is central to the Wisdom figure. Since this Wisdom figure exists only in a "syncretistic form," Conzelmann[23] asserts that it is "methodologically impossible to look for the ancestry of one goddess, 'Wisdom', and her myth." Instead we must look first for the "goddess with her myth" and then search "for the mythical revision of it" in Jewish-Hellenistic theology. The goddess most widely honored at the time is Isis. She and her myth are suggested as standing behind the wisdom hymn in Ecclus. 24. In short, the text of Ecclus. 24 shows "that personified Wisdom belongs not to a stage of *myth* but rather to *mythology*. Its predecessor is the syncretistic goddess which is most widely known under the name of Isis."[24]

The same distinction between mythic material or myth and "reflective mythology" can also be applied to Prov.

1–9.[25] Here we can observe "reflective mythology" appropriating a living myth, namely that of the Egyptian
goddesses Maat or Isis. Mythic material was added in Prov.
1:22f. and 8:1ff. to an older collection of Jewish wisdom
sayings that had no reference to a mythological figure of
Wisdom. What is the theological reason for such an addition? Such additions arose either to deal with the problem
of theodicy in the post-exilic Jewish wisdom schools or as
a result of missionary and apologetic efforts to offset the
appeal of the Isis cult. In the former case Wisdom was
objectified and separated from men and characterized as a
mythic person whom one must seek but who remains
difficult to find in this world.[26] At the same time the
continuing faith in the wisdom of Yahweh as Lord of
creation and redemption was affirmed by characterizing
wisdom as belonging closely to Yahweh and as being
present in this world. In this context elements were borrowed from the myth of Maat or Isis and adapted to
Jewish theological purposes. The relationship between the
original living myth and the wisdom mythology in Judaism
is therefore not that of "background" or "influence" as it
is usually seen but that of theological reflection which uses
the language and features of myth in the mode of "reflective mythology."

The suggestion that the material from the myth of Isis
was taken over for the sake of combatting the revived Isis
cult finds its support in an analysis of the structure of the
Wisdom of Solomon.[27] The author of the Wisdom of
Solomon apparently patterned his book according to the
structure of the Isis aretalogies. In addition, he used titles
and concepts found in the hellenized Isis cult. In this way
he was able to deal with the craving of men and women in
the Hellenistic age for the unification with God and the
salvation of the soul. Since human reason was inadequate
to direct man's life he turned to mysticism, philosophical
contemplation, and the mystery religions in order to gain
union with a transcendent reality. This religious atmosphere presented a challenge to the believing Jew. The
author of the Wisdom of Solomon wanted to give his

fellow believers an expression of their revealed beliefs that could match the depth of the religious sentiments of the Isis literature and cult. The apologetic and missionary needs of Hellenistic Judaism compel the author of the Wisdom of Solomon to incorporate concepts and materials of the Isis myth and cult into his theological reflection.

Although the complexity of Philo's theology prohibits any summary reference, it is generally agreed that in his wisdom speculation Philo not only uses concepts from the Jewish tradition, Platonism, and Stoicism, but also appropriates elements from the myth of the goddess Isis and her cult.[28] For Philo, God is so transcendent that a qualitative difference exists between him and the world. Man on his own is not able to know God and to transcend his world and to achieve union with God. He needs figures of mediation between himself and God.[29] Such mediatory figures for Philo are Wisdom, the Logos, Moses, and Israel. These mediatory figures of Philo are clearly cosmological figures and exhibit mythological features. Philo can therefore not only interchange the feminine figure of Wisdom with that of the masculine *Logos-Eikon* but can also identify the Logos with the cosmologically conceived figures of Moses, the Patriarchs, or Israel as a corporate entity.[30] Philo introduces such cosmological mediatory figures, whose features he adapts from the Isis-Osiris myth, in order to preserve the majesty of the transcendent God and at the same time to retain the notion that God is working and in touch with the world and the human soul. The mediation between the transcendent God and the created world is the reason why Philo appropriates concepts and materials from the Isis-Osiris cycle for the formulation of his theology. These elements are fused with traditional elements of his Jewish faith to a systematic theology.

The methodological distinction between myth and reflective mythology has also been applied to the analysis of gnostic texts.[31] The following basic features of this mythological material in gnostic texts have been worked out: Sophia who belongs to the Pleroma because of a sexual fault gives birth to a son, the demiurge, without a sexual partner. Her sexual fault or violation is the cause for the cosmic fall. Sophia recognizes her sin, does penance, and is redeemed and exalted back to the heavenly spheres. The guiding principle of this mythological narrative is, as in Jewish wisdom literature, soteriological in character. Sophia and her fate exemplify the true gnostic who through the knowledge of his fall and redemption can himself be set free from his imprisonment in the world and restored to his true divine nature.

The mythic material concerning Sophia is found in different gnostic texts and has parallels and connections with the Wisdom figure in the Wisdom literature of late Judaism. Since the gnostic myth in its basic structure shares common features with the Wisdom figure, its roots are supposed to lie in one basic Jewish wisdom myth. [32] Yet common mythical features do not say anything about a substantive connection since the "gnostic mythology" has different meanings in the different gnostic systems. The question of dependency or background can be answered only after one has defined the kind of dualism that is decisive for the system. This is true of both the different gnostic texts and the different historical-religious "parallels." Although there exist mythical elements common to both Jewish Wisdom mythology and to the gnostic mythology, these elements have a different function in their respective theological contexts and these differences are of decisive importance.

The concept of preexistence provides an example illustrating this point. Although it is present in Ecclesiasticus chapter 24, John's Gospel, and gnostic writings, it does function differently in different contexts. In Ecclus. 24 the concept of the preexistence of Wisdom serves to prove the absolute authority of the *Nomos* (Ecclus. 24:23). In John 1:1 (17:5, 24) the concept of the preexistence exemplifies the intimate relationship between the Son and the Father. In gnostic writings the preexistence of a heavenly being is the beginning of a series of events that lead to the origin of evil. The mythological feature of the descent of Wisdom is here transformed into a cosmic fall and catastrophe. Thus a comparison of parallels in terminology and motifs does not lead to a specific result as long as their theological context is overlooked since the same motifs and mythologoumena function differently and are interpreted differently in distinct theological systems.

The concept of a "basic Wisdom myth" which underlies the different accounts in Jewish, Jewish-Hellenistic, and gnostic literature does not appear to be helpful in defining the function of the different Wisdom motifs that are employed in the various theological texts and systems. The category of a "basic myth," which is reconstructed from the different mythological elements that are found in various theological contexts, does not suffice to provide an understanding of their function and of their meaning in the specific contexts. Such a "basic myth" is a systematic reconstruction and reflects more the concern of the reconstructing scholar than that of the texts. It appears therefore to be a more useful task to conceive the problem not in terms of a "basic myth" but to distinguish living myth from "reflective mythology." As recent research indicates there existed in Jewish-Hellenistic and gnostic thought a trajectory[33] not of a single wisdom or redeemer myth or a trajectory of a developing myth but that of "reflective mythology" which uses the language and concepts of myth for theological reasons. Such theological reasons are the post-exilic community's problem of theodicy and its missionary interests in the face of the renewed Isis cult, Philo's concern for the transcendence of God, or the gnostic's longing for salvation. The mythological elements found in these writings should not be reduced to one basic myth but should be seen in their different functions within distinct theological contexts.

The Christological Hymns of the New Testament

In the first two sections of this essay I have sought to demonstrate that the categories used in the form-critical and *religionsgeschichtlich* discussions of the New Testament christological hymns are inadequate. Static categories such as the distinction between Jewish-Hellenistic parallels, background or influence, or the construction of a basic myth or a single developing myth are neither appropriate to define the Christian communities in which these hymns originated nor to describe their relationship to their *religionsgeschichtlich* milieu. The theological question behind these methodological deliberations is: Why do these hymns speak about Jesus in mythological language? This question cannot be answered by opting for a basic wisdom myth within Jewish-Hellenistic theology or by positing the anthropos-redeemer myth of gnostic religion or by reconstructing a "developing myth." This question can be answered only if we recognize that there already existed in Hellenistic Judaism a trajectory of "reflective mythology" or a theology employing mythical materials and concepts. This trajectory originated in the theology of the post-exilic wisdom schools and moved through Hellenistic Judaism and Gnosticism. As a trajectory of "reflective mythology" it appears to have borrowed primarily from the myth of Isis-Osiris though it could have also taken over elements from the myth of Tammuz-Adonis. The New Testament christological hymns have their place on the curve of such a trajectory.

The conjunction of this wisdom trajectory with the New Testament christological hymns appears to have been prepared by Philonic theology where the feminine figure of Wisdom had already been identified with that of the masculine Logos. Philo also had already identified the Logos with historical figures such as Moses, Isaac, or Israel. Moses is depicted as having been exalted from his death and having been enthroned as a god and as ruler over the cosmos. Philo, however, transforms the cosmological mythology derived from the Isis-Osiris cycle into psychological realities. The Logos as priest and king of the cosmos becomes the priest of the soul. The historical figures of Moses or Isaac are transformed into archetypes or virtues. The history of Israel becomes a psychological paradigm. [34]

In contrast to the Philonic transformation of cosmological elements of the Isis-Osiris myth into psychological realities, the New Testament christological hymns evidence a great interest in the motif of cosmic, worldwide rulership. The exaltation and enthronement of Jesus Christ to universal kingship is clearly the climax of the hymnic proclamation in 1 Tim. 3:16. The chiastic form[35] of this hymn is defined by spatial patterns: heaven-earth, spirit-flesh. The hymn proclaims in spatial patterns the epiphany, enthronement, and acclamation of Jesus Christ as a universal saving event.[36] The worldwide nature and universality of the salvation in Jesus Christ is also stressed in Heb. 1:3; 1 Pet. 3:22; Col. 1:15–20, and Phil. 2:6–11. Through his exaltation and enthronement Jesus Christ has received his supreme rulership over the whole cosmos, over heavenly and earthly powers. He is the *kyrios* (Phil. 2:11).[37] The *kyrios* title is found as a title in Hellenistic religions.[38] The gods of these religions were the lords of their communities but they proved their power in cosmic dimensions. For instance, Isis is called "rerum naturae parens, elementorum omnium domina" (Apuleius, *Metamorphoses* 11.5), and has the titles "regina manium" (11.5) and "regina coeli" (11.2). Isis is praised in the prayer of Lucius: "Te superi colunt, observant inferi, tu . . . regis mundum, calcas Tartarum" (11.25). According to F. C. Grant,[39] Isis virtually took the place of all the other gods and goddesses and she claimed that their names and functions were only names and various titles and functions of her own. Like Isis, Jesus Christ is in the hymn Phil. 2:6–11 given a name which is "above all names" and venerated by those "in the heavens and on earth and beneath the earth." The allusion to Isa. 45:23 does not speak against this. Whereas in Isa. 45:23 "every knee and tongue" refers to all men, in Phil. 2:6–11 the *proskynein* is rendered by all powers in the cosmos.[40] Furthermore: As Isis's true name is "Isis the queen" (*kyria*, sometimes *kyrios*), so the true name of Jesus Christ is lord (*kyrios*).

This proclamation of the universal lordship of Jesus

Christ is addressed to people of the Hellenistic world who believed that the world is ruled by merciless powers and above all by blind fate or destiny.[41] The desires and longings of the Hellenistic person are concentrated upon the liberation from the cosmological powers of this world and upon participation in the upper, divine world. In this religious milieu the Christians proclaim Jesus Christ as the ruler over the principalities and powers that have previously dominated the world. Just as the Jewish-Hellenistic wisdom speculation appropriated elements from the Isis myth and cult, so too does the Christian proclamation of the cosmic lordship of Jesus Christ borrow its language and categories from the Hellenistic religions, perhaps from Isis myth and cult.[42] In this milieu where the hymns and aretalogies of Isis are found the Christian community conceives hymns in praise of Jesus Christ as the preexistent one who appeared on earth and is now exalted and enthroned as lord of the whole cosmos. These Christians believe that they are already liberated from the bondage of death and freed from the cosmic powers. They believe that they already participate in the dominion of Jesus Christ.

This proclamation of Jesus Christ as the preexistent one and as the cosmic lord, at first expressed in mythological language, functions in the Christian community as a living myth in its own right and constitutes its own cult.[43] The exaltation and enthronement of Jesus Christ to cosmic sovereignty and reconciliation are the central contents of this myth. The theologoumena about the preexistence and mediatory activity of Jesus Christ in the creation of the world underline his cosmic sovereignty. This myth, however, lives from the knowledge that this preexistent cosmic lord is the same as the Jew Jesus. This knowledge is expressed in the categories of humiliation and incarnation or with reference to the death of Jesus. The mythical features, however, are so strong that these references to the human life of Jesus Christ are in danger of being swallowed up by them, as can be seen in later gnostic writings.

Paul already saw this tendency. Against this tendency of the Christ-myth he emphasized the humanity of Jesus Christ by stressing his death on the cross.[44] Against its implied realized eschatology he maintained the "eschatological reservation." This mythological tendency is also counteracted in the manner in which the New Testament christological hymns are used by Paul and the Deutero-Pauline writers. Their new setting is no longer the hymnic proclamation but the dogmatic argumentation and paraenetic exhortation.[45]

Conclusion

As we have seen, the basic theological question underlying the study of the New Testament christological hymns is: Why do these hymns use mythological language to speak of Jesus Christ who was a historical person? This question can be answered only if we recognize that the christological hymns are part of a trajectory of "reflective mythology" in Hellenistic Judaism and Gnosticism. This trajectory employs the language and elements of various myths or mythologies for the sake of apologetic or missionary purposes. Just as Philo identifies Moses with the preexistent Logos and stresses his exaltation as king and god, so too do the early Christian hymns speak of Jesus Christ in mythological language in order to emphasize his universal importance. Although each christological hymn of the New Testament should be separately analyzed in order to define the theological interest which led to the employment of mythological language, I have attempted to delineate the theological interest that is prevalent in the case of Phil. 2:6–11 and 1 Tim. 3:16. Both hymns are interested in proclaiming the universal and cosmic rulership of Jesus Christ as *the kyrios*. They attempt therefore to show, each in a different way, that Jesus Christ is not only equal but superior to all the gods and lords of the Greco-Roman world and that he is acknowledged as such not only by the Christians but by the whole world. The mythological language which they employ can not be derived from a single basic myth or from a developing redeemer myth. Instead, as in Jewish-Hellenistic wisdom speculation, this mythological language is probably developed in dialogue with various mythic beliefs and thought-contexts of the time. In other words: Neither the background nor the parallels define the theological content and aim of the New Testament christological hymns, but rather the theological interest of these hymns determines the mythological language and material which is appropriated and accentuated.

NOTES

1. The exegetical and theological interest in the New Testament christological hymns is evidenced by the appearance of several monographs in the last ten years (Neufeld, Schille, Kehl, Gabathuler, Martin, Deichgräber, J.T. Sanders, and Wengst), the reprinting of older words on the problem (Seeberg, Lietzmann, Kroll, Norden, Lohmeyer), and not least by the publication of various articles dealing with single hymns and their *religionsgeschichtlich* milieu (Bultmann, Käsemann, Haenchen, Schnackenburg, Schweizer, Bornkamm, Jeremias, Georgi, Robinson, Strecker, Feuillet, J.A. Sanders, and Stenger). For a discussion of the literature cf. also the short review of M. Rese, "Formeln und Lieder im Neuen Testament. Einige notwendige Anmerkungen," *Verkündigung und Forschung. Neues Testament* 2 (1970), pp. 75–95.

2. Some authors add Col. 2:13–15; 1 Pet. 2:21ff. or Ign. Eph. 19:2f. The studies of J. Kroll, *Die christliche Hymnodik bis zu Klemens von Alexandreia* (repr. Darmstadt, Wissenschaftliche Buchgesellschaft, 1968), and E. Norden, *Agnostos Theos* (repr. Darmstadt, Wissenschaftliche Buchgesellschaft, 1956) are still basic for the form-critical discussion.

3. R. Deichgräber, *Gotteshymnus und Christushymnus in der frühen Christenheit. Untersuchungen zu Form, Sprache und Stil der frühchristlichen Hymnen*, SUNT, no. 5 (Göttingen, 1967), p. 120: "Nun interessieren im Zusammenhang unserer Aufgabenstellung in

erster Linie die form- und stilgeschichtlichen Probleme unseres Textes. . . ."

4. K. Wengst, *Christologische Formeln und Lieder des Urchristentums,* SUNT, no. 7 (Gütersloh, 1972).

5. Ibid., pp. 179, 208.

6. Ibid., pp. 164f.

7. J. T. Sanders, *The New Testament Christological Hymns: Their Historical Religious Background,* SNTS Monograph Series, no. 15 (Cambridge Eng., 1971).

8. Ibid., p. 24.

9. Ibid., pp. 24f.

10. Ibid., p. 25.

11. D. Georgi, "Der vorpaulinische Hymnus Phil 2:6–11," in *Zeit und Geschichte,* Dankesgabe an Rudolf Bultmann zum 80. Geburtstag (Tübingen, 1964), pp. 263–293.

12. Sanders, *Christological Hymns,* p. 269.

13. Ibid., p. 120.

14. Ibid., p. 132.

15. Cf. the discussion of the literature by E. Lohse, *Colossians and Philemon* (Philadelphia, 1971), pp. 41–61.

16. S. Mowinckel, "Psalms and Wisdom," in *Wisdom in Israel and in the Ancient Near East,* Supplement to Vetus Testamentum, no. 3 (Leiden, 1955), pp. 205–225.

17. Sanders, *Christological Hymns,* p. 141.

18. L. Wittgenstein, *Philosophical Investigations* (New York, 1968), 34ef.

19. L. Dürr, *Die Wertung des göttlichen Wortes im Alten Testament und im Antiken Orient,* Mitteilungen der vorderasiatisch-ägyptischen Gesellschaft XLII.1 (Leipzig, 1938), p. 51, maintains that the hypostatization of the Word has been found mostly in hymns and prayers. H. Ringgren, *Word and Wisdom: Studies in the Hypostatization of Divine Qualities and Functions in the Ancient Near East* (Lund, 1947), uses Dürr's work very extensively, but does not limit his study to Israel. He suggests "that the general idea of a goddess has influenced the shaping of personal Wisdom, whether it be from a Hellenistic Isis religion, from an Astarte influenced by Isis, or from a general Semitic Ishtar-Astarte" (p. 147).

20. For a survey see G. Fohrer, and U. Wilckens, "*Sophia,*" *TDNT* VII, 465ff. and 489ff., and U. Wilckens, *Weisheit und Torheit,* BHTh, no. 26 (Tübingen, 1959), pp. 193ff.

21. R. Bultmann, "Der religionsgeschichtliche Hintergrund des

Prologs zum Johannes-Evangelium," in ΕΥΧΑΡΙΣΤΗΡΙΟΝ, Festschrift für Hermann Gunkel, FRL, no. 36 (Göttingen, 1923), II, 10.
22. Cf. H. Conzelmann, "The Mother of Wisdom," in J. M. Robinson, ed., *The Future of Our Religious Past*, Essays in Honor of R. Bultmann (New York, 1971), pp. 230–243.
23. Ibid., pp. 232f.
24. Ibid., p. 243.
25. C. Kayatz, *Studien zu Proverbien 1–9*, WMANT 22 (Neukirchen, 1966); R. N. Whybray, *Wisdom in Proverbs*, SBT, no. 45 (London, 1965).
26. B. L. Mack, *Logos und Sophia. Untersuchungen zur Weisheitstheologie im Hellenistischen Judentum*, SUNT, no. 10 (Göttingen, 1973), pp. 106f.
27. J. M. Reese, *Hellenistic Influence on the Book of Wisdom and Its Consequences*, AB, no. 41 (Rome, 1970), pp. 33–50.
28. Cf. C. Colpe, "Philo," *RGG* V. 343ff. H. Feldman, *Scholarship on Philo and Josephus (1937–1962)* (New York, 1963), and H. L. Goodhart and E. R. Goodenough, "General Bibliography of Philo," in E. R. Goodenough, *The Politics of Philo Judaeus* (New Haven, 1938), pp. 127–318.
29. Cf. H. Hegermann, *Die Vorstellungen von Schöpfungsmittler im Hellenistischen Judentum and Urchristentum*, TU 82, (Berlin, 1961).
30. Mack, *Logos und Sophia*, pp. 158–161, and H. Windish, *Die göttliche Weisheit*, pp. 227–229, point out that the concept of Messiah is tied closely to the concept of Sophia in the later psalms and in the apocalyptic literature.
31. L. Schottroff, *Der Glaubende und die feindliche Welt; Beobachtungen zum gnostischen Dualismus und seiner Bedeutung für Paulus und das Johannesevangelium*, WMANT 37 (Neukirchen-Vluyn 1970).
32. Wilckens, *Weisheit und Torheit*, pp. 160–196.
33. For the category "trajectory" cf. J.M. Robinson, "The Dismantling and Reassembling of the Categories of New Testament Scholarship," in J.M. Robinson and H. Koester, *Trajectories through Early Christianity* (Philadelphia, 1971), pp. 8–14.
34. Mack, *Logos und Sophia*, p. 195.
35. Cf. E. Schweizer, "Two New Testament Creeds Compared," in *Neotestamentica. Deutsche und Englische Aufsätze 1951–1963* (Zürich, 1963), p. 126; W. Stenger, "Der Christushymnus in 1 Tim. 3:16," *TTZ* 78 (1969), 35f.

36. Schweizer, pp. 125–127.

37. Cf. for the *kyrios*-acclamation see Wengst, *Christologische Formeln,* pp. 131–135. An extensive review of the literature on Phil. 2:6–11 is given by R.P. Martin, *Carmen Christi: Philippians II.5–11 in Recent Interpretation and in the Setting of Early Christian Worship,* SNTS Monograph Series, no. 4 (Cambridge, Eng., 1967), pp. 63–95.

38. Cf. W. Bousset, *Kyrios Christos* (Nashville, 1970) pp. 138–147.

39. F.C. Grant, *Hellenistic Religions: The Age of Syncretism* (Indianapolis, 1953), pp. 128ff.

40. E. Käsemann, "Kritische Analyse von Phil 2, 6–11," in *Exegetische Versuche und Besinnungen* (Göttingen, 1960), I, 85–90.

41. Cf. K. Prümm, *Religionsgeschichtliches Handbuch für den Raum der altchristlichen Umwelt* (Rome, 1943), p. 436ff.

42. Cf. M. Dibelius, "Die Isisweihe bei Apuleius und verwandte Initiationsriten," in, *Botschaft und Geschichte* (Tübingen, 1956) II, 30–79; Wengst, *Christologische Formeln,* p. 134.

43. Cf. Bousset, *Kyrios,* p. 136.

44. This is especially evident in the phrase "even death on a cross" of Phil. 2:8, which is according to most exegetes a Pauline addition.

45. Deichgräber, *Gotteshymnus,* pp. 188–196.

3: Hellenistic-Jewish Wisdom Speculation and Paul

Birger A. Pearson

IT IS WIDELY RECOGNIZED THAT PAUL, IN PROVIDING A conceptual framework for the Christian faith as he taught it in his missionary activity, appropriated concepts and literary forms developed in the wisdom schools of Hellenistic Judaism. But Paul's method of using the traditions of Hellenistic-Jewish wisdom, and his own attitude toward the speculative theology of his Jewish and Christian contemporaries, are a matter of on-going discussion and debate.

In this essay I want to take up for brief discussion the views of Hans Conzelmann regarding Paul as a teacher of wisdom,[1] and then to explore in some exegetical detail the only passage in Paul's letters which deals in a systematic way with the theme of "wisdom," viz. 1 Cor. 1:10–4:21. On this basis some conclusions can be drawn with regard to Paul's method in dealing with speculative wisdom traditions and the theological stance reflected in his arguments.

Paul as a Teacher of "Wisdom"

In discussing the role of Paul as a "wisdom teacher" it is essential at the outset to deal with Hans Conzelmann's seminal article "Paulus und die Weisheit." In this article Conzelmann claims to detect an organized school-operation behind Paul's use of traditional "wisdom." He notices that one cannot find any direct literary appropriation of Jewish wisdom in the Pauline letters. What one discovers, instead, is a reworking of wisdom theology and wisdom traditions, a fact which suggests the existence of a "school."[2] What is involved in Paul's letters, according to Conzelmann, is an active encounter on the part of Paul (and his pupils) with Christian tradition as well as Jewish tradition, and to understand him one must posit a school operation organized by Paul wherein "wisdom" was methodically taught and discussed. The existence of such a school fits very well into what we know of Paul's missionary activity, Conzelmann says, for Paul did not constantly move from place to place but established centers of operation. The location of Paul's "wisdom school" was probably Ephesus, he suggests, referring to Acts 19:9. Paul is thus the founder of Christendom's first school of theology.

Conzelmann very cogently accounts for the existence of the Deutero-Pauline letters as products of Paul's school, which presumably continued in operation after the apostle's death. These documents especially reflect the style of a school operation (p. 234). In my view this is the strongest part of his argument. More relevant to the point at issue here, though, is the question that Conzelmann raises as to products of this school-activity in Paul's genuine letters. As criteria for isolating these units in the epistles Conzelmann suggests the occurrence of unusual concepts and expressions which do not fit well into the total context of the letter, or passages which literarily do not fit the context.[3] Conzelmann discusses several passages which he suggests are products of the Pauline school in which Hellenistic-Jewish wisdom was approximated and reworked: 2 Cor. 3:7–18 (p. 235f.); 1 Cor. 1:18ff. (pp. 236–238); 1 Cor. 2:6ff. (pp. 238–240); 1 Cor. 10:1ff. (p. 240); 1 Cor. 11:2ff. (p. 240); 1 Cor. 13 (p. 241f.); Rom. 1:18ff. (p. 243f.)

Conzelmann's suggestion concerning a "school of Paul" is I think interesting and cogent, especially insofar as it provides a plausible context for the continuation of Pauline tradition in the post-apostolic period out of which the Deutero-Pauline letters emanate. As to the possibility of seeing a "school" at work behind certain passages of Paul's own letters, this will have to be judged on the basis of a detailed analysis. And for this purpose there is no better place to begin than the one place in Paul's correspondence where he deals at all systematically with the term *sophia*, in the opening section of 1 Corinthians. Although Conzelmann isolates two passages from this section, 1 Cor. 1: 18ff. and 2:6ff., as products of the school of Paul, it is advisable to see these passages in the larger context of the entire section, 1:10–4:21.

Paul and "Wisdom": 1 Cor. 1:10–4:21

Within this section the first reference to "wisdom" is at 1:17, in the last sentence of the opening *parakalō* passage dealing with the Corinthian factionalism; the last occurrence is at 3:19, in the midst of a passage dealing with Paul's position as apostle in the Corinthian church, a passage which in its turn closes with a second *parakalō* in which Paul as the Corinthians' sole "father" urges them to become "imitators" of him. The material bound by the first and last occurrences of the term *sophia* has been taken as a "homily" in genre, whose main theme is the judgment of God against all human wisdom.[4] However it is also important to observe that this theme is intimately bound up with the problem of the Corinthians' community strife and, most importantly, with their "declaration of independence" from Paul, items to which the opening and closing *parakalō* passages are especially directed.[5] The entire passage, 1:10–4:21, constitutes, therefore, an *apologia* in which Paul defends his apostolic authority against his opponents.

The elaborate discussion of "wisdom" precisely in this context, especially the way in which this discussion is constructed, shows that it was a major concern of the Corinthian Christians. It also shows that Paul was considered by them to be somewhat deficient in this aspect of his ministry among them, that he had held out on them (cf. 3:1ff.) or, worse yet, that other teachers were better qualified as teachers of "wisdom" than he (e.g. Apollos). It is apparent from Paul's argumentation in 4:3–5 that he is the subject of considerable criticism. It is also interesting to see how Paul expresses his relationship to Apollos in 3:5–4:5.[6] On the one hand he wants to underscore his sense of collegiality with Apollos, but on the other hand he makes it clear that he, Paul, is after all the one who "laid the foundation" for the Corinthian church (3:10). He even holds out the possibility that that which has been subsequently "built upon" (ibid.) may not only be silver and gold but also wood and straw, the latter to be burnt away in the Day of Judgment! And, in the final analysis, no matter how many "pedagogues" the Corinthians might have they still have but one father, Paul.[7] Indeed, he will not shrink from using the "rod" against them if need be (4:21).

In directing his remarks to the Corinthian cultivation of "wisdom" Paul sees that not only his own apostolic authority is being undermined in Corinth, but also the very heart of the Christian message itself. In their concern for "wisdom" the Corinthians were neglecting the centrality or even the relevance of the cross of Christ, as is clear from 1:17 ("that the cross of Christ be emptied of its power"). Paul's initial attack against "human wisdom" or "worldly wisdom"—as though he were up against mere philosophers or rhetoricians—does not yet indicate the scope or the claims of the Corinthian "wisdom."[8] The dismissal of Corinthian *sophia* as "worldly" must be seen as part of Paul's own polemical rhetoric, for it is clear from 3:1ff. that some of the Corinthians were claiming to be a spiritual elite and living on a level of eschatological realization

(4:8). This much can be said of the opponents' position even without recourse to the controversial passage, 2:6ff., a passage to which we must return.

The combination of a claim to an elitist "wisdom" coupled with a claim to be (already) "reigning" is reminiscent of the Stoic conception of the ideal wise man as a type of "king."[9] But it is most probable that we should see operative in the background of Paul's discussion the Hellenistic-Jewish conception of the sage as one who is treading the "royal way" of wisdom, whose goal is "companionship with the bountiful God" (Philo, *Migr.* 28).[10] Involved in this conception of the "royal way" of wisdom is, according to some scholars, a type of "wisdom mystery" analogous to the Isis mystery as experienced by Apuleius (*Metamorphoses* 11).[11]

The "wisdom" document entitled *The Teachings of Silvanus,* which is part of the Coptic library from Nag Hammadi (*Cairensis Gnosticus* VII,4),[12] contains a number of sayings which illustrate the idea of kingship by virtue of the possession of "wisdom":

> If it is good to rule over the visible things, as you see it, how much better is it for you rather to rule over everything, since you are great above every group and every people, and exalted in every respect, (possessed of) divine reason (or "speech," *logos*). [87:33–88:4] Clothe yourself with wisdom (*sophia*) as a garment, and put understanding (*epistēmē*) upon yourself as a crown; sit upon a throne of perception (*aisthēsis*). For these things are yours; [and] you will receive them again above. [89:20–26]

As W. Schoedel has observed elsewhere in this volume, Silvanus represents a Christianized form of Hellenistic-Jewish wisdom speculation.[13]

From other sections of 1 Corinthians outside of the passage under consideration, the Corinthian Christians were enthusiastic devotees of "freedom" (6:12; 10:23), cultivated ecstasy (chapters 12–14), and rejected the doctrine of resurrection in favor of a doctrine of immortality

(chapter 15). All of this complements what we know from
the opening chapters and provides us with a basis for
referring to the Corinthian spirituality as a kind of "wisdom mysticism."[14]

Paul sees the wisdom claims of the Corinthians resulting
in the "emptying" of the cross of Christ, and in "boasting"
(Paul's word for "hybris") as a style of life, accompanied
by strife amongst the brethren and overweening independence vis-a-vis the apostle himself. Paul attacks their position by asserting the judgment of God over all forms of
human wisdom (1:18ff.), and by showing them with biting
irony that the wisdom of God revealed through himself is
unfortunately beyond their ken thus far, judging from
their behavior in the congregation (2:6—3:4). It is crucial
for an understanding of Paul's argument to notice his
heavy use of irony. It should also be observed, however,
that Paul's arguments are themselves based largely on conceptions and traditions at home in the Jewish schools of
wisdom,[15] whether of the Hellenistic Diaspora or of Palestine, and especially apocalyptic conceptions of various
sorts.[16] The use of scripture, especially of prophetic literature, is especially noticeable. The traditional "wisdom"
conception that God alone is wise and the source of all
wisdom[17] is very prominent in 1:18ff., and this is coupled
with a theme derived from the prophetic writings of Scripture that human wisdom stands under the judgment of
God.[18] Paul's arguments in chapters 1—2 bear a considerable resemblance, taken as a whole, to Bar. 3:9—4:4, a
passage which has been interpreted as a homily composed
for reading on the Jewish fast day, the ninth of Ab.[19] The
Haphtorah text for that day is Jer. 8:13—9:24, and it is to
be noted that Jer. 9:23 (22 LXX) is quoted by Paul in
1:31. In Bar. 3:9f. it is stated that God has hidden Wisdom
from the "rulers of the nations" (3:16) and the mighty,
but has given it in the form of his Torah to Israel, his elect.
Paul uses a similar tradition—he probably knows the Baruch passage—but for him the "Wisdom of God" is not
Torah, but Christ crucified (1:23f., 30).[20] This Wisdom of

God stands over and against all forms of human wisdom and self-assertion.

In developing the theme of God's judgment against human wisdom Paul has recourse to a number of prophetic passages in scripture containing critiques of court wisdom or scribal wisdom. The point is made very forcefully in 1:19 with a quotation from Isa. 29:14 (but *athetēsō* possibly comes from Ps. 32:10 LXX), followed by an allusion to Isa. 19:11 and 44:25 in 1:20, a quotation from Jer. 9:22 in 1:30, and a quotation from Isa. 40:13 in 2:16. The theme is recapitulated in 3:19ff. with quotations from Job 5:12f. and Ps. 94:11. It is possible that Paul was using a Jewish *florilegium* of scripture quotations warning against Greek wisdom.[21] In expositing this theme Paul also utilizes the standard apocalyptic dualism, "this-age/age-to-come," categorizing all human wisdom as "wisdom of this age" (or of "the world") or of the "rulers of this age" (1:20; 2:6, 8; 3:18f.). For Paul, all who belong to "this age," adhering to the standards of the world, are "perishing" (1:18; cf. 2 Cor. 2:15; 4:3) together with their wisdom (1:19).

Also distinctly reflected in 1:18ff. is the ancient and ubiquitous Jewish tradition that God humbles the high and mighty and exalts the lowly (cf. e.g. the "Song of Hannah," 1 Sam. 2:7ff.; the "Magnificat," Luke 1:51ff.), a theme that is especially developed in apocalyptic literature (e.g. 1 Enoch, *passim*). Concomitant with this theme is the idea that God hides himself and his wisdom from the wise (i.e. the "worldly-wise") and offers revelation to "babes," a typically apocalyptic conception given classic expression in the dominical Thanksgiving saying in Matt. 11:25, "I thank thee, Father, Lord of heaven and earth, that thou hast hidden these things from the wise and understanding and revealed them to babes"[22] (RSV). This apocalyptic reversal of values is given expression especially in the paradoxical contrast between "wisdom" and "folly," a contrast that pervades the entire passage. For Paul, God's wisdom=folly to the world; worldly wisdom="folly" before

God. The essential point that Paul makes is that the cross of Christ—which Paul sets up as the keystone of Christian faith—is "folly" to men who belong to this perishing world, for God in his wisdom has so ordained it (1:21),[23] but is wisdom, power, and righteousness for those who are being saved (1:30).

As the argument develops Paul seems to disclaim "wisdom" for himself, and that is a special problem in view of what is subsequently said in 2:6ff. Paul makes a statement of his apostolic policy of preaching in 1:23: "We proclaim Christ crucified," which, to be sure, is equated with the "wisdom of God" in the next verse (the "we" certainly referring to Paul himself). But then, in a statement pertaining to his personal experience in Corinth, he disclaims the use of "lofty words of wisdom" (2:1), "persuasiveness of wisdom" (2:4 $\pi\epsilon\iota\theta o\hat{\iota}\varsigma$ $\sigma o\phi\iota\alpha\varsigma$)[24] and "wisdom of men" (2:5). What he disclaims, actually, is only a certain type of "wisdom": high-flown rhetoric and, especially, anything that would smack of human wisdom instead of divine, anything that might be grounds for "boasting." Thus there is no essential contradiction between 1:18ff. and 2:6ff. Up until 2:6ff. Paul deals generally with "human wisdom" as contrasted with divine, pointedly suggesting that the Corinthians' cultivation of wisdom belongs in the former category. Why he suggests this is an important point, but can be discovered only with reference to his further remarks in 2:6ff., wherein something of the Corinthian "wisdom" teaching can be discerned.

In 2:6ff. a striking shift in language takes place, a phenomenon which has occasioned considerable debate amongst scholars. R. Bultmann's argument that Paul here is reflecting the position of his opponents has had a lively influence in the discussion,[25] and has been carried to great lengths by U. Wilckens, according to whom the Corinthian opponents of Paul are gnostics whose theology Paul here borrows in order to combat it.[26] Lührmann has modified this approach somewhat, suggesting that Paul in 1 Cor. 2:6ff. is taking over a piece of his opponents' esoteric

preaching and emending it, mainly by means of additions,
to make it conform to his own theology.[27] But now
Conzelmann suggests that the dramatic shift in language in
2:6ff. can be accounted for with reference to the use of
school material from the Pauline school. He claims that
this passage does not fit the context, nor is it polemically
directed.[28]

In my view this passage fits its context and situation
very well indeed, and it, together with the whole passage
(1:10–4:21), is assuredly polemically oriented. The shift in
language is due to Paul's use at this point of certain key
expressions taken from the terminology of his opponents.
Since they, as a "spiritual" elite, deal in esoteric "wisdom," Paul will now adopt the same mode of speech; but
in so doing he does not—contrary to Bultmann and Wilckens—capitulate to his opponents' position. In the course
of his argument he allows us a glimpse of the opponents'
theology, but he speaks of a wisdom which turns out to be
nothing other than the "wisdom of God" that he had
referred to earlier, the wisdom of God's salvific plan centering in the cross of Christ!

Throughout the passage, with the possible exception of
v. 12 (a parenthetical expression), the "we" is Paul himself.[29] There is in this respect a parallel in structure to be
observed between 2:6– 3:1 and 1:23–2:1: *"But we* [i.e., I,
Paul, in my apostolic office] preach Christ crucified . . . *and
I, brethren,* when I came to you . . ." (1:23–2:1). *"But we*
[i.e., I, Paul, in my capacity as an apostle)] speak wisdom
amongst the mature . . . *and I, brethren,* was not able to
speak to you as to spiritual men . . ." (2:6–3:1).[30] The
implication here in 1 Cor. 2:6ff. is that Paul is just as
capable of speaking in an esoteric fashion as anyone in
Corinth, and indeed as their apostle and the special recipient of revelation is the only one really qualified to do so!
For he has the "mind of Christ" (2:16, cf. Isa. 40:13) and
is, therefore, not subject to the criticism of the Corinthians
(2:15, cf. 4:3 and 9:3).[31]

We are reminded in this connection of such other pas-

sages in Paul's correspondence as 2 Cor. 11:18ff., where he
says that if his opponents can boast of their credentials he
can do the same only more so, and Phil. 3:3: "if anyone
else thinks he has ground for confidence in the flesh, I do
even more so . . ." (his *curriculum vitae* follows!).[32]

In 1 Cor. 2:6ff. Paul uses his opponents' terminology at
key points in his discourse, but turns it back against them.
Thus his opponents' terminology remains—enabling us to
reconstruct something of their arguments on the basis of a
history-of-religious analysis—but the essence and content
of the "wisdom" here discussed is Paul's own. In this
passage the terms *teleios* (v.6, opp. *nēpios*) and *pneumatikos* (v. 15, opp. *psychikos*) relfect the usage and self-
understanding of the opponents. Their claim to "perfection" and "spirituality" was doubtless based on their
achievement of "wisdom," a wisdom which evidently put
them in touch with the "glory" of the exalted Christ, the
"Lord of glory" (v.8), and consisted of heavenly things
"which eye has not seen, nor ear heard, nor has occurred
to the heart of man" (v. 9).

The *teleios-nēpios* terminology which Paul wrests from
his opponents[33] was derived by them from the usage of
Hellenistic-Jewish wisdom speculation, of which Philo is the
best representative.[34]   For Philo *teleios* is one who has
achieved the highest religious attainments, especially "wisdom." The metaphor is that of "adulthood" over against
"infancy": Those who have achieved "wisdom" have ar-
rived at a higher plane of existence, in contrast to the
"babes" who still need to be fed a milk diet (e.g., *Migr.* 28
ff.). The "solid food" of wisdom is for the *teleioi* who live
according to the propensities of the "mind" or "spirit"
within them, the heavenly nature given to Adam in creation (cf. *Leg. Al.* 1.90ff; *Agr.* 8 ff.). Translating this usage
to the situation of the Corinthian church it is easy to
imagine that Paul's emphasis on the cross of Christ would
have been regarded as, at best, part of the "milk" given to
"babes" but certainly outgrown by "mature," "spiritual"
persons.

Closely related to the *teleios-nēpios* terminology is the

contrast *pneumatikos-psychikos,* also arising out of Hellenistic Jewish wisdom speculation, specifically a tradition of scripture-exegesis. I have shown elsewhere[35] that the standard Hellenistic anthropology which divides the soul of man into a lower soul and a higher soul (usually called *nous*)[36] is taken over in Hellenistic Judaism and is read out of Genesis 2.7 (LXX): καὶ ἔπλασεν ὁ Θεὸς τὸν ἄνθρωπον χοῦν ἀπὸ τῆς γῆς καὶ ἐνεφύσησεν εἰς τὸ πρόσωπον αὐτοῦ πνοὴν [sometimes read πνεῦμα as in Philo, *Leg. Al.* 3.161; cf. Josephus *Ant.* 1.34] ζωῆς, καὶ ἐγένετο ὁ ἄνθρωπος εἰς ψυχὴν ζῶσαν. Thus man is a trichotomy of body from earth, a vital principle (*psychē*) that he shares with the animals, and a "spirit" (*pneuma*) which is derived from God's "inbreathing" in creation. The *pneuma,* in Hellenistic Judaism, comes to be equated with the *nous* or "higher soul" of commonplace Hellenistic anthropology, and is understood to be immortal due to its heavenly origin.

The *pneuma-psychē* contrast, derived from this exegesis of Gen. 2:7, is the basis for the contrast of adjectives *pneumatikos-psychikos* used in 1 Corinthians, chapters 2 and 15 (and nowhere else in Paul's writings).[37] In 1 Corinthians, chapter 15, it is clear (especially in 15:44–49) that Paul is arguing against a doctrine of immortality, and the exegesis of Gen. 2:7 is at the center of the controversy.[38] The same complex of ideas lies in the background of the discussion in chapter 2. In addition to the affirmation of man's immortality, i.e., that of his "mind" or "spirit," Hellenistic Jewish exegesis of Gen. 2:7 taught that the very possibility of knowing God and appropriating his wisdom is resident in man himself by virtue of the created "inbreathing."

Two Philonic texts will illustrate this doctrine. In *Det.* 86 Philo uses scriptural exegesis to express a Greek philosophical commonplace regarding man's "mind":[39]

> Let us, therefore, the pupils of Moses, no longer be in doubt as to how man has attained a conception of the invisible God. For Moses himself learned the means by a divine oracle and has communicated it to us, putting it

thus. The Creator prepared for the body no soul sufficient of itself to perceive its Maker, but considering
that it would be of great benefit for his creature if he
could attain a conception of the One who made him—
since this is the determining factor in achieving happiness and blessedness—breathed into him from above of
his own divinity.

In what follows Philo explains that this is why so small a
thing as the mind of man has room for the whole of the
universe in its conceptions, for it is a "fragment" of the
Deity (*Det.* 90). The crucial scripture text, for Philo, is
Gen. 2:7, the "oracle" to which he refers in the passage
quoted above.[40]

Again, Philo (*Leg. Al.* 1.36) interprets the word ἐνεφύσησεν in Gen. 2:7 as involving three things: τὸ ἐμπνέον,
τὸ δεχόμενον, and τὸ ἐμπνεόμενον:

That which inbreathes is God, that which receives is the
mind (*nous*), that which is inbreathed is the spirit (*pneuma*). What, therefore, follows from these premises?
There comes to be a union (*henōsis*) of the three, as God
extends the power from himself through the mediating
spirit until it reaches the subject. And for what purpose,
except that we might receive a conception of him? For
how could the soul have thought of God, if he had not
inbreathed it and grasped it with power?

Thus, for Philo, man has within him, breathed into him
by God, the capacity for knowing God and the higher
truths of the universe. This ability does not belong to
man's natural soul (*psyche*) but is given him by God in
creation by virtue of the divine spirit breathed into man.
Thus man's higher soul, his "mind" or "spirit," enables
him to rise above the level of his earthly and sense-
perceptive soul and to receive impressions from the heavenly
sphere. Cultivation of the higher self by means of "wisdom" results in man's becoming *teleios* (*Agr.* 8 and *Leg.
Al.* 1.94, noted above). In this arena of Hellenistic-Jewish
wisdom speculation, presupposed as the background of the
theology of the Corinthian opponents of Paul, possession
of "wisdom" is a form of self-realization.

Thus for the Corinthian devotees of wisdom, the basis of man's ability to receive the divine wisdom is his own pneumatic nature given him in creation (Gen. 2:7). In 1 Cor. 2:13b–14 Paul utilizes the Corinthians' language, with its principle of "like known by like" and its distinction between pneumatic and psychic natures, but radically re-interprets it. For Paul the "spiritual" man is the one who walks according to the Spirit of God, whose gifts he has received from God (2:12; cf. Romans, chapter 8) apart from any created potentiality in himself.[41] The gift of the Spirit is a gift of free grace, and is an eschatological event. The "psychic" man, for Paul, is the one who has only natural possibilities apart from the eschatological gift of the Spirit, and cannot attain to "the things of the Spirit of God" by virtue of anything within himself. To such a man, who has not received the Spirit, the things of the Spirit are "foolishness" (2:14).[42] Paul thus affirms the radical break between God and natural man, a break which can be bridged only from God's side, by his love and by his decisive act in Christ. Any kind of mysticism which dissolves the gulf between the heavenly world and the earthly is absolutely excluded in Paul's theology.

For Paul the term *pneuma* is understood in apocalyptic fashion (as is the case also with the term *sophia*). The Spirit is the divine eschatological gift which has been poured out among the elect of the last times. In no case can it be said—in Paul's view of the matter—that man has a divine or "spiritual" element within him. This Paul explicitly denies in 2:11, where he distinguishes between the "spirit of men" (with its ability to know "the things of man,") and the Spirit of God who alone has natural knowledge of "the things of God." The supernatural and eschatological gift of the Spirit God gives to whom he will, frequently to the "fools" and "base-born" of this world (1:27–29). He who has received this gift can be proleptically referred to as *pneumatikos*,[43] though man's full attainment of the "spiritual" existence is yet to be realized in the future, in the resurrection from the dead (1 Cor. 15:45ff.).

For Paul the gift of the Spirit of God has consequences not only for the "spirit" of man, or for the elated experiences he can have (1 Cor. 12–14), but for his entire existence now in the historical present, especially his conduct in the body. So Paul stresses that the Christian's *sōma*, not only his *nous*, is the "temple" of the Spirit of God (6:20).[44] He states in a passage heavy with irony that his opponents in Corinth evidently cannot be called "perfect" or "spiritual" because their conduct in the community is dominated by jealousy and strife, a sign that they are still "babes," still fleshly (3:1, 3).[45]

It has been determined that Paul, in Corinthians 2:6ff., has skillfully used the language of his opponents against them, reinterpreting their categories in a direction suited to his own apocalyptically-oriented theology. It yet remains, however, to establish what the nature of the Corinthian "wisdom" was, and Paul's evaluation of it. Having perceived that in Hellenistic-Jewish wisdom speculation (especially Philo) the use of such terms as *teleios* and *sophia* involves a kind of mystical orientation that certainly goes beyond any conventional philosophical usage, and having suggested that such a background fits the situation in Corinth, we still have to inquire how their specifically *Christian* "wisdom" fits into such a framework and what the nature of this "wisdom" might have been. To this point, as was suggested above, the phrase "Lord of glory" (2:8) and the reference to heavenly things in 2:9 may provide some clues.

The exaltation christology which must be presupposed in the christological title, "Lord of glory" (a title used in Jewish literature to refer to God),[46] has its most important New Testament witness in the pre-Pauline hymn in Phil. 2:5–11. However, the error of the Corinthians, from Paul's point of view, would not have been in christology itself—with which he is in basic agreement—but the conclusions they were drawing from it vis-a-vis their own self-understanding: they were applying the exalted state of Christ to themselves, considering that they were "already reigning" with Christ (cf. 4:8), and in possession of such things as "eye has not seen, nor ear heard, nor has occurred to the heart of man."

Paul, for his part, means to apply to the life of the community a criterion other than the "glory" of the exalted Lord, namely his *cross,* which the Corinthian "wisdom" was "emptying" (1:17) of its salvatory force. Indeed Paul even goes so far as to suggest that true "wisdom" is, in fact, nothing else than an understanding of the cross, the center of the Christian kerygma.

Paul's arguments in 1 Cor. 2:6–8 reflect a Jewish apocalyptic background,[47] and a preaching form developed in the primitive church: "once, but now" (here: once hidden, but now revealed).[48] Paul understands the crucifixion of Christ to be the center of a "mystery" belonging to God's redemptive plan (his "wisdom"). This plan none of the "rulers of this age" knew, for if they had known this mysterious "wisdom" they would not have crucified the "Lord of glory," thus bringing defeat upon themselves and opening the way of salvation to God's elect.

The "rulers of this age" are demonic powers, understood by Paul as standing behind the human, political rulers of the world.[49] Paul does *not* say that the "rulers" did not recognize the Lord of glory and therefore crucified him.[50] The *hēn* in 2:8 clearly precludes this, for the relative pronoun refers not to the "Lord of glory"[51] but to the hidden plan of God by which the "Lord of glory" was to be crucified in order thereby to defeat the demonic powers and redeem the elect. According to Paul, the "rulers" crucified the "Lord of glory" knowing full well who he was; what they did not know was God's redemptive plan.

Paul has thus taken an enthusiastic christological affirmation of his opponents, "Lord of glory," and has emphasized that the decisive point is his crucifixion. The implication of this for the Christian life in the present is that the cross of Christ is the decisive factor now, and the glory— the experience of heavenly verities (2:9)—is promised for the future (cf. 1 Cor. 15:43; Phil. 3:21; Rom. 5:2; 8:18; etc.), prepared for the future possession of "those who love God."[52] Two very different ways of understanding the Christian existence are in evidence here, one characterized by a type of mysticism (the opponents), [53] the other characterized by historical realism and an "eschatological reservation."[54]

One question yet remains: Why does Paul contemptuously refer to the mystical and heaven-oriented "wisdom" of the Corinthians as "human wisdom," "wisdom of this world" (1:20ff.; 2:5; 3:18f.)? The answer to this is that Paul, rightly or wrongly, regards any kind of claim to self-transcendence as a manifestation of human arrogance over against God. But Paul goes even further! He refers to their "wisdom" as that of the (demonic!) "rulers of this age" (2:6), a linguistic hyperbole that would seem to go beyond any kind of logic one can think of (though we must remember the apocalyptic reversal of values that Paul reflects in the whole passage). Paul perceives that the Corinthians were attempting to side-step the cross, thinking to attain to "glory" without reference to the salutary power of the cross and without being willing to apply its criterion to their life in the present. That Paul would regard this as "demonic" is easily understood when it is recalled that the Lord himself, when Peter attempted to turn him away from the cross, rebuked him with the chilling words, "Get behind me, Satan! For you are thinking the thoughts of men rather than of God!"[55]

Conclusion

The following conclusions are suggested by the foregoing discussion:

1. Paul's argument from 1:10 to 4:21, including 2:6ff., is to be understood as an integral unit, polemically directed. Conzelmann's view that "school traditions" have been inserted by Paul at 2:6ff. cannot be maintained. But

Paul reveals himself in the total passage as a master of the use of "traditions," even those that are foreign to his own theological orientation, as in 2:6ff. In that case he turns his opponents' language and "traditions" back against them.

2. The passage studied reflects a high level of theological discussion in the Corinthian church. Paul's arguments provide hints that Apollos was the one who introduced the Corinthians to their "wisdom" speculations,[56] including the Hellenistic-Jewish traditions of scriptural exegesis which we have noted. We may thus speak of a "school of Apollos" in Corinth.

3. Though Paul probably did have a "school of theology" as part of his operations in Ephesus (whence 1 Corinthians was sent), it is clear that Paul does not regard himself primarily as a "sage" or a "teacher," but especially as an *apostle,* as the special recipient of revelation which he is to mediate to the Gentiles (Gal. 1:12, 15, with allusion to the prophetic call of Jeremiah). As such he represents in himself all three of the divine offices given by God to the church (apostles, prophets, and teachers—1 Cor. 12:28), and as the apostolic founder of his churches he is a "father" who will brook no opposition, no theological dissent, from his "children."

4. Though Paul is thoroughly familiar with the traditions, speculations, preaching and teaching styles, etc., of the Hellenistic-Jewish Diaspora, his own theology is *critical* of "Hellenistic-Jewish wisdom speculation." Paul's theology reflects the influence of an apocalyptically-oriented Pharisaism and is at home in the apocalyptic Christianity of the primitive Palestinian church.

NOTES

1. H. Conzelmann, "Paulus und die Weisheit," *NTS* 12 (1965–66), 231–244; cf. also his commentary, *Der erste Brief an die*

Korinther (Göttingen, 1969), soon to appear in English in the Hermeneia series (hereafter it is referred to as Conzelmann's commentary). For another important perspective on the relationship between Paul and Hellenistic-Jewish wisdom, see D. Georgi, *Die Geschichte der Kollekte des Paulus für Jerusalem*, Theologische Forschungen no. 38 (Hamburg, 1965), pp. 66ff.

2. *NTS* 12, p. 233. Cf. Georgi's remark: "Paul is our first literary evidence for an encounter between wisdom-schools and Pharisaism, scribal training and Pharisaic piety"—*SBL Proc.* 1 (1972), p. 532.

3. One problem with this—which Conzelmann briefly notes (p. 235, n. 2)—is the possibility of later editorial interpolations. E.g., for a possible interpolation at 1 Thess. 2:13—16, see Pearson, "1 Thessalonians 2:13—16: A Deutero-Pauline Interpolation," *HTR* 64 (1971), 79—94. Of course, the editing of Paul's letters is itself further evidence of an on-going Pauline "school."

4. See W. Wuellner, "Haggadic-Homily Genre in 1 Corinthians 1—3," *JBL* 89 (1970), 199—204. That Paul in his letters frequently reflects the style and forms of synagogue preaching is not surprising. For a discussion of Diaspora synagogue preaching and Paul's relation to it see H. Thyen, *Der Stil der jüdisch-hellenistischen Homilie*, FRL 65 (Göttingen, 1955), esp. pp. 119ff. H. Conzelmann refers to the passage, 1:18—3:23, as a "ring-composition," marked by considerably stylistic skill. See his commentary, p. 53.

5. See esp. N. Dahl, "Paul and the Church at Corinth according to 1 Corinthians 1—4," in *Christian History and Interpretation: Studies Presented to John Knox*, ed. W. Farmer *et al.* (Cambridge, Eng., 1967), pp. 313—335.

6. This was already perceived by F.C. Baur; cf. Dahl's discussion in the aforementioned article, p. 313. For 1 Cor. 1—4 as an apostolic *apologia* cf. also R. Funk, *Language, Hermeneutic, and Word of God* (New York, 1966), pp. 277ff.

7. Paul's claim to "fatherhood" vis-a-vis the Corinthians (4:14f.) may at first glance be related to the Wisdom tradition wherein the wise teacher instructs his pupils as "children" (cf., e.g., "my son" in Prov. 3:11; 6:3; 23:19, 26; 24:21; 27:11; Eccles. 12:12; etc.). But Paul here is speaking not as a "sage" but as the apostolic founder of the Corinthian congregation.

8. Against J. Munck, *Paul and the Salvation of Mankind*, trans. F. Clarke (Richmond, 1959), pp. 148ff.; also R. Scroggs, "Paul: Σοφός and Πνευματικός," *NTS* 14 (1967—68), 33ff.

9. E.g. *SVF* III, 599, etc. Cf. R. Grant, "The Wisdom of the Corinthians," *The Joy of Study,* Festschrift F.C. Grant, ed. S. Johnson (New York, 1951), pp. 51—55.

10. Cf. *Migr.* 197: σοφὸς βασιλεύς. Many other passages from Philo could be cited; cf. the literature referred to in n. 19.

11. See esp. J. Pascher, ΒΑΣΙΛΙΚΗ ΟΔΟΣ. *Der Königsweg zu Wiedergeburt und Vergottung bei Philon v. Alexandreia,* SGKA 17.3—4 (Paderborn, 1931); E. Goodenough, *By Light, Light: The Mystic Gospel of Hellenistic Judaism* (New Haven, 1935); U. Wilckens, *Weisheit und Torheit. Eine exegetisch=religionsgeschichtliche Untersuchung zu 1 Kor. 1 und 2,* BHTh 26, (Tübingen, 1959), esp. 139ff.; cf. Wilckens, *TDNT* VII, 501.

12. For publication plans see J.M. Robinson, "The Coptic Gnostic Library," *NT* 12 (1970), 81—85. I am using here a trascription prepared by M. Peel of the publication team at work on the Nag Hammadi texts, a project of the Institute for Antiquity and Christianity of the Claremont Graduate School, J.M. Robinson, Director.

13. *Silvanus* is a non-gnostic—at places even anti-gnostic— document. Schoedel's argument that it represents a bridge between the Hellenistic-Jewish wisdom of Alexandria and the Alexandrian Christian fathers is quite convincing.

14. It is common nowadays to refer to the Corinthians as "gnostics." The chief proponents of this view are U. Wilckens, *Weisheit und Torheit* and W. Schmithals, *Gnosticism in Corinth,* trans. J. Steely (Nashville, 1971). I have dealt with their views in *The πνευμα-τικός-ψυχικός Terminology in 1 Corinthians. A Study in the Theology of the Corinthian Opponents of Paul and Its Relation to Gnosticism,* SBL Dissertation Series, no. 12 (Missoula, Mont., 1973).

15. This point is emphasized by Conzelmann, *NTS* 12, 234ff. Cf. also his commentary, p. 21. Cf. as well Wilckens, *Weisheit und Torheit,* esp. pp. 21ff.

16. The relationship between "wisdom" and "apocalyptic" is clearly established already with reference to the book of Daniel. See especially G. von Rad, *Wisdom in Israel* (Nashville, 1972), esp. pp. 263ff.

17. E.g., Tob. 12:13, Ecclus. 1:8, Dan. 2:20 LXX; 9:7 LXX; Wisd. of Sol. 9:9; cf. Conzelmann, *NTS* 12, 236.

18. See W. Wuellner, *JBL* 89 (1970).

19. See E. Peterson, "1 Korinther 1,18f. und die Thematik des jüdischen Busstages," *Frühkirche, Judentum und Gnosis* (Rome,

1959), pp. 43–50. Wisd. of Sol. 9:9–18 has also been seen in the background; see R. Scroggs, *NTS* 14, 48ff., referring especially to 1 Cor. 2.6ff.

20. Cf. Rom. 10:6ff. where Paul interprets Deut. 30:12–14 in terms of the Jewish wisdom tradition which identifies Wisdom with Torah (cf. Bar. 3:29f.) but again equates Wisdom with Christ. On this passage see esp. M.J. Suggs, " 'The Word is Near You': Romans 10:6–10 within the Purpose of the Letter," in *Christian History and Interpretation,* ed. Farmer *et al.,* pp. 289–312.

21. L. Cerfaux, "Vestiges d'un florilège dans 1 Cor. 1:18–3:24?" *Revue d'histoire ecclésiastique* 27 (1931), 521–534; cf. also Conzelmann's commentary, p. 57 and 59. For a fine discussion of the humiliation-exaltation theme and its relation to the development of Jewish doctrines of immortality and resurrection see G. Nickelsburg, Jr., *Resurrection, Immortality and Eternal Life in Intertestamental Judaism,* Harvard Theological Studies, no. 26 (Cambridge, Mass., 1972).

22. It is probable that Paul had this saying in mind in 1 Cor. 1:18–21. Cf. M.J. Suggs, *Wisdom, Christology, and Law in Matthew's Gospel* (Cambridge, Mass., 1970), p. 83. Cf. also J.M. Robinson, "Kerygma and History in the New Testament," in Robinson and H. Koester, *Trajectories through Early Christianity* (Philadelphia, 1971), p. 42.

23. This is my interpretation of the crux, ἐν τῇ σοφίᾳ τοῦ θ εοῦ, in this verse. God has ordained that man should not come to know God by his own wisdom, but by *faith* in the preaching of the cross. For other interpretations of this passage, cf. Conzelmann's commentary, pp. 60ff. For an analogous use of the phrase "in the wisdom of God," see 1 QS IV, 18b: "And God in the mysteries of his understanding and in his holy wisdom has provided an end to the existence of falsehood" (my trans., text ed. E. Lohse, *Die Texte aus Qumran* [Darmstadt, 1964], p. 14).

24. I prefer the minority reading πειθ οἱ σοφίας. Cf. G. Zuntz, *The Text of the Epistles* (London, 1953), pp. 23ff.

25. See "Karl Barth, *The Resurrection of the Dead"* [1926], *Faith and Understanding,* vol. 1, ed. R. Funk (New York, 1969), 66–94, esp. 68ff.

26. *Weisheit und Torheit.* For good criticisms see R. Scroggs, *NTS* 14, 33ff., and especially R. Funk, *Language, Hermeneutic, and Word of God,* pp. 277ff.

27. *Das Offenbarungsverständnis bei Paulus und in paulinischen*

Gemeinden, WMANT 16 (Neukirchen, 1965). For a critique of his position see Pearson, *The πνευματικός-ψυχικός Terminology,* chap. 4.

28. *NTS* 12, 238ff.; and his commentary, pp. 74ff.

29. Conzelmann misses this point altogether, as do Wilckens, Lührmann, and Bultmann.

30. Paul's use of the first person plural to refer to himself (usually in his capacity as apostle) is well known and frequent in his letters. See Stauffer's discussion in *TDNT* II, 356ff. A striking example, showing conclusively Paul's use of the plural with reference to himself, is 1 Thess. 2:18.

31. This connection between 2:15 and 4:3 establishes very clearly that 2:6ff. is an integral part of the argument in 1:10–4:21.

32. Cf. also 1 Cor. 14–18; 15:9f.; the latter passage is the basis for the Deutero-Pauline 1 Tim. 1:15f. Paul must have been one of the world's greatest masters of one-up-manship!

33. In Paul's own theology *teleiotēs* belongs to God (Rom. 12:2) and will belong to man only in the eschatological future (1 Cor. 13:10), having not yet been achieved even by Paul himself (Phil. 3:12). Outside of this passage in 1 Corinthians Paul nowhere makes a distinction between *teleioi,* capable of higher wisdom, and *nēpioi,* able to receive only elementary instruction. Heb. 5:14 reflects a provenance similar to that of Paul's Corinthian opponents.

34. The larger context of this usage is Hellenistic philosophical paraenesis, especially that of Stoicism, as shown long ago by J. Weiss, *Der Erste Korintherbrief* (Göttingen, 1910), p. 74.

35. See *The πνευματικός-ψυχικός Terminology,* chap. 2. To the material discussed there add the Hellenistic-Jewish texts in the *Teachings of Silvanus* referred to above (esp. 92:11ff.).

36. This doctrine, which amongst the Greeks is possibly of Orphic derivation, widely held amongst philosophers from Plato on; cf., e.g., *Timaeus* 69cd. (It should be remembered, too, that Plato's *Timaeus* ultimately came to function in Hellenistic philosophy as a Greek "book of Genesis," upon which numerous commentaries were written. Philo's *De opificio mundi* doubtless relies upon Hellenistic commentaries on the *Timaeus*). For an interesting discussion of the Hellenistic anthropology relating to the soul see, e.g., E.R. Goodenough, "The Divided Self in Greco-Roman Religion," chap. 2 in his book, *The Psychology of Religious Experiences* (New York, 1965), pp. 30–63.

37. Hence the likelihood that the use of this terminology arises in the context of Paul's discussion with his Corinthian congregation.

38. A number of Hellenistic-Jewish texts, especially from Philo, are referred to in connection with the background out of which the arguments of Paul's opponents derive (Philo, *Her.* 231; *Op.* 135; *Leg. Al.* 3:161; *Som.* 1:34; *Her.* 55ff.; *Spec. Leg.* 4:123; *Det.* 80; *Plant.* 18; *Wisd. of Sol.* 2:1–5, 23; 15:11). Paul for his part, reflects a Palestinian interpretation of Gen. 2:7 which relates this text to the promise of a future resurrection (Genesis Rabba 14.5; 2 Macc. 7:23).

39. This idea, according to Dörrie, goes back to Parmenides, and his equation of being and thinking. See H. Dörrie, "Emanation. Ein unphilosophisches Wort im spätantiken Denken," in *Parusia. Studien zur Philosophie Platons und zur Problemgeschichte des Platonismus, Festschrift J. Hirschberger* (Frankfurt, 1965), p. 132, n. 43.

40. In *Det.* 80ff. Philo had solved the apparent contradiction in Moses concerning the soul, that it is "blood" (Lev. 17:11) and that it is "spirit" (Gen. 2:7) with a discussion concerning the duality of the soul. Man's higher soul, his "rational" element, is a divine creation whose roots are in heaven (with a play on Plato, *Timaeus* 90A). Cf. also *Plant.* 17.

41. Paul is actually referring in v. 15 to himself, primarily, as a paradigm of the *pneumatikos* man.

42. Paul's own expression; cf. 1:18, 21, 23, 25, 27; 3:18f.; 4:10.

43. Cf. Paul's references to the eschatological gift of the Spirit as an *arrabon*, 2 Cor. 1:22; 5:5; retained in the Deutero-Pauline Eph. 1:14.

44. Philo in *Virt.* 188 refers to man's *logismos* or *nous* as the "temple" of God and of his Wisdom.

45. Cf. Gal. 5:20, where strife and jealousy occur side by side in a list of the "works of the flesh." It is clear that for Paul *sarkikos* and *psychikos* mean the same thing, and that *sarkikos* is Paul's own term; cf. also Funk, *Language, Hermeneutic, and Word of God*, p. 296.

46. E.g. 1 En. 22:14; 25:3; 27:3,5; 36:4; 40:3; 63:2; 83:8. It is used elsewhere in the NT as a christological title only in James 2:1.

47. On the Jewish apocalyptic background of Paul's use of μυστήριον and σοφία see, e.g., A. Fridrichsen, "Gnosis. Et Bidrag till Belvsning av den paulinske Terminologie og Erkjennelsesteori," in *Religionshistoriska Studier Tillägnade Edvard Lehmann* (Lund, 1927), pp. 85–109, esp. p. 92. On the term μυστήριον see especially

R. Brown, *The Semitic Background of the Term "Mystery" in the New Testament,* Facet Books, Biblical Series 21 (Philadelphia, 1968).

48. Cf. R. Bultmann, *Theology of the New Testament,* vol. 1, pp. 105f.; N. Dahl, "Formgeschichtliche Beobachtungen zur Christusverkundigung in der Gemeindepredigt," in W. Eltester, ed., *Neutestamentliche Studien für Rudolf Bultmann, ZNW* 21 (Berlin, 1954), pp. 3–9.

49. The Jewish-apocalyptic background of the phrase "the rulers of this age" has been thoroughly discussed by M. Dibelius, *Die Geisterwelt im Glauben des Paulus* (Göttingen, 1909), pp. 90ff. For further background material from Qumran see D. Flusser, "The Dead Sea Sect and Pre-Pauline Christianity," *Scripta Hierosolymitana* 218ff. 4 (1972).

50. Cf. *Ascension of Isaiah* 11:19; *Epistula Apostolorum* 13.

51. Against Wilckens, *Weisheit und Torheit,* pp. 71ff. He equates the "Lord of glory" with a personified Sophia. See the criticism of Funk, *Language, Hermeneutic, and Word of God,* pp. 292, 295, who stresses that what is hidden from the powers and from the "uninitiated" is the mystery of the cross.

52. Paul emphasized the last part of the citation, "what God has prepared for those that love him." Cf. the *Gospel of Thomas* 17, where the last part of the quotation is missing. The use of this apocryphal saying in Thomas—there attributed to Jesus—and by Paul's opponents is probably similar.

53. The position of the opponents reconstructed here can be taken as a kind of mysticism according to the criteria set forth, e.g., by G. van der Leeuw, *Religion in Essence and Manifestation* (London, 1938, reprint New York, 1963), pp. 493ff.: the break-down of the barriers between the self and the external world in a kind of self-transcendence, involving a theory of knowledge which can be summed up in the principle "like by like" and a mystic practice, which in the case of the Corinthians would involve their cultivation of "wisdom" and of ecstasy (1 Cor. 12–14).

54. The apt expression "eschatological reservation" to characterize the apocalyptically oriented theology of Paul is used by E. Käsemann, "On the Subject of Primitive Christian Apocalyptic," chap. 5 of his *New Testament Questions of Today* (Philadelphia, 1969), p. 128; cf. J.M. Robinson, *Trajectories,* p. 31.

55. Cf. in this connection the fear of Ignatius lest the "ruler of

this age" tempt him away from his martyrdom (Ignatius, *Romans* 7.1).

56. So also, with reservations, C.K. Barrett, *A Commentary on the First Epistle to the Corinthians* (New York, 1968), p. 43. Cf. the tantalizing description of Apollos given in Acts 18:24ff (and the D reading in v. 25).

4: The Transformation of Wisdom in the World of Midrash

Henry A. Fischel

I

IF AN APPROPRIATE SUBTITLE WERE TO BE GIVEN TO THIS chapter it might be either "The Impact of Greco-Roman Rhetoric on Rabbinic Literature" or "The Westernization of Midrash." Only a few decades ago such titles would have aroused heavy if not emotional opposition among many scholars. In recent years, however, it has become quite acceptable to treat Palestinian Jewry and with it earlier rabbinic civilization as a sector of the partly hellenized world.[1] It is of course true that wide areas of midrashic wisdom are indigenous and perhaps unaffected by Greco-Roman culture, yet much of the area we wish to treat here, Midrash on *ḥokhmah* and *ḥakhamim,* seems to have developed in contact with the West[2] and represents a synthesis of indigenous and Western materials.

"Eastern" or indigenous would in the context of this chapter refer not only to a possible continuation or reuse of biblical and apocryphal wisdom situations in Midrash but also to certain new developments, among them novel observations on biblical texts, new evaluations and explorations of wisdom, the interpretation of biblical history under its aspect, and some (but not all) demonstrations of its part in creation, revelation, and redemption. All these

67

appear frequently without any perceptible traces of Greco-Roman culture.

II

1. The theme of wisdom is prominently represented in the tannaitic liturgy, one of the characteristic creations of the piety of this age. The very first of the petitions of the *'Amidah*[3] asks for *de'ah*, *binah* and *haskel*, discernment, understanding and reasoning, all near-synonyms of wisdom. The Sephardic version, indeed, has *hokhmah:*

> You bestow on man discernment in grace
> And teach the mortal one understanding.
> [And][4] grace us from (before) you (with) wisdom,
>   understanding and discernment.
> Praised are you, O Lord, in grace bestowing
>   discernment.

"How great are your works, in wisdom you have made them all" (Ps. 104:24) in the morning prayer and "in wisdom you open the gates" in the evening prayer, both preceding the *Shema'*, refer again to divine wisdom.[5] The second in a litany of morning benedictions, following that of the ritual hand washing, refers to the Deity "who created man in wisdom."[6]

2. The tannaitic prayer, however, is by no means totally indigenous. Unfortunately, the comparative study of it has been sadly neglected. Elias Bickerman alone has made the bold attempt of analyzing the *'Amidah* (which, indeed, has a minimum of biblical allusions) as a variant of the Greek civic prayer. Regrettably, his initiative has not been taken up by others.[7] Yet the importance of Hellenistic piety and prayer, especially those of the *sophos* class, is inestimable. One only has to think of Alexander's Prayer, Aristotle's *On Prayer*, Cleanthes' *Hymn to Zeus*, and Cicero's prayer-hymn to Philosophy, *Tusculan Disputations* 5.5, to gauge their exemplary character.

In the tannaitic morning liturgy the well-known three-fold thanksgiving, on being not a "barbarian," not a slave, and not a woman,[8] has long been suspect of stemming from other Sage cultures, possibly Eastern, but more likely Western, since a very similar version circulated in Greece, known as the Prayer of Thales, or Socrates, or Plato.[9]

3. The liturgy of the Eve of Passover, the Seder, which developed into a ritual of the home in the Hellenistic period, had adopted important aspects of the symposium and the sympotic literature of the Greco-Roman Sages, as Siegfried Stein has demonstrated. In the Seder the place and function of such genuinely Jewish prayers as the *Kiddush* and the *Hallel* must be seen against the background of comparable items in the Greco-Roman symposium; and the *Nishmath,* besides, shows traces of the rhetorical *logos basilikos.*[10]

In the instance of the *baraitha* of the four sons of the Passover Haggadah the problem of the precise origin, character, and purpose of a possibly wisdom-related item is particularly vexing: "Vis-à-vis four (types of) sons the Torah makes (its) statement (Exod. 13:14 or Deut. 6:20–24): one wise (*hakham*), one wicked, one innocent, and one unable to ask. . . ."[11] Whereas David Daube is inclined to assume a Hellenistic pattern on the grounds of the fourfold division, Siegfried Stein points out its closeness to a Philonic typology of children.[12] Fred O. Francis, on the other hand, traces the wording, structure, and setting of this item to biblical and apocryphal wisdom literature but agrees with Louis Finkelstein's suggestion that the passage witnesses to the encounter of Judaism with Hellenism.[13] Typologies of this kind, however, including the antithesis Sage/Fool and the connection of morality and wisdom, are as common in, for example, Stoic popular philosophy as they are in wisdom literature.[14] It seems to the present writer that this typology originated in and is patterned after one of the popular activities during the Western symposium: the *eikazein,* i.e., the characterization of those present by entertaining comparisons with animals, special people, or historical and mythological personalities and their various properties.[15]

4. Finally, the mysterious macarismus of Shime'on b. Zoma (*fl. c.* 110 C.E.), *barukh ḥakham ha-razim*, "praised be the 'Discerner of Secrets,' "[16] understood in the amoraic context as referring to the Deity, may be a descendant of Cicero's formula *investigat occulta, Tusculan Disputations* 1.25.61f., said in praise of the inventor. B. Zoma's subsequent "Blessed be Who created all these to serve me," may represent Seneca's *"veneror itaque inventa sapientiae inventoresque, . . . mihi laborata sunt. . . ."* "I venerate therefore the inventions of wisdom and the inventors, . . . (all) these have labored for me" (*Epistles* 64.7). Even the benedictory formula "blessed" is found in Plutarch's *Moralia, de esu carnium* 1.2, "O blessed ones and god-beloved," all four items, Greek, Latin, and Hebrew alike, dealing extensively and in similar fashion with the progress of civilization and the ensuing division of labor.[17] This rabbinic passage can easily be mistaken for an indigenous creation and a continuation of earlier wisdom situations. It is, rather, a modified standard *topos* of Greco-Roman rhetoric.

III

1. Some indigenous wisdom-related material may have been created in reaction to the Greco-Roman environment. Thus, the well-known teaching that wisdom is identical with Torah[18] frequently includes the belief that wisdom-Torah is a vital instrument of survival for the individual as well as the collective (cf. Eccles. 7:12),[19] an interpretation which is perhaps not independent of the tragic historical events in the Roman period.[20]

Disappointment with the world and its ways is, furthermore, reflected in statements which demonstrate that (human) wisdom may make for increased anger, sorrow, and suffering in the world, in contradistinction to divine wisdom,[21] and that subtlety, craftiness, even destructiveness entered the world through wisdom.[22] There are qualities higher than wisdom, such as devotion, piety, obedience, fear of Heaven, mercy, repentance.[23] Only as an "inheritance," i.e., a tradition, is wisdom positive.[24] True wisdom is Halakhah and its practice rather than secular skills, poetic inspiration,[25] or even morality and speculation.[26] The Messiah will teach final wisdom;[27] even the Torah is an incomplete form of heavenly wisdom.[28]

2. Undoubtedly, these contrasts, limitations, and distinctions amount to a comparative devaluation of wisdom, a phenomenon that is best explained by the impact the Greco-Roman civilization made on the Eastern world through its challenging technology, science, art, and administration, i.e., a dominant and domineering type of wisdom. This becomes evident in midrashic statements which frankly admit that *ḥokhmah* is with all the nations[29] or that theirs is superior.[30] Even Haman is some sort of hakham.[31] Yet "Should someone tell you that there is wisdom among the nations, believe it (Obad. 8), but if he tells you there is Torah among the nations, do not believe it."[32] Israel's Torah is here seen as a unique spiritual or divine phenomenon and contrasted with worldly wisdom of whatever type.

IV

1. Other midrashic wisdom materials which at first glance appear to be indigenous reveal their Western affinities only through detailed comparative analysis.

Thus, Shime'on b. Azzai, a contemporary and companion of b. Zoma, seems to be squarely within Eastern wisdom tradition in his often repeated warning "Run to a light precept [as to a weighty one] and flee from transgression. . . ."[33] The imperatives "choose" and "flee," and occasionally "run," however, are quite common in the ethic of both Epicureans and Stoics. The Hebrew pair of

imperatives has no precise biblical precedents and involves
the mishnaic style, i.e., composite verbal form with auxil-
iary verb: *hawe raṣ* [*hawe*] *boreaḥ* [variant: *beraḥ*]. The
antithetical title of Epicurus' lost work *On Choices and
Avoidances (Flights), peri haireseōn kai phugōn,* is typical
of this sort of Western wisdom.[34] The diatribe and the
rhetorical epistle likewise use such imperatives.[35] Cicero,
Tusculan Disputations 5.24.68, states clearly that it is the
specific task of the *sapiens* to engage in *discriptione ex-
petendarum fugiendarumque rerum,* paralleling b. Azzai's
sequence and antithesis.

   2. The use of the proverb, one of the characteristic
ingredients of wisdom literature, is another point in question. In rabbinic literature proverbs no longer appear in
extensive collections and as "abstract" raw material for
instruction but rather in isolated instances in the setting of
individual life situations, usually climaxing or introducing
an anecdote, especially in the rabbinic parallels of the
Greco-Roman *chria (exemplum),* the (often burlesque and
cynicizing) Sage anecdote. The proverb appears here as a
spontaneous creation of the Sage at the decisive moment
in the narrative, as its punchline, as it were, or as the
concluding moral. This spontaneous creation of the Sage is
called *sententia* by the critics but is frequently a true
proverb, as also in the fable.[36] Thus Acher, i.e., Elisha b.
Abuyah, a contemporary of b. Zoma and b. Azzai, when
seeing an observant man lose his life over the fulfillment of
a biblical precept, utters the proverbial phrase

>   *Zo Torah we-zo sekharah?*
>   This is Torah and this its recompense?[37]

The *chriae* on Hillel the Elder culminate in proverbs or
proverblike ethical *sententiae.*[38] Frequently, both Sage
ancedote and the concluding proverb are of Western provenance.[39]

   Another use of the isolated proverb occurs in diatribes,
i.e., rhetorical-eristic passages such as the controversy between Cain and Abel "in the field" before the fratricide, as

in all Palestinian Targumim on Gen. 4:8 (and with Philo). The proverbial coinage used in the former is the well-known "there is no Judgment and there is no Judge," reused in many a midrashic passage and talmudic controversy. Again, the skillful employment of the proverb is recommended by Aristotle whose view is followed for centuries in the Greco-Roman *rhetorica,* handbooks, *progymnasmata,* and literary tracts on style and grammar, including Christian works.[40]

3. How well some Western elements have been hidden in the framework of seemingly indigenous wisdom passages is illustrated by the instance of b. Zoma's teaching in *Pirke Aboth* 4.1 (4.1–4 Taylor) which to this day has never been recognized as representing the well-known Stoic paradoxa *([ad]mirabilia, inopinata).* The four rhetorical questions of b. Zoma:

> Who is wise (or: a Sage)?
> Who is mighty (or a strong man)?
> Who is rich? Who is honored?

represent four of the usually three to seven *paradoxa,* i.e., extreme statements on the ethical properties of the Sage for which the Stoics were praised (as well as ridiculed): Only the Sage is strong, rich, kingly, free, sane, honored, etc.[41] The rhetorical question is one of a variety of possible formulations of these propositions[42] which are often enriched by Epicurean and Cynical items. B. Zoma's answers are in line with the pattern: whoever learns from anyone is a Sage (originally Cynical); whoever conquers his impulse is strong; whoever rejoices in his portion is rich; whoever honors others is honored (a variation of an Epicurean belief! *Gnomologium Vaticanum* 32). All propositions are effectively formulated and well structured but the biblical proof texts, whether added later or supplied by b. Zoma himself,[43] distract from the original intent of the pattern.[44] In spite of the partial cleavage between the text and the proof texts the passage represents an intriguing amalgamation of Eastern and Western elements.

4. Even a phenomenon as well established in biblical and apocryphal literature as the hypostatization of wisdom and, rabbinically, of the Torah, is not necessarily a continuation of the biblical situation in the Midrash: it was also a popular and recommended device of Greco-Roman rhetoric. Just as the Torah can speak and address the Israelites so the Sea can address the Athenians (Hermogenes). Other such recommended hypostatizations are poverty, jealousy, envy, strife, and, not to forget, insomnia. Seneca casts Sapientia in the role of speaker in his ninety-fourth and ninety-fifth letters.[45]

5. The explicit or implicit involvement of biblical wisdom in creation (Prov. 3:19f.), revelation,[46] and redemption remains, of course, a major concern of indigenous Midrash on wisdom.[47] Wisdom is involved in the creation of the world, the Tabernacle, the Temple, and the Temple to Come.[48] And although wisdom in the "Land of Israel" is infinitely greater than at any other place, it is acknowledged that wisdom is ubiquitous. It is not impossible, however, that this latter, biblically based belief would have have remained dormant or weak had not the philosophy of the Stoics, spread abroad by the rhetoricians, become very influential in the ancient world and encouraged indigenous beliefs of a similar nature. The Stoic teaching of the all-pervading divine *pneuma*, as *logos*-reason, *nomos*-law, and *physis*-nature, was particularly effective and may have activated the dormant potential of the earlier Eastern position. The instances of rabbinic acquaintance with the teachings of the Stoics are, of course, numerous.[49]

V

1. Perhaps the most frequently misclassified instance of a Western Jewish literary genre as Eastern wisdom are the *Pirke Ab(h)oth.*

There are some strong reasons for reclassification. First and most serious, the *PA* collection does not ascribe the authorship of its materials to one name in the manner of biblical and apocryphal wisdom literature but to a great many. Second, sequels in time do not play a role in biblical wisdom collections of proverbs in contradistinction to *PA*, in the basic chapters of which they are of the essence. Third and finally, the traditional style elements which ancient wisdom literature shared with all biblical poetry have been abandoned, among them the *parallelismus membrorum* and the alphabetic acrostic. Biblical language has given way to mishnaic language.

All these are indications that the literary genre and the purpose of *PA* also differ. There are two recognizable aims in the basic chapters of *PA:* (1) to establish a chain of tradition, i.e., a succession from teacher to student, or tradent to tradent, paralleling the diadochic works of the Greco-Roman world regarding philosophers, jurists, and physicians, i.e., any class of Sages;[50] and (2) to introduce the most important or best known teachings and opinions of these authorities, paralleling the doxographic works of the Greco-Roman world.[51] In fact, this combination of both the diadochic and the doxographic is found in the West. Except for the biographical additions, Diogenes Laertius' *Lives and Sayings of the Eminent Philosophers* is precisely such a type of work, composed reasonably close to the time of the redaction of the Mishnah. *PA* is thus hardly the "New Testament of Judaism," as it has been incongruously called, but rather its Diogenes Laertius.[52]

2. Indeed, it is highly probable that whoever composed the initial chainlike statement of *PA*, the sorite, was aware of the rhetorical uses of the Homeric instance from the *Iliad* 2.102ff. which likewise establishes a *diadoche* of transmission, occasionally omits the direct object (as in AdRN A) and lets the last link of the chain break into speech. This Homeric sorite became the principal model for the use of the sorites in many handbooks of rhetoric from Quintilian to the Middle Ages.[53] It is thus highly probable that the compiler(s) of *PA* were acquainted with diadochic and doxographic models, at the very least

through quotation by orators. Moreover, Greek instruction, Greek science, and diplomatic activity, intermittently carried on at the academies (courts) of the Hillelite dynasty would tend to confirm this conclusion.[54]

VI

1. The demise of the larger literary genres of biblical wisdom literature in mainline Judaism was inevitable vis-à-vis the ascending and soon dominant literary forms of Midrash and talmudic discussion. Late collections of psalms, reformulations of biblical history, patriarchal testaments, apocalypses, and others did not survive long. They had become marginal to the talmudic procedure, non-canonical and non-authoritative, often because of their origin in sectarian groups.

There are, however, larger accumulations within rabbinic works, some of them dealing with wisdom or including wisdom-related materials. The problem of their classification and derivation is still unsolved, as is the principle of their collection: were they recited and enumerated *ad hoc* whenever an evolving talmudic discussion touched upon their principal subject? Or were they part of previously existing collections, oral or written? Or are they later accretions that were added to a suitable keyword in the text of Talmudim and Midrashim? Is their material Eastern or Western, or an amalgamation of both? A brief mention of some of these wisdom-related accumulations must here suffice.

2. A cluster of stories centering around Alexander the Great is thus unmistakably foreign, dealing, as it does, with themes known from the Alexander *bioi* and romances, Cynical *chriae*, and various bits from other sources.[55] Just as in the evaluation of the Cynics, Alexander is also here shown as a fool.[56] The elders, the women, and the Rabbis (!) confronting Alexander appear as Sages, teach him true wisdom, and win a battle of wits over him. *Aporiae* (near-

unanswerable questions) and Stoic *paradoxa* mark some of
this material as Western. The "story of the eyeballs,"
illustrating Prov. 27:20, however, may be indigenous wisdom material.[57]

3. A rather extensive collection of stories is found in
Lam. R. 1:1, Nos. 4–19, illustrating Lam. 1:1b, "great
among the nations." In some fifteen to twenty literary
units (depending on the method of counting) "great(ness)"
is interpreted as referring to the "wisdom," or, more
accurately, acumen, of Israelites. Here quite a few Athenians and some Samaritans lose their battle of wits with
Jerusalemites, but also Jewish Sages are taught a lesson by
a simple woman and even by children. R. Joshua sum-
marizes: "Happy are you, O Israel, for you are all wise
from the oldest to the youngest," No. 19. Question and
answer, the battle of wits, *aporiae,* riddles, and quite a few
oneirocritical items make up the collection. There are
parallels to an Ahikar motif (No. 8), a Diogenes *chria* (No.
7), and the (usually Cynicizing) Prodicus "Fable" (of the
Two Ways, No. 19, second item), all of which appear in
related forms also in the Aesop romance. This collection
needs further exploration.[58]

4. Extensive oneirocritical materials are collected in BT
Berakhoth 55a–57b. From 57a (end) on, the collection
changes almost imperceptibly into a related category, that
of the prognostic meaning of "signs," first in dreams,
thereafter in reality, such as "six things are a good sign
(*siman*) for a sick person: sneezing, perspiration," etc.[59]
Both dream interpretation and the exploration of "signs"—
perhaps "semiotics" would be a servicable term for the
latter discipline—are not totally unrelated to some aspects
of wisdom literature. They play a much more prominent
role, however, in the West where they developed a literature and literary form of their own. An extensive section
of the *Phaenomena* of Aratus, d. 276 B.C.E. (translated by
Varro and Cicero into Latin), represents semiotics, as do
passages of the Hippocratic *Aphorismoi.*[60]

5. The stories centering around the heretic Acher[61]

likewise form an accumulation of considerable length and coherence. They are partly Western, apparently following, consciously or unconsciously, the popular rhetorical biography of Epicurus (and its literary descendant, that of Arcesilaus). These stories do not employ the epithets *ḥakham* or *ḥokhmah* but are the portrayal of a Sage gone astray, an anti-hero.

6. Shorter accumulations will not be treated here, since the likelihood that they are parts of larger wisdom-related genres is still more remote. Among these shorter accumulations, however, there are several which begin uniformly with the stereotype "great is," e.g., "great is repentance," and praise the same virtue or sanctum several times in succession, employing various illustrations or proofs for each statement. Coinages of this type thus constitute the post-talmudic tractate *Perek ha-Shalom,* version A, part of B, and, as the title indicates, all of *Perek "Gadhol ha-Shalom,"* (Tractate "Great is Peace").[62] An example: "Great is Peace, for the Prophets ordained in the mouth(s) of all the creatures (to be) but (one greeting:) 'Peace' " (No. 5).

Are all these collections[63] the harbingers of the later medieval revival of large wisdom genres or the last satellites of the gigantic codification activity—culminating in the second to fourth centuries—by which antiquity stored its valued treasures, from law to philosophy, from folklore to myth, from grammar to science, from dream interpretation to magic? This question remains as yet unanswered.

VII

1. With the apparent demise of the larger ancient wisdom genres new smaller wisdom-related forms emerge in rabbinic literature and these are unmistakably Western. Most represent media by which the West describes the world of the *sophos,* among them *chria, aporia, akousma* (question and answer on ethical dilemmas), the *topos* (the rhetorical and often diatribic treatment of a theme),[64] the

altercatio (the dialoguic clash between Sage and Tyrant [Emperor] or between representatives of two opposite opinions);[65] the parody;[66] new uses of the sorite; the *paradoxon;* metaphorical descriptions of disciples;[67] the *exitus* of Sage or martyr;[68] the sympotic discussion of foods; (pseudo-) Hippocratic description of natural phenomena, and others.

2. Change of form is indicative of some change of content. A number of ethical propositions transmitted by these adapted forms is no longer identical with those of the Hebrew Bible, and others only marginal in Scripture are now emphasized. Among these new values or stresses are endurance, poverty, austerity, lowly toil, strenuous effort, health, and manliness.

3. Through the use of these Western forms and their accompanying ethic the concept of the early talmudic Sage has also become partly Westernized.[69] Although the Midrash still discusses Solomon as well as Job and some others, the true models of wisdom are now the Tannaim and Proto-Tannaim, especially Hillel the Elder, to a lesser degree Eli'ezer b. Hyrcanus, Joshua b. Hananiah, R. Meir, and R. Akiba. Their anecdotal portrait now resembles that of the Greco-Roman sage, in particular Socrates, Antisthenes, Diogenes, and Crates (all Cynics or Cynicized in much of rhetorical tradition, especially in the *chria*), the Stoics Zeno and Cleanthes (often listed as Cynics in Greco-Roman *diadochai*), Aristippus (a Cynic to Philo), and Pericles and Cato Minor Uticenses, all prominent in Western rhetoric and rhetorical literature. Most of the philosopher-Sages are founders of new schools or new movements within these schools. This may be true, too, of their Hebrew counterparts.

VIII

It is no wonder then that many early rabbinic treatments of wisdom are inspired by the West.

1. Contemporary discussants prefer to start with the

item by Hoshaya (Palestine, *c.* 225 C.E.) or Judah b. Ilai
(*c.* 150 C.E.) in *Genesis Rabba* 1.1 and its parallels.[70] We
are told to read (the still unvocalized) biblical text of Prov.
8:30 ("And I [wisdom] was with Him [the Lord], a
nursling,") as *'u/omman,* "craftsman" or "artist" (cf. Song
of Sol. 7:2) instead of the later masoretic *'amon,*
nursling, darling, ward, *Schosskind,* or Buber's *"Pflegling."*
The Midrash elaborates:

> The Torah says: I was the tool of God's craftsmanship.
> According to human custom, when a king of flesh and
> blood builds a palace, he does not build it by his own
> skill ("mind") but by the skill ("mind") of a craftsman.
> And the craftsman does not build it out of his imagina-
> tion ("mind") but (with the aid of) drafts and de-
> signs. . . . Thus God was looking at the Torah while
> creating the world. [Theodor-Albeck I, p. 2]

Precisely the complexity of the Midrash with its mixture
of similes for the aids of creation (tool, craftsman, craftsmanship, mind) betrays the interference of patterns. It is
not necessarily Plato's *Timaeus* 27f. (cf. Philo's *de opificio
mundi* 15–25), although the Platonic passage employs all
the decisive ingredients: "looks at pattern," "craftsman
(Demiurge)," "created," "looked at what is eternal," and
"copy." It is equally likely that rhetorical descendants of
the passage inspired the midrashic instance.

The suggestion that a naive native type of "Platonism"
may have existed in earlier Hebrew wisdom literature
which included preexistence and eternal forms[71] is, at
best, relevant only in part. If such a belief, indeed, existed,
it would have remained dormant had not Greco-Roman
fashion made it relevant again.[72]

2. Another wisdom-related teaching in the Midrash
seems to have been reinforced, if not provoked, by Stoic
doctrine. The wisdom of evil (or in evil) is mentioned in
the Midrash in connection with noxious and superfluous
animals which, although seemingly a mere nuisance, became nevertheless the agents of divine missions during the

Ten Plagues and are, in general, part of the "overall plan of creation."[73] Vermin and creeping things which God does faithfully maintain remind Him to have mercy, even more so, with man. Moreover, fly, bedbug, serpent, snail, and lizard have medicinal uses.[74]

Beside the "sceptics" of the Middle (Platonic) Academy it was above all the Epicureans who had singled out the noxious animals in one of their famous and forceful arguments against the belief in divine providence.[75] Their traditional opponents, the Stoics, had equally forcefully and repeatedly demonstrated the existence of *pronoia* regarding these self-same animals. Chrysippus, apparently the originator of the teaching of the providential usefulness of animals to man, thus had maintained that, for example, bedbugs do not let man indulge in too much sleep and "usefully" awaken him; mice warn him not to let things lie around in disorderly fashion;[76] and even "panthers, bears and lions" are "a school for training in bravery."[77]

Similarly, Seneca's proof for the teleology even of natural catastrophes (*divina exercentur*),[78] part of this general argument, is paralleled by a detailed passage in JT *Berakhoth,* which demonstrates in Judaic fasion the meaningfulness of earthquakes. The Jerusalem Talmud may participate here, as so frequently, in anti-Epicurean polemics, since the proof for the meaningfulness of the destruction of the Temple in the same passage apparently reacts to the frequently uttered observation of the Epicureans that if indeed Providence prevailed, gods would often destroy their own temples.[79]

3. The strange fact that Adam becomes an important Sage and inventor according to many midrashic passages and especially in the views of b. Zoma and Rab(h), may betray a similar tendentiousness. The Stoics, above all Posidonius, maintained that early man knew already the crafts taught by the early Sages, countering the evolutionary theory of the Epicureans according to whom early man was primitive and savage. Since Stoic reason and providence thus eliminated chance even in the history of early

man, a similar extension of the rule of *hokhmah* to Adam
must have helped the Rabbis in their struggle against
Epicurean views in their own environment.[80]

4. Similarly, in the rabbinic identification of Torah with
wisdom, a certain degree of Westernization can be observed. The content of Wisdom-Torah, especially the Oral
Law, includes now a number of contemporary Greco-
Roman intellectual disciplines. To Bar Kappara, *c*. 200
C.E., it is thus actually sinful not to apply astronomy if
one knows it, and R. Yohanan recommends calendric
knowledge (*mazzaloth u-thekuphoth*) and astronomical
mathematics (*hissubh*).[81] Beside the Solomic variety, wisdom implictly includes theosophy-mysticism (symbol:
Ezekiel), biblical wisdom literature (Proverbs, Ecclesiastes), halakhoth, codification, law (Judah ha-Nasi) and,
apparently, rhetorical and exegetical skill (b. Zoma). Significantly, the symbols of wisdom have been extended to
include two Tannaim![82] Occasionally we find the formula
that the true *talmidh hakham* knows Halakhah, Aggadah,
Mishnah, Midrash, and Scripture (*mikra'oth*) and also ar-
cane disciplines, the language of the animals, fables, in
short just everything knowable.[83] It was believed that the
members of the Sanhedrin knew the major languages of
the world as a prerequisite for their office.

Wisdom is thus encyclopedic and approximates the requirements of the contemporary rhetorical culture. This is,
of course, not contrary to expectation, since the social
function of the Tannaim and Amoraim was frequently
identical with that of their Western counterparts: to be
jurists, administrators, rhetoricians, academic teachers, literary critics, grammarians, theologians, "Seelenführer,"
moralists, fabulists, and folklorists in one person.[84]

5. The symbiosis of Western and traditional elements,
however, is not complete. Distinctions are made between
different types of wisdom. To Ele'azar (b.) *Hisma, c*. 110
C.E., calendric knowledge and geometry are merely the
spice(s) of *hokhmah* which latter is, in truth, difficult
Halakhah.[85] Gradations of *docta ignorantia*—the fear of

sin being highest—and even know-nothingness—Honi ha-Me'aggel, "the Circler"—survive. Besides, there are the well-known interludes of violent disgust with Greek wisdom, mostly after military and political clashes.[86] And Moses remains, of course, the greatest of all Sages, having received all fifty created measures of wisdom except that of Divine Wisdom itself.[87]

IX

1. Wisdom traditions also cluster around the concept of the Sage, his wisdom and his properties, and this material reflects, likewise, relations with the West.[88]

According to some beliefs, the Sage possesses a craft, often a lowly one; frequently he is or was a slave; according to others, to the contrary, a craft or business involvement would spoil the leisure and contemplation essential to the Sage's task. This contrast of opinion is also Greco-Roman.

2. The Sage is humble. The instances are numerous, and so are the Western parallels. The story of Hillel's patience while subject of a wager is also told of Pericles. Nevertheless, the Sage is strongly, occasionally even arrogantly, aware of his value and possesses a distinct class pride. Both Aristippus and Hillel are well worth the money lost on them.[89]

3. The Sage lives a life of asceticism. This is a frequent *topos* in rhetoric, reinforced by the convictions of the Cynical, Stoic and Epicurean schools, though for different reasons. Key themes are bread and water (bread and salt, bread and cheese, acorn and fig), distinct yet simple if not sub-standard garb, lowly bed, lowly (or no) house. The Sage is thus mostly poor or has renounced his possessions (Hillel, Crates). Whatever the motivation for this austerity—moral discipline, "shortcut" to virtue, avoidance of trouble, anti-vanity, anti-luxury, Boas-Lovejoy's Primitivism—it is not a dualistic dichotomy of flesh and spirit with the

aim of mortifying the former. Even the ascetic heroism in
the snow, of a Socrates, a Diogenes or a Hillel, is non-
dualistic. Wisdom is glorified in an "ugly vessel," so Socrates, so R. Joshua.[90]

4. The Sage—in this ideal projection—learns from all
(even a mouse: Diogenes). He is happy, outgoing, con-
versing and arguing with people, disdaining the ignorant
and the fool yet trying to convert them, believing that
virtue is knowable and teachable (whether for a fee or
without), surrounded by disciples, grateful and loyal to his
teachers (only Epicurus is the exception), pondering
whether theory or practice is higher, avoiding involvement
with governments (yet being more often himself scholar-
bureaucrat and counselor to rulers). He eats, mourns,
prays, and consoles as the Sage should. His attitude toward
love and marriage is ambiguous. He is witty, challenging,
non-conventional, intolerant of tyranny, thus frequently
meeting a martyr's death. He recognizes the authority of a
scriptural canon (even if only as an esthetic or traditional
model) and interprets it in a novel way, frequently applying parody, irony, and satire. He knows that wisdom is, in
some way, divine, yet with man and the world, and will try
to live in this cosmic symbiosis. His wisdom is therefore a
form of reverence if not piety, of ultimate concern, and a
road to fulfillment in accordance with an eternal pattern.

5. The Western-related material in rabbinic sources is
abundant and ubiquitous, and it will undoubtedly take a
generation of scholars to unearth it. Many situations will
always remain ambiguous and controversial owing to their
complexity and the involvement of a multitude of factors.

A final instance—though still classifiable—will illustrate
some of these difficulties. It has often been asserted that
the dimension of hope is stronger in Hebrew sources,
especially in rabbinic thought, than in the West, perhaps
through the workings of Messianism, a more substantial
and sustained belief in immortal life (in this period) and
the trust in an all-powerful, "interested," and personal
god. However this may be, the diffused pessimism, even

melancholy, that is palpable throughout the entire Ancient World, should not be underestimated even in rabbinic literature.[91] Best known among these "pessimistic" materials is the striking decision of the schools of Hillel and Shammai, after prolonged discussion, in favor of the position that it is better for man not to be born than to be born.[92]

The Western affinity of this item has rightly been asserted by a number of scholars.[93] To this assertion one must add that the earliest formulation of this thought, that of Theognis, *Elegies* 425–428, had a considerable afterlife in Greek tragedy and comedy,[94] as literal quotation or in variation, and both in affirmation and rejection:

> Of all things, indeed, to earthly *men* [pl.] *not to be born* and not to see the rays of the burning *sun*, is *best;* but *once born he* [sing.] should *as speedily as possible* pass the gates of Hades and lie low, having heaped together for him much earth. [Keywords in italics]

Still more relevant is the additional observation that by the early tannaitic period this theme had become a rhetorical *topos* and its key phrase, *mē phynai*, "not to be born," a commonplace.[95] Many of the Greco-Roman quotations thus hint at the traditional nature and wide distribution of these sentiments, their controversial message and their origin in the opinion of Sages. This then is apparently the framework for the emergence of the tannaitic controversy. The surprising final negative vote of the rabbinic schools is mitigated by "but now that he has been created" (or "once born"), "let him ponder [var. "screen"] his deeds." The thematic element "but once born" is common to all fully developed passages in the West as is, naturally, the use of a comparative or superlative in conjunction with the antithesis.

The first difficulty consists in assessing Eccles. 4:2–3.

> And I do praise the dead who already died more than the living who are still alive [pl.] but (still) more ("best") than both of them him [sing.] who has never

been,[96] who has never seen the evil action that is acted (out) under the sun.

Apparently there is a complete break in vocabulary between 'Erubbin and Ecclesiastes, and the remedial thought of the former is novel. And yet it seems that Eccles. 4:2–3 is also a descendant of Theognis on the grounds of the striking similarities in detail.[97]

Another difficulty consists in assessing "pessimism" in an isolated passage. Neither with Theognis and his satellites nor with Ecclesiastes is this pessimism absolute if the contexts are consulted (and considered to be by the same author).[98]

A last and final complication is the uncertain unity and dating of the Theognis materials. In no opinion are they later than the fifth century B.C.E.[99] Yet the question of their possible derivation from early Near Eastern wisdom literature has never been seriously raised.[100] Indeed, Theognis 411–466 read like early Near Eastern wisdom items as to thematic elements, keywords, and poetic parallelisms, and 373–382 are questions raised also by the Jobs of the Ancient Near East.[101] But then polygenesis, the independent but similar creations of certain general human themes with different cultures, is an ever present possibility unless monogenesis, the origin from one specific center, by precise material proofs, can be established.

However this may be and however significant to the historian of culture, to the exegete of early rabbinic sources the esprit du siècle, i.e., the atmosphere, problems, techniques, and fashions of the first or second century are the relevant background.[102] In spite of finer distinctions that can and must be made between the foreign pattern and the final form of its adoption, the recognition of the original pattern is decisive in the understanding of the texts.[103] The passage of 'Erubbin participates in relevant queries and experiences of the Western orbit and thus acquires an intercultural dimension.

Conclusion

The impact of the West on rabbinic belief was to recede
in the late Amoraic (350–500 C.E.) and in the Saboraic
(500–600 C.E.) and early Gaonic Periods (600–850 C.E.)
to see a rebirth only in medieval scholasticism, in concert
with the parallel developments in Christianity and Islam.
This openness to the West, brought about by political,
military, technological, and other social factors, was apparently facilitated by the existence of earlier indigenous
Sage-centered cultures in the Near East in general and in
pre-exilic and post-exilic Israel in particular. In any case,
wisdom literature seems always to have been an accepted
intercultural and interethnic coinage, appropriated as religiously neutral or non-committal.

As fruitful as this symbiosis of the Western wisdom and
rabbinic piety may have been, however, it harbored a
serious inner contradiction. As stated before, the Western
Sage of antiquity was non-conventional, controversial, perhaps radical. In the formative period of rabbinic culture
and in opposition to ancient polytheism and military occu-
pation, a place could be given to such an ideal figure. When
rabbinic culture had crystallized into its enduring form,
however, when polytheism had ceased with the progress of
Christianity, when the center of Judaism had moved to
Babylonia and the Jewish population of Palestine had
shrunk and was impoverished and without official representation, Judaism became increasingly a system of greater
conservatism and had recourse to indigenous resources. In
this development there was little room for a radical
Founder-Sage. Profound changes thereafter were effected
by different types of leaders, the Babylonian exilarch, the
ascetic saint of Ashkenaz, the mystic, the *shtadlan,* and
even the pseudo-messiah. Yet the abiding basis of the
talmudic culture made revivals of the *sophos* type possible.
Significantly, these revivals were no longer under the aus-
pices of a Socratic or Cynical pattern but under that of

that ancient *sophos* who (in spite of an *asebeia* process) had aimed at harmonization, reverence, and stability and who—relatively less important in Greco-Roman rhetoric—[104] became central if not dominant in medieval culture: Aristotle of Stagira.

NOTES

1. It can no longer be maintained that such a view is that of scholars who are strangers to or alienated from rabbinic culture, since some of the leaders in this endeavor are squarely at home in the world of traditional Judaism, among them David Daube, E. E. Hallewi (Halevy), and Saul Lieberman.

2. "East" and "West," as used in this study, do not imply any value judgments or modern associations evoked by these terms but are merely signals for a speedier orientation, avoiding the lengthy "Greco-Roman" or "Hellenic-Hellenistic" on the one hand, and "Near Eastern-Judaic" or "Hebrew-Aramaic" and occasionally "Judeo-Christian" on the other.

3. I.e., the so-called *Tephillah (par excellence),* or *Shemoneh-'esreh* ("eighteen," i.e., benedictions, in Saboric times extended to nineteen), recited at least three times daily. Cf. S. Baer, *Sedher 'Abhodhath Yisra'el,* rev. ed. (Berlin, 1937), p. 90, and J. H. Hertz, *The Authorised Daily Prayer Book,* rev. ed. (New York, 1948), pp. 136f., 138. Wisdom appears here as a gift of grace. Cf. 1 Kings 3:7; Jer. 9:23.

4. [ ] missing in the Ashkenazic text. ( ) added for the sake of style in the translation. Cf. S. J. Mansour, *Siddur Tephillath Yesharim* (Jerusalem, n.d.), p. 92.

5. Hertz, *Authorised,* p. 108 and p. 304. Baer, *Sedher,* p. 76 and p. 164. Introductions to the morning *Shema'* are called *Yosroth.*

6. Hertz, *Authorised,* p. 10; Baer, *Sedher,* p. 36. This item belongs to what could be called "toilet (lavatory) manners." Both Cicero and Talmud deal with this subject as does Herodotus.

7. E. Bickerman, "The Civic Prayer of Jerusalem," *HTR* 55 (1962), 163–185.

8. Hertz, *Authorised,* pp. 18f.; Baer, *Sedher,* pp. 40f. Cf. their footnotes *ad loc.* for variant readings.

9. Cf. H. A. Fischel, "Story and History, Observations on Greco-Roman Rhetoric and Pharisaism," in *American Oriental Society, Middle West Branch Semi-Centennial Volume,* ed. D. Sinor (Bloomington, Ind., 1969), pp. 74f. Paul in Gal. 3:28 seems to refer to this triple blessing. I. Elbogen, *Der jüdische Gottesdienst,* 3rd ed. (Frankfurt, 1931), p. 90, alludes to a possible Persian version. The post-Confucian Sages, indeed, used a similar pattern. Cf. Lactantius, *Divine Institutes* 3.19, for the fullest form of this prayer.

10. S. Stein, "Symposia Literature and the Pesaḥ Haggadah," *Journal of Jewish Studies* 8 (1957), 13–44. Recently, G. J. Bahr, "The Seder of Passover and the Eucharistic Words," *NT* 12 (1970), 181–202, has contributed further to this subject.

11. Text: M.M. Kasher, *Haggadah Shelemah* (Jerusalem, 1967), pp. 20–26 (Hebrew numerals). Cf. N. N. Glatzer, *The Passover Haggadah,* rev. ed. (New York, 1969), pp. 24f.

12. Stein, 'Symposia Literature," p. 35: *de ebrietate,* 30–33, 35, and 68, and *de congressu eruditionis,* 63–68.

13. Fred O. Francis, "The Baraita of the Four Sons," *SBL Proc.* 1 (1972), 245–283. Cf. Francis for the quotations of Daube and Finkelstein.

14. Cf. the massive material on Sage and Fool in H. von Arnim, *SVF* III, nos. 544–684.

15. On the *eikazein,* the *eikones* of the comedy, and Plato's more serious use of this genre, cf. Josef Martin, *Symposium. Die Geschichte einer literarischen Form,* SGKA, no. 17 (Paderborn, 1931), pp. 10ff., 56, 61. It can be shown, so the present author believes, that the Seder follows several partly playful, partly serious (*spoudaiogeloiic*) situations of the ancient symposium.

16. Tosephta *Berakhoth* 6 (7). 2; S. Lieberman, pp. 33f.; Babylonian Talmud (BT) *Berakhoth* 52a; and Jerusalem Talmud (JT) *Berakhoth* 13c, IX.2 (Krotoshin; New York-Vilna: 67b, IX.1).

17. Treated in detail in H. A. Fischel, *Rabbinic Literature and Greco-Roman Philosophy: A Study of Epicurea and Rhetorica in Early Midrashic Writings,* Studia Post-Biblica no. 21 (Leiden, 1973), 51–65.

18. *Lev. R.,* beginning, *et al.* Very frequent. Thus, the English translation of *Midrash Rabba* (Soncino), *Index Volume,* by J. I. Slotki, ed. H. Freedman and M. Simon (London, 1939), lists no less than twelve instances of this identification.

19. BT *Yoma* 83b, Yohanan, Pal., d. 279. Tannaitic anecdotes: *Eccl. R.* 7:12, No. 1.

20. Explicitly applied to the siege of Jerusalem and the rescue of R. Yohanan b. Zakkai in *Lam.. R.* 1:5, No. 31.

21. *Gen. R.,* 19.1.

22. BT *Sotah* 21b.

23. *Pesikta de Rab(h) Kahana* 25, 158b; BT *Berakhoth* 17a, amoraic; Mishnah *Sotah,* end.

24. *Eccl. R.* 7:11. No. 1.

25. BT *Megillah* 7a, Shime'on b. Menasia, *c.* 180.

26. *Ab(h)oth de R. Nathan (AdRN),* version A. chap. 29, Schechter.

27. *Gen. R.* 98.9 on 49:11.

28. *Gen. R.* 17.5, end.

29. BT *Sotah* 35b.

30. Cf. the admission of Yehudah ha-Nasi (Judah the Prince, redactor of the Mishnah, d. 217 C.E.) that in astronomical wisdom the opinion of the foreign sages is preferable, BT *Pesahim* 94b. Cf. BT *Niddah* 22b regarding medicine. The endorsement of the latter is anticipated by b. Sirah who was subject to the same pressures.

This situation apparently led to the creation of two benedictions: on seeing the Sages of Israel and on seeing the Sages of the nations, BT *Berakhoth* 58a. This distinction is still valid in contemporary usage: "Blessed . . . who imparted of His wisdom to them that fear Him," versus "Blessed . . .,who gave of His wisdom to flesh and blood," Hertz, *Authorised,* p. 992.

31. BT *Megillah* 16a.

32. *Lam. R.* 2.8–10, No. 13. Cf. *Sifra* 86af., Weiss; *Sifre Dt.* 74a, end, Friedmann.

33. *Pirke Ab(h)oth* 4.2 (4.5 Taylor). Henceforth *PA.*

34. Diogenes Laertius, *Vitae,* 10.27 Cf. E. Schwartz, *Die Ethik der Griechen* (Stuttgart, 1951), p. 196: *ta hairetea kai pheuktea.*

35. Epicurus, Cicero, Seneca, cf. "run," Marcus Aurelius, *Meditations,* 4.51, as in *PA, supra.*

36. The fable, perhaps also a wisdom genre, is, of course, very active in our period. Talmudic literature includes at least twenty-two instances, many paralleled in Western literature (Aesop, Babrius, etc.), but also quite a few without known parallels. In both the East and the West the political use of the fable is strong, i.e., some of the midrashic instances are resistance literature against assimilation, e.g., Akiba's famous "fox and fishes on dry land." Cf. "Hellenism," sub-section "Spiritual Resistance," *EncJ* (H.A.F.). Different observa-

tions in H. Schwarzbaum, "Talmudic-Midrashic Affinities of Some Aesopic Fables," *Laographica* 22 (1965), 446—483. The use of the fable is recommended in Aristotle's *Rhetoric* 2.20.5—8, 1393bf.

37. Cf. several related formulations and their common Western pattern in Fischel, *Rabbinic Literature,* pp. 35—43.

38. Thus, Hillel, upon seeing the skull of a drowned man of violence, exclaims the proverbial "measure for measure" in the vernacular Aramaic, *PA* 2.6 (2.7 Taylor).

39. This may include even the Golden Rule of Hillel and Akiba. Cf. Fischel, "Story and History" pp. 65—70, and "Studies in Cynicism and the Ancient Near East: The Transformation of a *chreia*," in *Religions in Antiquity: Essays in Memory of Erwin Ramsdell Goodenough,* ed. J. Neusner, *Numen, Suppl.,* no. 14 (Leiden, 1968), pp. 372—411.

40. Some of the earlier more influential extant works of this kind are Aristotle's *Rhetoric;* [Ps.-Aristotle] *Rhetorica ad Alexandrum; Rhetorica* [or *Auctor*] *ad Herennium* (Ps.-Cornificius or Ps.-Cicero, apparently written between 88 and 82 B.C.E.); Cicero, *de oratore; Brutus, et al.;* Quintilian, *Institutio oratorica;* Dionysius of Halicarnassus, *Ars rhetorica, et al.;* [Ps.-] Demetrius of Phalerum, *On Style;* [Ps.-] Longinus, *On the Sublime;* Rutilius Lupus (first century C.E.), *de figuris sententiarum et elocutionis;* Hermogenes, *peri ideōn* and his *Progymnasmata* as well as those of Theon (both second century (C.E.), and of Aphthonius of Antioch (*c.* 400 C.E., particularly influential and reprinted to Shakespeare's time and beyond). Among the Christians: [Ps.-] Zonaius; Augustine; Isidor of Seville (sixth century). Caecilius of Calacte (works lost) and his critic Ps.-Longinus (Augustan period) may have been Jews (or proselytes or sympathizers); the issue is still controversial.

41. Details in Fischel, *Rabbinic Literature,* pp. 70—73, 147—150. Cf. also D. L. Sigsbee, "The Ridicule of the Stoic Paradoxa in Ancient Satirical Literature," (Ph.D. diss., Univ. of Mich., 1968). Cf. Cicero's *Paradoxa Stoicorum.*

42. Paradoxical in the literal sense of the word are the formulations of 2 Cor. 6:6—10; Lucian's *Nigrinus* 1, and BT *Tamidh* 31b—32a (66a in some editions).

43. The latter case is less likely: b. Zoma's entire Midrash is close to Western patterns, and the *paradoxa* appear again in BT *Tamidh* (cf. the preceding note) without proof texts.

44. The proof texts are taken from biblical wisdom passages: Ps.

119:99; Prov. 16:32; Ps. 128:2; 1 Sam. 2:30 (a prophetic wisdom-related oracle in form and intent). Prov. 16:32 does fit its proposition well.

45. Cf. the extensive articles in W. H. Roscher's *Ausführliches Lexikon der griechischen und römischen Mythologie,* III.2 (Leipzig, 1902–1909), *s.v.,* "Personifikationen (Dichtung)," 2094–2110, and in Pauly-Wissowa's *Real-Encyklopädie der classichen Altertumswissenschaft,* new ed., vol. 37 (Stuttgart, 1937), *s.v.,* "Personifikationen," 1042–1058 (F. Stössl). The usual Greek term is *prosopopoeia.* Cf. also the still valid Part II, "Diatribe and Haggadah" of A. Marmorstein's "The Background of the Haggadah," reprinted in *The Arthur Marmorstein Memorial Volume, Studies in Jewish Theology,* eds. J. Rabbinowitz and M. S. Lew (London, etc., 1950), pp. 56f. Marmorstein anticipated the Western affinity of midrashic personifications in the wake of one of Rudolf Bultmann's early works *Der Stil der paulinischen Predigt und die kynisch-stoische Diatribe,* FRL 13 (Göttingen, 1910).

46. Through identification with the Holy Spirit, e.g., BT *Pesahim* 66b.

47. BT *Hagigah* 12af., Rab(h), Pal. and Bab., d. 247); BT *Berakhoth* 55a, tannaitic, *et al.*

48. *Ex. R.* 48:4, i.e., macrocosm and microcosm?

49. Cf. "Stoics and Stoicism," *EncJ* (H.A.F.). The Stoic position that freedom is freedom through and under Law, a by-product of these specific Stoic equations (cf. *SVF* III, 360), is paralleled by Joshua b. Levi's equating *haruth,* "engraved," (i.e., the Law) with *heruth,* "freedom," *PA* 6.2 (6.2), Pal. *c.* 250. Other Stoic teachings, *infra,* VIII.2.

50. Such diadoches were composed by Sotion of Alexandria (between 200 and 170 B.C.E.); Sosicrates of Rhodes (*fl.c.* 140 B. C. E.?); Alexander Polyhistor (b. *c.* 105 B. C. E.). Pertinent detail in E. (J.) Bickerman, "La chaîne de la tradition pharisienne," *RB* 59 (1951), 44–54.

51. The *physikōn doxai* of Aristotle's pupil Theophrastus (372/69–288/85 B.C.E.) set the pattern. Influential: Diocles of Magnesia, b. *c.* 75 B. C. E., and Aëtius, *c.* 100 C.E.

52. The extra-canonical *AdRN* which largely parallel *PA* and are enriched by such biographical materials are thus still closer to the type of compilation which Diogenes Laertius produced.

Chapters V and VI of *PA* are, of course, of a different order. Being largely anonymous they incorporate numerical sayings, coinages of the "great is ..." type, and diverse materials of a folk character. For these some afterlife of wisdom literature could perhaps be claimed. Too little comparative research, however, has been done on these chapters. It seems that even they are paralleling certain literary tastes and habits of the West. Thus the very popular literary form which the anthologies of Aelian (*c.* 170–235 C.E.) and Aulus Gellius (*c.* 130–180 C.E.) represent and which could variously be called Miscellania, Memorabilia, Paradoxographa, Curiosa, or Varia are not too remote from the last chapters of *PA*. This literary genre puts together reminiscences, personal experiences, startling facts, remarkable situations, folk science, numerical catalogues, all accompanied by religious or moralistic comments by the compilers. Chapter VI, moreover vaguely resembles the genre *protreptikos logos,* the exhortation to philosophy (or politics or the sciences). The protrepticus has an extensive history from the Sophists to Aristotle to Cicero to Galen (*c.* 165 C.E.) to Iamblichus (*c.* 280 C.E.) and the usual Stobaean excerpts (*c.* 425 C.E.).

53. Details in H. A. Fischel, "The Uses of Sorites (*climax, gradatio*) in the Tannaitic Period," *HUCA* 44 (1973), 119–151.

54. Cf. "Greek and Latin, Rabbinical Knowledge of," *EncJ* (H. A. F.).

55. BT *Tamidh* 32a–b: Alexander and the Gymnosophists [Elders of the South] ; Alexander and the Amazons [Women of Africa] ; etc.

56. So expressly in his own words: BT *Tamidh* 32b, top.

57. Treated in L. Wallach, "Alexander the Great and the Indian Gymnosophists in the Hebrew Tradition," *Proceedings of the American Academy for Jewish Research* 11 (1941), 47–83. Wallach is inclined to assume an Eastern basis for this material. Cf. also Fischel, *Rabbinic Literature,* pp. 73, 151f.

58. The motif of the young children who perplex the Sage by their riddles (some carry food) is also found in the *Certamen Homeri et Hesiodi* (cf. n. 95, *infra*) where Homer is the target of the young fisherboys (carrying their catch), 326 and 315. For the present view on the earlier sources and parallels of this *Certamen . . . (Agon)* legend as well as its Hadrianic interpolations, see Arnaldo Momigliano, *The Development of Greek Biography* (Cambridge, Mass., 1971), p. 26f. and "Introduction," p. xli, and "Addition to Appendix," pp. 624–627 (D. L. Page) in H. G. Evelyn White, ed., *Hesiod,* Loeb Classical Library (London, Cambridge, Mass., repr. 1970).

59. BT *Berakhoth* 57b, second mnemonic list.

60. The former: 733–1154 ("*Diosēmiai*"); the latter: 4.56, 74,

78, 81, 83; 7.10. Hippocratic materials were known to the Rabbis and appear, e.g., in the story of Hillel and the Wager, BT *Shabbath* 30af. More semiotics in Tosephta *Berakhoth* 3.4, Lieberman, p. 12, and parallels, cf. Seneca, *Epistula* 66.45. The Greek term for "sign" is *sēma* or *sēmeion*. The Hebrew *sīmān* is a loan-word from the Greek.

61. BT *Hagigah* 14b; JT *Hagigah* 77b, II.1; Tosephta *Hagigah* 2.3–4; and also *Cant. R.* on 1:4, No. 1. Cf. Fischel, *Rabbinic Literature,* pp. 12ff., 19f., 113f.

62. *Massekhtoth Ze'iroth,* ed. M. Higger (repr., Jerusalem, 1970), pp. 99–117.

63. Some of the *chriae* on Hillel the Elder come in clusters, e.g., those portraying his patience, BT *Shabbath* 30bf.

64. E.g., the praise of the inventor, etc., by b. Zoma, *supra,* 2.4, patterned after a considerable number of treatments in Greco-Roman rhetorical literature. E. E. Hallewi has traced other such *topoi* in the Midrash in his numerous writings in *Tarbiz.* Cf. also his recent *Olamah shel ha-Aggadah* (Tel Aviv, 1972).

65. One to be defeated or—perhaps a new development—both of equal strength, i.e., no longer between Sage and Fool but between Sage and Sage. The *altercatio* appears in a variety of sub-forms, some still bearing traces of their possible origin in juridical court procedure.

The literary terms in this section have been chosen from a variety of parallel terms that exist, both with the ancient critics and their modern heirs. This paper follows mostly R. Volkmann, *Die Rhetorik der Griechen und Römer* (repr., Hildesheim, 1963); less E. Norden, *Die antike Kunstprosa,* 5th ed., 2 vols. (repr., Darmstadt, 1958), and H. Lausberg, *Handbuch der literarischen Rhetorik,* 2 vols. (Munich, 1960).

66. In rabbinic literature this involves native as well as foreign texts or styles which are being parodied; the former: JT *Pesahim* 30b, III.7, Krot. (Abbahu, the Greek speaking wit, Amora, *c.* 300 C.E., of Caesarea); JT *Nedharim* 40a, VI.13, Krot., tannaitic, both parodying Scripture; the latter: Caesar's *veni, vidi, vici;* Epicurean ecstatic speech, and others, cf. Fischel, *Rabbinic Literature,* index, *s.v.,* "Parody."

67. Already Platonic. Cf. Fischel, "Story and History . . . ," p. 70.

68. Cf. Fischel, *Rabbinic Literature,* pp. 90f.

69. Both the total concept and the historical reality of the talmudic Sage are admirably portrayed in the now classical work of E. E. Urbach, *The Sages, Their Concepts and Beliefs* ([Hebrew] Jerusalem, 1969). For a summary see "Sages" in *EncJ.* The Sages are here seen in the light of the final and enduring amalgamation of East and West without distinction of components. Professor Urbach, of course, is aware of and mentions historical contacts and a number of parallels between rabbinic and Greco-Roman beliefs.

70. Especially *Tanḥuma,* ed. Buber, *Bereshith* No. 5, on Prov. 8:30.

71. W. D. Davies, *Paul and Rabbinic Judaism* (London, 1951), p. 171, quoting Bonsirven, *et al.*

72. The use of this Platonic item may have been partly polemical, i.e., claiming Wisdom-Torah as the eternal pattern rather than Plato's ideas or, perhaps, in the way of Hellenistic Judaism, asserting their identity. The introductory (and perhaps later) "tool of craftsman-ship" may try to ward off associations with the Gnostic Demiurge suggested by the wording and imagery of the similies. Professor Josephine M. Ford has raised the question whether such items could have been helpful in, or even initially aimed at, proselytizing.

73. *Gen. R.* 10.7; 79.5ff., Theodor-Albeck, tannaitic. Cf. paral-lels and similar Midrashim in the notes, *ad loc.* This particular Midrash mentions expressly flees, gnats and flies, and thereafter snake, scorpion, gnat, and frog.

74. JT *Berakhoth* 13b. IX.3, Krotoshin, tannaitic. A slightly different list of pests and their uses by Rab(h) in BT *Shabbath* 77b with equal stress on the purposefulness of all creation.

75. Lucretius, *de rerum natura,* 5.194–234; 2.167–181. Cf. the Epicurean spokesman Velleius in Cicero's *de natura deorum* 1.23 and *Academica* 2.120 (Sceptical).

76. Plutarch in *de Stoicorum pugnantiis* 21 and in Fragment 193 (Sandbach, 145 Bernardakis) tries to refute him, mentioning (in the latter source) also "flies, mosquitos, bats, dung-beetles, snakes."

77. Plutarch, *Fr.* 193 (145). Similarly, Marcus Aurelius, *Medita-tions* 1.6.23–26 regarding Heracles' exploits. The still unknown usefulness of other noxious animals and plants has yet to be discov-ered: *SVF* II, 1172, quoted by Lactantius *de ira Dei.*

78. *De ira* 2.27f. JT, *Yebhamoth* 9c, bottom, VIII.3, Krot., early amoraic, reports that a plague, in eliminating among others also all bastards, concealed the sins of that generation. JT comments that

thus "even the evil which the Holy-One-Blessed-Be-He brings into
the world, in Wisdom he brings it." The biblical support is seen in
Isa. 31:2, "and yet He is the Wise one, and brings about evil."

79. Most wittily in Lucian, *Timon* 10, when an angry Zeus by
mistake hits his own temple with his thunderbolt. P. H. DeLacy,
"Lucretius and the History of Epicureanism." *Transactions and
Proceedings of the American Philological Association,* 79 (1948),
12–23, has shown how these controversies increasingly used popular
("half-literary, half-philosophical") media (pp. 20ff.).

Interestingly enough, even such Western elements often appear in
clusters in rabbinic literature. JT *Berakhoth* thus offered the syn-
drome "earthquakes," "temple destruction," "noxious animals."
The section by b. Zoma, BT *Berakhoth* 58a, discussed *supra,* offers
"variety of physiognomies and minds from one pattern" (Aristotle,
Pliny the Elder) and the two detailed *topoi* on the "praise of the
inventor," etc., and the "grateful and ungrateful guests" (the latter
from Seneca, cf. Fischel, *Rabbinic Literature,* pp. 65–70).

80. *Gen. R.* 24.7; *Eccl. R.* 7:17, No. 1; BT *Pesahim* 54a, Jose b.
Halaphta, *c.* 150; *Nu. R.*19.3. In detail: Fischel, *Rabbinic Literature,*
pp. 64f. and notes. Rab(h) skillfully midrashizes Isa. 44:11, *we-
harashim hemmah me-'adam,* the craftsmen, being (only) human,"
into "the craftsmen, from Adam they (stem)." These sources must
be distinguished from those in which Adam resembles a prophet or a
cosmic giant (possibly with Iranian or gnostic affinities).

81. BT *Shabbath* 75a. These disciplines are, to be sure, useful if
not indispensable for indigenous ritual requirements, such as the
fixation of the calendar. Nevertheless, the formulations of these
principles go far beyond indigenous necessities.

82. BT *Berakhoth* 57b, beg., tannaitic, an oneirocritical-semiotic
passage. Significant, too, is the fact that in this passage desirable
qualities and happenings include various types of piety, miracles, and
well-being, i.e., indigenous values. The meaning of b. Zoma's wisdom
is here conjectured. He appears frequently as a skillful and powerful
Darshan and profound exegetical halakhist in the sources. Were his
contemporaries aware of the fact that his entire Aggadah is Western-
inspired? Was this the reason for the voices critical of him? Cf.
Fischel, *Rabbinic Literature,* pp. 86–89.

83. Claimed, e.g., for Yohanan b. Zakkai and Jonathan b.
Uzziel: Add: the (secret) language of plants, demons and angels,
minutiae of Scribes (Masorah?), hermeneutics, the parables of fullers
or washers (they figure in the Roman comedy), and theosophy.

Some of these have magical connotations. BT *Babba Bathra* 134a. Cf. I. Epstein's note *ad loc.* in the Soncino translation.

84. Perhaps with the Greeks and Romans and with Philo there still lingered the memory of a living embodiment of such universal knowledge: surprisingly enough not Aristotle but the Near Easterner Posidonius to whom Cicero and Pompey had made pilgrimages at his school at Rhodes (d. 50 B.C.E.).

85. *PA* 3.18 (3.28 Taylor). The underlying consonants of the usual readings *peripheriyoth,* "peripheries," or *parpera'oth,* "side dishes," may perhaps be yet unrecognized derivatives of the Latin *palpamenta,* "spices," the *resh* being interchangeable with the *lamedh* in Hebrew, Aramaic, and Arabic. Strangely enough the halakhic portions, i.e., "bird offerings," and "onset(s) of menstruation," which according to Ele'azar are "the essentials of Halakhah" (and not merely "spices") seem to be based on Alexandrian logical patterns. If Ele'azar was aware of this, his statement would reflect Greco-Roman leanings throughout.

86. Cf. "Greek and Latin, Rabbinical Knowledge of," *JE.*

87. Rab(h), BT *Rosh ha-Shanah* 21b.

88. For details and some sources for this survey cf. Fischel, "Story and History," *passim.*

89. Thus according to their own statements. Diogenes Laertius, *Lives,* 2.77, end and *AdRN,* B, chap. 29, p. 60f. (S.), using similar formulations. The later amoraic self-evaluation of the Sage agrees: the *locus classicus,* BT *Babba Bathra* 12a, claims that authority was taken from the Prophets and given to the Sages (Abhdimi of Haifa, c. 280). The ensuing Babylonian discussion of the statement attempts to show that Wisdom is superior to Prophecy, that authority had always belonged to the Sages (who were Prophet-sages in biblical times) and that some form of presage is still found with them. Of course, all would agree that the writing of inspired Scripture had ceased.

90. Joshua b. Hananiah and the Emperor's daughter, BT *Ta'anith* 7a. Both humility and austerity are expressly connected with *hokhmah* in BT *Sotah* 21b. Judah ha-Nasi reads here Prov. 8:12 midrashically "I, Wisdom, dwell (in) nakedness," and Yohanan reads Job 28:12 "and Wisdom will be found (with whoever makes himself indistinguishable) from nothing."

91. Some talmudic sources which (superficially) could be classified as pessimistic have been (uncritically) collected by J. Günzig, "Pessimistische Gedanken in Talmud und Midrasch," in *Festschrift,*

Prof. Dr. [Sigmund] Maybaum ... [70th Birthday] (Berlin, 1914), pp. 148–156. Cf. also Stobaeus, vol. V, chap. 34, 824–856 (Wachsmuth-Hense), for a collection of such Greco-Roman sources.

92. BT *'Erubbin* 13b, end of Gemara, tannaitic. The anthithesis of the two basic positions is fully spelled out there as well as in almost all classical sources cited hereafter. The question whether there was, indeed, such a historical session is, of course, inessential for the purpose of this study.

93. Thus briefly by Robert H. Pfeiffer, "Hebrew and Greek Sense of Tragedy," in *The Joshua Bloch Memorial Volume*, ed. A. Berger, *et al.* (New York, 1960), pp. 54–64 (60f.), and elaborately by E. E. Hallewi, *Sha'are ha-Aggadah*, pp. 247–249.

94. Best known is Sophocles, *Oedipus Coloneus* 1225–1228. A considerable number of others (at least twelve) are listed in W. C. Greene, *Moira* (New York, 1963) p. 42, no. 189, and related notes (cf. *mē phynai*, Index, p. 449).

95. Hallewi rightly quotes Epicurus *apud* Diogenes Laertius, 10.126, Sextus Empiricus, *Outlines of Pyrrhonism*, 3.231, and Plutarch, *Moralia* 758 A (*Dialogue on Love*), who all reject Theognis' proposition. Greene adds *The Contest of Homer and Hesiod (Certamen* ...) 73f. (or Evelyn-White after Goettling: 315, end); (PS.-?) Plutarch, *Moralia* 115C ff. (*Consolatio ad Apollonium*), and Cicero, *Tusculan Disputations* 1.48.114, the latter two quoting an Aristotelian fragment (Silenus before Midas, from *Eudemus* or *Of the Soul*). *Moralia* 109 D is only remotely related. All these accept this "pessimistic" proposition.

To this list, however, must be added Pliny, *Natural History* 7.1.4, and Cicero *apud* Lactantius, *Divine Institutes* 3.19 (Cicero's strange *conflagratio* may be a survival of the original keyword "sun" in a new application). It is a methodological necessity in instances of suspected Western relations of an Eastern passage to list as many uses of a Western item as possible, preferably from rhetoricizing literature (as the most likely medium of transmission), in order to establish fully its prominence at the time of the Eastern occurrence. One or two early *loci classici* are too slim a basis for the comparative analysis of a much later Eastern item.

96. Literally: who has not yet been born. This, however, does not make sense in the light of the author's own feelings, for the man yet unborn still has to face "the evil action that is acted (out) under the sun." Perhaps the difficulty of the author to express himself, also in his use of the comparatives, points to a *Vorlage*.

97. Both begin with a plural and continue with a singular. They use, of course, evaluative comparisons, state the antithesis in full, stress the death motif strongly, and use poetic parallelisms. The Hebrew lacks the advice to veer toward death "as soon as possible" but achieves the same length with the tripartite division.

98. Greene, *Moira*, p. 46, claims that Theognis' work demonstrates "the need for activity and endurance." Eduard Schwartz, *Ethik der Griechen* (posthum.), ed. W. Richter (Stuttgart, 1951), cautions us not to mistake such passages as pessimistic but to see in them admonitions to master life (p. 64). This seems to be true also of the negativist position of 4 Ezra 4.12 and, *expressis verbis,* the rabbinic formulation. Ancient Near Eastern wisdom texts, however, may remain totally negative, cf. "The Dialogue of Pessimism" (Pritchard: "A Pessimistic Dialogue Between Master and Slave"), in W.G. Lambert, *Babylonian Wisdom Literature* (Oxford, 1960), pp. 145–151. Yet final abandonment of pessimism is also found, cf. "Counsels of a Pessimist," p. 108. Cf. the general survey, p. 17, ibid.

99. *Oxford Classical Dictionary*, 2nd ed., 1970, *s.v.* (C. M. Bowra).

100. Sympotic uses, themes for bards, Attic *skolia* (in parts), ethics for an Athenian aristocratic circle, and a mere gnomology, are the usual suggestions for their true property.

101. For other early Greek wisdom materials such as Phocylides, the fragments of Semonides (*sic*), the Maxims of Chiron, *et al.,* for Hesiod—not to mention Herodotus—the suggestion of Eastern connections has been made. Cf. recently P. Walcot, *Hesiod and the Near East* (Cardiff, 1966). Cf. J. Kerschensteiner, *Platon und der Orient* (Stuttgart, 1945). In Ps.-Phocylides and Aristeas the Hellenistic-Jewish symbiosis is, of course, obvious.

102. In characterizing the armament of modern mainland China or the publishing business of modern Taiwan, it is irrelevant to go back to the historical fact that the gunpowder and the printing press were invented in the Far East earlier than in the West.

103. Although this is not the occasion of a full study of such distinctions, it should be pointed out here and now that this task, too, will present equally vexing problems. Thus, in the instance of *'Erubbin,* it seems that the tannaitic discussion raises doubts about the value of man's creation as such, i.e., a one-time, universal event (involving the creative action of the Deity) whereas the Western statements (including Eccles.) allude to the perennial tragic lot of individuals (eclipsing, at least temporarily, the involvement of any

gods). The Hebrew uses *nibhra'*, "was created," throughout the
passage instead of *noladh*, "born," which latter would be the equivalent of the Greek *mē phynai*. Even if the choice of the Hebrew "was
created" is accidental and serves to convey the Western pattern fully
("to be born"), the question arises whether any Hebrew listener
would be able to eliminate the theological overtone of Creation from
this verb *nibhra'*. It so happens that the answer to this question is
positive: an anonymous rabbinic critic before Samuel b. Naḥmani
said of Job: "he never was and never existed" (*lo' nibhra'*), BT
Babha Bathra 15a, end, Pal. *c.* 260; i.e., the verb *nibhra'* did lose its
specific theological meaning and became identical with "being born,
exist," (assuming, as we must, that this usage is older than the
amoraic occurrence, especially in view of the clear, Mishnaic-Hebrew
style of the quotation, which is in contrast to the Aramaic context).
It is, of course, too fanciful to assume that "once created" refers to
the belief that each individual birth is part of an ever renewed
creation. The amoraic formula "Who renews every day continually
the Work of Creation," BT *Hagigah* 12b, finally added to the
introduction of the morning *Shema'* (Hertz, p. 108 *et al.*), refers to
the drawing of a Heavenly Curtain and does not yet represent the
medieval speculation of a perpetual divine re-creation of the All.

Strangely enough, the finale, "let him then ponder [screen] his
deeds," fails to allude to the Law as man's last resort in his dilemma
(although the traditional commentaries earnestly try to see such an
allusion in the text), but rather recommends man's thoughtfulness,
the consciousness of his precariousness, quite in line with the atmosphere of the Western contexts. A traditionalist might be tempted to
see the entire talmudic item against the belief of a higher form of
existence after death, which by that time must have prevailed among
the Tannaim. This seems, indeed, to be young Aristotle's interpretation of the Greek formula, accepted by (Ps.-) Plutarch (*Moralia*,
115E). Yet the Hebrew source fails to allude to this belief directly,
thus making the Western provenance of the formulation more likely.

What remains of possible Eastern elements is thus only a detail in
the narrative framework, i.e., that two opposed factions "vote" on a
question of belief. However, even this could be merely a matter of
style paralleling the acknowledgement of a Cicero or Seneca that on
a specific doctrine the major philosophical schools agree. But then,
again, a Ciceronian or Senecan statement is not binding on the
reader whereas a unanimous opinion of the "Houses" is obligatory.
This obligation, however, does not pertain to doctrinal matters with

the same degree of authority as it does to halakhic matters. The total Western provenance of the passage is thus reasonably sure.

104. I.e., his biography, his students, and startling formulations of his teachings as oratorical material. His theory of rhetoric was, of course, all-important.

5: Philo in the Tradition of Biblical Wisdom Literature

Jean Laporte

IN THIS CHAPTER[1] I WISH TO IDENTIFY IN PHILO IDEAS and images which belong to the biblical literature of wisdom, especially to Proverbs, Ecclesiasticus, and the Wisdom of Solomon. To a lesser extent the book of Deuteronomy and the Letter of Aristeas will be considered. My purpose is not make a thorough study of wisdom in Philo, but to show the importance of the wisdom literature in shaping his way of thinking. Earlier studies[2] such as those of E. R. Goodenough, H. A. Wolfson, and R. A. Baer have discussed wisdom in Philo but have not shown the importance of the wisdom literature in their assessment. I would like to call attention to the importance of this literature for Philo and to draw some conclusions about his method of thought as it stands in continuity with that of the biblical books of wisdom. I have particular reference to certain central images. Such an approach to his writings may provide a key to the understanding of Philo as well as an impetus for new research on him. It could also prevent scholars from denouncing the so-called contradictions in his thinking or from scolding him for his lack of originality, without realizing how his distinct approach, especially in his use of biblical materials, enables him to counterbalance seemingly contradictory ideas, to purify, and to give a deeper meaning to what he has received.

Did Philo Know the Biblical Books of Wisdom?

To begin with, did Philo know the biblical books of wisdom? The indexes mention only fourteen refereences,[3] most of which are to Proverbs, one is to Ecclesiastes, one to Song of Solomon, one to Wisdom, none to Ecclesiasticus. One passage, *Cont.* 25ff., is given as a possible reference to Proverbs, Ecclesiastes, and Song of Solomon, for the reason that these books seem to be included in the expression "anything else." "In each house there is a consecrated room or closet (*semneion kai monasterion*). . . . They (the Therapeutae) take nothing into it . . . but laws and oracles delivered through the mouth of prophets, and psalms, and *anything else (ta alla)* which fosters and perfects knowledge and piety. . . . They have also writings of men of old, the founders of their way of thinking, who left many memorials of the forms used in allegorical interpretation. . . ." This reference is, of course, very vague. The other references are citations or close verbal parallels: *Aet.* 19, according to Bernays,[4] refers to Wisd. of Sol. 11:7, "which created the world out of formless matter"; *Hypoth.* 7:6 is connected by Colson with Prov. 19:7 concerning the precept of love; and *Hypoth.* 7:8 with Prov. 11:1 and 16:11 concerning the wrong scales and measurements.[5] The three latter instances, however, can be contested, since the first two of these do not necessarily mean a borrowing from these books, and the third one may refer to Deut. 25:13–16 or to Lev. 19:35. The reference of *Prob.* 38ff. to Prov. 17:2, "A wise man rules a foolish master" (LXX) is supported by Ambrose who read Philo and even knew some of his lost treatises.[6] The reference of *Congr.* 177 to Prov. 3:11–12, concerning the father who chastises his beloved son, mentions Solomon, and is unquestionable. The following ones also are certain: *Ebr.* 31ff. quotes Prov. 8:22 concerning preexisting Wisdom, mother and nurse of creation, and *Virt.* 62ff. is an implicit reference to the same text. *Ebr.* 84 cites Proverbs three times:

Good also, I think, is that saying in Proverbs (*paroi-miais*): "Let them provide things excellent in the sight of the Lord and men" (cf. Prov. 3:4), since it is through these that the acquisition of excellence is brought to its fullness. For if you learned to observe the laws of your father, and not to reject the ordinances of your mother (Prov. 1:8), you will not fear to say with pride, "For I too became a son obedient to my father and beloved before the face of my mother" (Prov. 4:3).

We added to this list *Q.G.* 4. 129 citing Prov. 19:14, "The self-taught man, of whom it is said in Proverbs, 'From God is woman suited to man.'"

Fifteen references is a small crop, and they are not all certain. However, it seems that other less explicit references or allusions can be included, as when Philo speaks of wisdom as the daughter and delight of God, as nurse ranked with the divine powers, motherless and virginal, providing the sage with instruction and opening her house to him, being for him a mother and a bride, or when wisdom is compared to gold, to the tree of life, to the Law, to Eden and to the land promised to Abraham. There are also references to the Spirit of God as associated with wisdom, pervading the world and man, source of light and sanctification. And there are references to the Two Ways, the coupling of opposites, and panegyrics of Ancestors, which offer striking parallels to the wisdom books, particularly to Ecclesiasticus. The idea that God is not the author of evil but the cause of every good thing, a point Philo never wearies of repeating, is also a theme of Ecclesiasticus and of Wisdom of Solomon. The connection between wisdom and kingship also is represented in Philo.

From actual citations we see, then, that Philo definitely knew Proverbs, but in the case of the other books direct evidence is lacking. Can we, therefore, be certain that Philo knew these books? My purpose is to show that he knew, and made use of, their ideas and images, developing them according to his own views, often altering their meaning. But does this presuppose that he knew and used these

books? C. Larcher says no for Wisdom of Solomon[7] and
the same is possible for Ecclesiasticus and Ecclesiastes. It
seems to me that these scholars who argue that Philo did
not know these books are looking for explicit citations.
But Philo is not likely to cite these books, since he does
not write commentaries on them and he does not grant
them divine authority. May I add that Philo is so different
from what scholars are used to seeing, in the field of
Scripture as well as of philosophy, that he is at once so
Greek yet so biblical, that few are willing to be lost in him
in order to discover him. Therefore, if the reader of this
chapter finds that the ideas and images of the books of
wisdom are developed in Philo, he may conclude together
with me that there is a remarkable parallel as well as
continuity of ideas and language between wisdom literature and Philo. This conclusion is even more certain if one
does not reject the hypotheses that Philo knew not only
the legend but also the *Letter of Aristeas,*[8] and that Philo
was influenced by earlier Jewish allegory in Alexandria.[9]

Wisdom and Knowledge

Let us begin with the association of wisdom and knowledge which we find both in the books of wisdom and in
Philo, and which is as important as the connection between wisdom and virtue. The wise man looking for
knowledge may turn his mind in the direction of the
knowledge of God, or he may turn it to human matters,
i.e., anthropology, cosmology, letters, the sciences of nature, philosophy, briefly, to *paideia.* For Philo wisdom
includes all these areas of knowlege, because wisdom is the
science of things divine and human and their causes (*Q.G.*
3.43). This idea also belongs to the books of wisdom. The
theme of the wise man looking for knowledge is found in
the books of wisdom. In the prologue of Proverbs, for
instance, we read (1:5), "The wise man increases in learning, and the man of understanding acquires skill to under-

stand a proverb and a figure." The book of Proverbs already manifests an interest in practical, theoretical, and literary reflection. Ecclesiasticus (39:1–11) praises the scribe who possesses both practical and theoretical knowledge and is also a man of prayer. These same ideas reappear in Philo: wisdom is a divine light filling the soul of the wise man when he comes near to God; the wise man is a man of prayer, a teacher who communicates his knowledge without dissimulation, jealousy, or gain, and who can be considered as an intermediary between God and the ignorant or the fool.[10] The parallel between Philo and wisdom literature is also evident in Ecclus. 42:15–43:33, where the glory of God is celebrated in nature and in history, and in Wisdom of Sol. 7:17–21, where we find not only the apologetic concern for the demonstration of God's existence from the spectacle of the cosmos, and of the defense of the chief "truths" concerning man and his destiny, but also the following description:

> For it is He who gave me unerring knowledge of what exists, to know the structure of the world and the activity of the elements; the beginning and end and middle of times, the alternations of the solstices and the changes of the seasons, the cycles of the year and the constellations of the stars, the natures of animals and the tempers of wild beasts, the powers of spirits and the reasoning of men, the varieties of plants and the virtues of roots; I learned both what is secret and what is manifest, for wisdom, the fashioner of all things, taught me.

Wisdom here embraces nature and man. Of course, the literary fiction prevents the author from introducing Solomon engaged in a discussion of the Greek philosophy and *paideia*, but the ideas and schools can be identified in his book.[11]

In Philo, the association of wisdom and *paideia* becomes a major theme. Moses and Abraham, but not Solomon, are given, respectively, as the great witness and the great representative of *paideia*, a difference which reflects Philo's intention to consider only the Torah and not the other books. Yet Philo subordinates *paideia* to philosophy and insists on the importance of faith in God in all his discussion of these matters. This hierarchy of values is both a result and a guide for study for the wise man who is in danger of being charmed and distracted by the sciences, or of being seduced by the beauty of the cosmos and of the heavens, and failing to discover the transcendent and living God. His attitude toward secular learning is basically positive as reflected in his description of Moses' education,

> Arithmetic, geometry, the love of metre, rhythm and harmony, and the whole subject of music as shown by the use of instruments or in text-books and treatises of a more special character, were imparted to him by learned Egyptians. These further instructed him in the philosophy conveyed in symbols, as displayed in the so-called holy inscriptions and in the regard paid to animals, to which they even pay divine honors. He had Greeks to teach him the rest of the regular school course, and the inhabitants of the neighboring countries for Assyrian letters and the Chaldean science of the heavenly bodies. This he also acquired from Egyptians, who give special attention to astrology. [*Mos.* 1:23] [12]

Philo goes far beyond Wisdom of Solomon in the appropriation of Greek philosophy and *paideia*. In dealing with the relation between *paideia* and philosophy he uses allegory, a method used only sparingly in the books of wisdom. But his purpose is to explain how *paideia* should be dealt with and evaluated, which would reflect not merely a Greek spirit but also the biblical tradition. Both Philo and Wisdom of Solomon realize that a noble mind may be charmed by *paideia* and by the beauty of the world to the point of missing the discovery of philosophy and of God himself.[13] Both Wisdom and Philo also observe that the demonstration of the Creator is possible on the basis of the order of the universe, and, more particularly, from the "spectacle" of the heavens.[14] This theme was widespread after Xenophon in the cosmic religion of the Hellenistic times, as represented, for instance, by Cleanthes' *Hymn to Zeus,* the pseudo-Aristotelian treatise *De Mundo,* and Cicero, without mentioning the large influence of the now lost treatises of the young Aristotle.[15] The image of Plato's Demiurge was joined with proof of God's existence from the order of the world, and thus was brought into agreement with the biblical faith in the Creator.[16] We can even find in both Philo and Wisdom of Solomon the notion of creation out of formless matter.[17]

Another common theme is vindication of the ways of God in physical and moral evil. This problem was a matter of deep concern to the authors of Proverbs, Ecclesiasticus, Wisdom of Solomon, and to Philo.[18] The wise man should be indifferent to physical evil, or regard it as a chastisement from a God of justice and mercy; and death is seen either as a gift of liberation or as the action of a contrary power, the Devil. Moral evil, however, is ascribed to the free will of man and to the passions of which he has made himself a slave, not to God Himself. God can only be the cause of good. We may wonder whether all these ideas came to Philo through the books of wisdom and the Bible or directly from Greek *paideia.* In this regard the comment of R. Hammerton-Kelly is very much to the point: "I must confess that I am no longer convinced that the attempt to separate 'Jewish' and 'Hellenistic' material in Philo is profitable; it is as difficult and as profitless as trying to separate the Jewish and American elements in the psyche of a Beverly Hills Jew."[19]

The Two Ways

In this section, we shall deal with the wisdom theme of the Two Ways, one which leads to life and happiness, and the other to disobedience and death. The theme of the Two Ways is well known in the Bible under the form of a choice offered by God to man between good and evil,

obedience and disobedience, life and death. It is one of the
chief teachings of Deuteronomic paranesis (30:15–20),
and it appears often in the books of wisdom. We need to
cite only one example of this formula, "The path of
righteousness is life, but the way of error leads to death"
(Prov. 12:28). It also finds expression in images such as
those of the mother, of the hostess, and of the harlot. In
Philo, the theme of the Two Ways appears either in the
logic of the commandments with the idea of the obedience
to God and His Covenant,[20] or in the consideration of
virtue and vice as the fruit of grace and liberty.[21] Let us
point out a few parallels between Philo and the books of
wisdom. A good example is the father and mother who
teach the way of justice to their son and do not hesitate to
chastise him since they want his improvement. In the
books of wisdom, this image is already transposed from
the human parents to God and to personified Wisdom.[22]
The role of chastisement in education appears often in the
Law (Deut. 8:5), in the books of wisdom,[23] and in Philo.
The Father is God who corrects His son Israel or those
who transgress His commandments. See for example Deut.
8:5 and Prov. 3:11–12, "My son, do not despise the Lord's
discipline or be weary of his reproof, for the Lord reproves
him whom He loves, as a father the son in whom he
delights." The master is also the sage who teaches wisdom
to other men (Ecclus. 3:1), or Wisdom herself, who advises
and exhorts her son and does not hesitate to rebuke him
when he disobeys her precepts. Not only is she the mother,
but Solomon chose her as his wife in Wisdom of Sol. 9:1ff.
Philo insists on the duties of parents and children, particularly in *Dec.* 106–120, where parents have, in some ways, a
divine role vis-à-vis their offspring. He reaffirms the respect due to father and mother in *Ebr.* 84, where he
quotes Prov. 3:4 and 4:3, but, in the same place, he
allegorizes: the father becomes the *Logos,* and the mother,
Paideia, "Their father, right reason, has taught them the
honour of the Father of all; their mother, instruction, has
taught them not to make light of those principles which

are laid down by convention and accepted everywhere" (*Ebr.* 81). A list of the disciplines pertaining to encyclopedic *paideia* follows (91–92):

> Under the name of piety and holiness it deals with the attributes of the Really Existent; under that of nature study, with all that concerns the heavens and the heavenly bodies; as meteorology, with the air and the consequences which result through its changes and variations both at the main seasons of the year and those particular ones which follow cycles of months and days; as ethics, with what tends to the improvement of human conduct, and this last takes various forms: politic, dealing with the state; economic, with the management of a house; sympotic, or the art of conviviality, with banquets and festivities; and further we have the kingly faculty dealing with the control of men, and the legislative with commands and prohibitions.

Let us observe that, in this list, the primacy is ascribed to piety and holiness, which connect the sage with God.

The image of the Hostess is important in the books of wisdom and in Philo. This image is twofold, since the Hostess can be either Wisdom or the Harlot, and her teaching can be wine of spiritual delight or the wine of folly. We find this coupling of opposites in Proverbs (9:1–18, cf. 8:6), where both Wisdom and Folly make a speech and invite men to visit their house and to share their bread and wine. The idea of drinking the wine of folly reminds us of the wine of Sodom and Gomorrah in Deut. 32:32ff. The theme of the banquet, with indulgence in violent passions, greediness, and carnal pleasure, is developed in Proverbs, Ecclesiasticus, and Wisdom of Solomon.[24] Hesitating between Wisdom and Folly, men can be compared to the man at the crossing of the ways who is solicited by the strange woman but reminded of his duty by virtue. (Prov. 1:11; 5:1; 8:1).

In Philo, the theme of the two kinds of women representing good and evil reappears in many kinds of spiritual conflicts, and we also find the images of the house of wine, of wisdom and of folly.[25] This image has a biblical root, but Philo develops it according to the Greek example of Heracles at the crossing of the ways, solicited by two women representing virtue and pleasure. The story is told by Xenophon (*Memorabilia* 2.1), but is much older. Philo refers to it again and again, either naming Heracles himself (*Prob.* 99–104), or substituting the biblical figures of the hated woman (Leah, or asceticism) and of the loved woman (Rachel, or pleasure), the two wives of Jacob, the biblical hero of virtue, for the figures of the Greek story. Philo makes use, in this interpretation, of the law of Deut. 21:15–17 concerning the inheritance of the son of the hated woman. The most remarkable development on this subject is *Sacr.* 19–44, which includes two long discourses, one from Pleasure and the other from *Ponos* (effort), and two long lists of virtues and vices. For the present purpose let us notice that Philo uses the Greek example, yet he gives it a biblical character. We are not too surprised to see Philo using the story of Heracles at the crossing of the roads and even mentioning the Greek hero by name, because Philo delights in stories which can be allegorized, whatever their origin, as we see for instance when he uses the story of the Muses, which, like that of Heracles, was a commonplace of moral teaching and had lost all its pagan connotation. But Philo transposes this story into biblical language: Heracles is now Jacob; and piety towards God is mentioned first on the list of virtues in the same text.

In considering the theme of the Two Ways, we still have to deal with retribution. Just as in Deuteronomy and in the books of wisdom, retribution is earthly, since the practice of good is a "way of life" which embraces happiness and success. Wisdom of Solomon, however, insists on the reward and life in the hereafter. Since, in the earthly reward, prosperity is the recompense of justice, it becomes easy to conceive of the reward as either a divine blessing or curse, or as self-retribution. The idea that self-reward, in itself and in its consequence, is temporal success is very Greek,[26] but the biblical books of wisdom also lay stress on it. A couple of examples are enough as evidence: "Go to the ant, O sluggard; consider her ways, and be wise" (Prov. 6:6), and, "My son, do not forget my teaching, but let your heart keep my commandments; for length of days and years of life and abundant welfare will they give you. . . . So you will find favor and good repute in the sight of God and man" (Prov. 3:1–2, 4). Prudence is often seen as a companion of wisdom, but prudence is an earthly virtue. Philo derives prudence and the other cardinal virtues from wisdom as does the Wisdom of Solomon (8:7).

Philo believes in the immortality of the soul and in eternal life,[27] but he does not postpone retribution to another world, since he holds it to be immediate in the form of self-reward according to the teaching of Plato and of the Bible. The rewards for virtue are the good working of the senses and of the functions of the body, temporal blessings, the esteem of one's countrymen, social virtues and influence on neighbors, even the ability to become a good statesman or a citizen of the world. The opposite, the bondage of the passions, leads to the ruin of the body and soul and can become disastrous for our neighbor. Wisdom can be used as a remedy, since it makes one into a free man and a friend of God and purifies one from passions.[28] Healing of the soul is necessary, since there is nobody who has lived without tasting evil.[29] However, more than purification, the essential reward for virtue is the growing of virtue in our soul, and perfection, especially when virtue comes to be loved for itself, quickened by divine grace, and thus being more divine than human. Virtue itself becomes a source of divine joy and energy (*Leg. Al.* 3.166–168).

The reward for justice in the hereafter, or the idea of immortality, is not developed in Proverbs and Ecclesiasticus, although it may be underlying the pair death-life and the image of the tree of life. But it is a characteristic teaching of Wisdom of Solomon; for instance, "God created man for incorruption, and made him in the image of his own eternity, but through the Devil's envy, death

entered the world" (Wisd. of Sol. 2:23–24); "The souls of
the just are in the hand of God, and no torment will ever
touch them" (3:1); "Why has (the just) been numbered
among the sons of God [the angels?], and why is his lot
among the saints?" (5:5); "Wisdom brings about incorrup-
tibility, and leads to immortality and an eternal reign"
(6:17–21).[30]

Philo depends on Plato for his notion of the "unending
death." Immortality properly speaking is immortal life, as
in Plato, the fruit of virtue and of contemplation, because
of the essential immortality of the archetypes of virtue in
which men share.[31] The tree of life in Philo represents
virtue, goodness, or wisdom, as a source of everlasting
life.[32] However, it would be wrong to reduce Philo's
doctrine of spiritual life on earth and of immortality to
that of the Greeks, since he teaches that the life of the soul
depends on a gift of God's word and spirit (*Leg. Al.*
3.162–176). In addition, as in Wisd. of Sol. 5:5, the soul
of the wise, on her departure, is translated to God, being
added to a genus in the case of Moses, and to a race in the
case of other men.[33] We should also remember that Philo
is an interpreter of Scripture before being an exponent of
Greek philosophy, and that, faithful to the inclination of
the books of wisdom,[34] he lays emphasis on spiritual
goods, and even interprets in this sense the material blessings of Deuteronomy (*Praem.* 104).

Preexisting Wisdom

The theme of the preexisting Wisdom is very rich in
Philo. Wisdom appears as a divine power in connection
with the image of Woman rather than with that of Logos.
She is considered a source of fecundity in the soul rather
than as an agent of creation for the physical world although she is associated with the Logos in the work of
creation. She is also associated with the Spirit of God, with
the Law, Tabernacle, Eden, and the Land promised to
Abraham.

Merely enumerating these topics seems to promise an interesting comparison between the teachings of the books of wisdom, where these attributions are scattered and not brought together systematically. Philo recasts these materials, presenting a more coherent and systematic account of preexistent wisdom.

What do we find in the books of wisdom? The great test, unquestionably, is Prov. 8:22–31. J. T. Foreste[35] points out the most important features of this famous text: wisdom is from God and absolutely prior to the visible creation; the preexistence of wisdom is developed according to the plan of biblical cosmogony; wisdom has a role to play in creation, but Proverbs is content to assert her presence at creation with only a vague suggestion of an active role; the sense of companionship is not clear, and wisdom can be considered either as the architect or as the nursling of God.[36]

Philo knows Prov. 8:22ff and the Wisdom prior to creation. He writes (*Ebr.* 31), "Thus, in the pages of one of the inspired company, wisdom is represented as speaking of herself after this manner: 'God obtained me first of all his works and founded me before the ages' (Prov. 8:22). True, for it was necessary that all that came to the birth of creation should be younger than the mother and nurse of the All." In the context, Wisdom is called knowledge (*epistēmē*) of the Father and Maker of the universe. Their son is this veritable world, for she received the divine seed and became a mother. Philo combines the idea of mother to that of nurse (*tithēnēs*) of the universe, which may reflect in the active mode (the one who nurses) the nuance of the Hebrew. He also uses the middle voice *ektesato* (He obtained me) instead of *ektise,* the active (He created me) of LXX, thus once more being closer to the Hebrew.[37] Philo refers to Prov. 8:22 implicitly in *Virt.* 62 and explicitly in *Det.* 54, in the same sense of the preexisting Wisdom.

There are many references in Philo to Wisdom as prior to the visible world and as creative. We even find the notion of creation out of formless matter in *Aet.* 19, reminding us of Wisd. of Sol. 11:17, and perhaps *Timaeus*

51a. Wisdom is the companion of God because of her extra-temporal and divine origin, and we might say that God has never been without his Wisdom. But Wisdom is also posterior to .the creation of the world, which seems to contradict what we said before. We read in *Q.G.* 1.6, "But after the world wisdom came into being, since after the creation of the world Paradise was made in the same manner as the poets say the chorus of Muses (was formed), in order to praise the Creator and His work." Paradise here means wisdom, which is defined in the context as the knowledge of things divine and human and their causes. Muses are created in order to inspire poets, that is to say the men who perceive the beauty and order of the world, and who acknowledge and praise the Creator in hymns (cf. *Plant.* 126–129). Here (*Q.G.* 1.6), wisdom is found in both the praise of creation and in the inspiration leading to the perception of its order and beauty, for wisdom can be seen in only its own light, "for it is impossible for nature to see nor is it possible without wisdom to praise the creator of all things."[38] This teaching relies on the Philonic (and Platonic) theory of exemplarism, where the archetypes are naturally endowed with light and energy, and is complemented by the doctrine of prophetic inspiration, which is substantially that of Plato in *Banquet* and *Phaedrus*.[39]

However, reconciliation between the wisdom prior and the wisdom posterior to the visible world is not a difficult task. The bond is found in the theory of exemplarism itself, since, through the archetypes, we reach the divine power which unites them and is their source, God's wisdom. In this sense, divine Wisdom is close to the Logos of God, who is the architect creating the city in his mind before planting it on the earth (*Op.* 23–25). But, if divine Wisdom presents an intellectualistic aspect, her character is, first of all, moral and mystical. In one word, she is the daughter of God, the spouse of man, for she is the divine source of virtue.

Let us begin with wisdom as the daughter of God in her extra-temporal existence. The idea in its fullest expression is found in the life of Isaac (*Praem.* 49–59). Isaac is the man who is naturally perfect, that is, he is by nature in full communication with God and needs only to persevere in this state. His mother is Sarah, who represents sovereign or divine Wisdom. His name is Isaac, which means "laughter," i.e., the joy accompanying virtue. In Isaac this joy is divine, and so evil has no attraction for him. Rebekah, his only wife, is the "Constancy" which is his only need, but she is also in some regards a rejuvenated Sarah, transformed from the old woman (philosophy) who receives the sage who has grown old in the course of *paideia* and gives him a belated posterity in a bride who is radiant with youth and charm—Wisdom in love with the sage. According to *Q.G.* 4.188 (cf. 145–146), Isaac is playing a divine game with Rebekah-Wisdom when Abimelech sees them and covets Rebekah. Abimelech, however, is the man who is still "in progress," imperfect, and the imperfect man cannot love Wisdom and have her as his wife. When Woman is the symbol of virtue in the life of the Patriarchs and saints of the Old Testament, she appears as the virtue of the ascetic which disciplines and purifies the passions of man, or as philosophy welcoming the man coming to her from *paideia;* but when she is the symbol of divine Wisdom or Generic (absolute) Virtue, she gives to the wise in a mystical intercourse a divine posterity, the virtue born from God, joyful and invincible. In contradistinction to Hagar, who is a figure of *paideia,* or Leah, who is a figure of effort or asceticism, and who both are still very "human," women such as Sarah, Rebekah, Sipphorah, and Hannah figure divine Wisdom in the mystery of her fecundity in the wise man. Philo refers to a mystery, to which Jeremiah, Hosea, and some exegetes of his own time, who practice allegory, are initiated.[40]

What is this mystery, this divine game? Let us re-examine *Q.G.* 4.188:

It is said that even the Father and Creator of the universe continually rejoices in His life and plays and is joyful, finding pleasure in play which is in keeping with the divine and in joyfulness. And He has no need of anything nor does He lack anything, but with joy he delights in Himself and in His powers and in the worlds made by Him. . . . Rightly, therefore, and properly does the wise man, believing (his) end (to consist in) likeness to God, strive, so far as possible to unite the created with the uncreated and the mortal with the immortal, and not to be deficient or wanting in gladness and joyfulness in His likeness. For this reason he plays this game of unchangeable and constant virtue with Rebekah, whose name is to be interpreted in the Armenian language as "Constancy." This game and delight of the soul the wicked man does not know. . . . But the progressive man, as if looking from a window, sees it but not the whole of it and not the mingling of both alone.

Herewith we again meet Wisdom as the daughter of God and the mother of all things. We read in *Q.G.* 4.97, "[Rebekah] was born to 'Bethuel,' which should be interpreted as 'daughter of her God.' And who is to be considered the daughter of God but Wisdom who is the firstborn mother of all things and most of all of those who are greatly purified in soul?" We also read that the house of Bethuel is "the household of wisdom" (*Q.G.* 4.116), that God is "the housemaster of wisdom" (*Q.G.* 4.59), that Isaac's mother was "motherless wisdom," whose house was changed into a Bridal chamber for him so as to be a unity of betrothal and a partnership of the self-taught kind with ever virginal Constancy" (*Q.G.* 4.145). The divine Graces, who also are "virgin daughters" and powers of God, seem to offer a parallel to divine Wisdom (*Q.E.* 2.61). It is possible to enlarge on the sexual imagery of this mystery which is the fecundation of virtue. Wisdom is made pregnant by God, and impregnates man while herself remaining a virgin. Feminine in regard to God, Wisdom becomes masculine with regard to man, who is made masculine by her, and begets, but who should not affirm his fatherhood of this offspring which is the work of God in him. The defilement of virtue in a soul is remedied by intercourse with wisdom, which restores the pristine condition of virginity to deflowered virtue.[41] Good examples of developments of this kind can be found in *Fug.* 48–52 and *Cher.* 42–52. Philo, therefore, founds this mystery of Wisdom on the biblical notion of the preexisting Wisdom and on what is said in Scripture of Wisdom as the divine light of the soul and as woman; but he gives this theme a broad development and extends its use to the analysis of the life of virtue, which is his favorite topic. These speculations have antecedents and parallels in Greek philosophy and in Egyptian and Persian myths.[42] The problem of Philo's sources is complex, especially in this case, and perhaps such an inquiry is not truly relevant and fruitful, in the sense of Hammerton-Kelly cited above.

The Spirit of God

We shall not enlarge on the theme of the Spirit of God in Philo, since this topic has been studied recently.[43] The Spirit of God includes both the prophetic and the creative Spirit. The books of wisdom provide scant materials concerning the prophetic Spirit. Philo grants it a larger place: he considers Moses as inspired, and also the Patriarchs, Hannah, Jeremiah, the Therapeutae of Lake Mareotis; and he explains prophecy by the theory of ecstasy, in which the soul is drawn out of itself and moved by God.[44] Can we say that Philo conforms to the teaching of Wisdom of Solomon (7:21–8:1) concerning the Spirit of God? Wisdom of Solomon interprets Wisdom as a subtle, pure, intelligent spirit, originating from God and penetrating everything like the light coming from the sun. But above all Wisdom is a spirit which enters holy souls and makes them into friends of God and prophets. The ideas and terminology of Stoicism in this text have been noticed by scholars, as well as has the negation of the Stoic Pantheism by the affirmation of the Spirit of Wisdom as a gift of God.[45]

In Philo, all these features reappear, although we cannot affirm that he refers to this text, and we find in him all the aspects of the Stoic teachings on the *Pneuma* (Spirit).[46] Philo also maintains the association between Wisdom and Spirit.[47] But, just as Wisdom finds her favorite field of activity in the sage and the virtuous, the Spirit of God finds its own in the structure of the soul, of which it becomes a component. The Spirit of God in Philo seems to be confined to anthropology (and in some regards to cosmology) to such an extent that, except concerning prophecy, we do not find it mentioned in Philo's developments on virtues and good deeds which belong to the field of ethics. The reason for this silence is that the operation of the Spirit of God is found not on the moral but on the metaphysical level as the communication to man of divine light and energy.[48] The presence, or rather the almost complete absence of the Spirit of God in us, is the result of the original drama, when man renounced the Spirit of God in Adam, and, as a consequence, was enslaved by the passions in the first age of individual life.[49] When Adam woke up to sense-perception, symbolized by the woman, he became one flesh with her, and thus, her slave not her master. From then on, he expected from her the gift of knowledge, which is the most essential function of the soul. Therefore, he has renounced the contemplation of the archetypes and divorced life-giving Wisdom, and the Spirit of God no longer inspires him with the impetuosity of a wind. Only a breath of it is left in man, just enough to make him aware of his choice of evil instead of good, and to fit him for repentance and punishment. Adam, and all those who are under the domination of the flesh, need to be purified, to repent, to struggle against the passions, and to come back to God with the help of His grace.[50] Thus we are at once the representatives of the man created according to the divine image and of the man fashioned out of clay, who is flesh. For this anthropological interpretation, Philo relies on the comparison of the two narratives of the creation of man,[51] and also on Gen. 6:3, "The Lord

God said, My spirit shall not abide for ever among men, because they are flesh" (*Q.G.* 9). Of course, this reminds us of Wisd. of Sol. 9:13–18 concerning the "earthly tent burdening the thoughtful mind," and of Wisd. of Sol. 1:4–5, "Wisdom does not enter a deceitful soul, nor dwell in a body enslaved to sin; for a holy and disciplined spirit will flee from deceit" (cf. Ecclus. 1:19).

The Tabernacle, Law, and Eden

Three images complete the theme of preexisting Wisdom: the Tabernacle, the Law, and Eden. Ecclesiasticus, chapter 24, weaves a crown for wisdom with all her identifications and functions: she comes from the mouth of God, dwells in the heavens, elected Israel as her resting-place, ministered in the holy tabernacle; she is likened to several kinds of trees, to the plants productive of incense, and to the vine; she is the hostess, the Law, the rivers of Eden, the dawn. Let us focus on Ecclus. 24:10, "In the holy Tabernacle I ministered before Him, and so I was established in Zion." This tabernacle is the heavenly one existing from eternity, and Wisd. of Sol. 9:8 clearly distinguishes between the temple of Solomon and the holy tent which God prepared from the beginning.

In Philo, the Tabernacle is a figure of wisdom since it is identified with wisdom itself, or with its copy, or with its house. On the basis of Exod. 31:2, "I have called by name Bezaleel . . . and I have filled him with the divine spirit of wisdom (*sophias,* LXX), and intelligence, and craftsmanship," Philo compares Moses, the wise man *par excellence,* to Bezaleel. Of course, Moses is far superior in wisdom to Bezaleel, since he sees the patterns of the Tabernacle, whereas Bezaleel, whose name means "in the shadow of God," and who is the artificer of this fabric, which is a counterpart of the universe, sees the universe only, and not the archetypes (*Plant.* 26–27). But Philo is more interested in the Tabernacle as the figure of man—the microcosm—

and of the soul of man, for instance, in *Leg. Al.* 95,
"This . . . is the reason of God's proclaiming Bezaleel by
name, and saying that He has given him wisdom and
knowledge, and that He will appoint him artificer and
chief craftsman of all the works of the Tabernacle, that is
of the soul. . . . We must say, then, that here too we have a
form which God has stamped on the soul as on the tested
coin." Bezaleel, the lover of wisdom, is introduced elsewhere (*Som.* 1.205–206) as weaving together grammar,
music, rhetoric, and philosophy into a single work, i.e., the
fruitful combination of culture and philosophy.[52]

The Tabernacle and its contents are a symbol of wisdom
(*Her.* 112). The "ten curtains" (Exod. 36:1), according to
Congr. 116–117, include the whole of wisdom, which is
God's dwelling place, or palace. This dwelling consists of
the intelligibles and of the sense-perceptibles, that is, of
the whole soul, mind, and senses, as receptive of knowledge. However, the tent which Moses received from God
and fixed outside the camp (Exod. 33:7) figures wisdom as
abiding in a purified soul, and not in the disturbing company of the body and passions, according to *Leg. Al.*
3.46–48.

The Law

Ecclesiasticus (15:1–10) offers a meditation on the Law
which reminds us of the Philonic images of Wisdom as a
mother and as a virginal bride: "The man who fears the
Lord will do this, and he who holds to the Law will obtain
wisdom. She will come to meet him like a mother, and like
the wife of his youth she will welcome him. She will feed
him with the bread of understanding, and give him the
water of understanding to drink. . . ." But the chief text is
Ecclus. 24:23, "All this is the book of the covenant of the
Most High God, the law which Moses commanded us as an
inheritance for the congregations of Jacob. . . ." The truth
is that this image can hardly be isolated from the two

others, since the three, the Tabernacle, the Law, and Eden, are contained in the same chapter 24. To these speculations, we may also add the references made to particular laws, and the meditations on the Fathers (Ecclesiasticus, chapters 40–50, and Wisdom of Solomon, chapters 10–19). A good example of a particular law recalled in the books of wisdom is the precept of justice in bargaining, i.e., the divine obligation to make use of exact scales and of weights and measures which conform to law. This example reappears in Philo, with a special emphasis.[53] More generally, Philo comments on the letter of the laws in his four long books *On special laws,* in such a way that E. R. Goodenough has been able to substantiate the hypothesis that Philo exercised a public office in his community of Alexandria.[54] Philo also writes on the commandments, which he considers as the ten general principles of religious ethics, from which all special laws derive (*Dec.* 154–178), and on virtues, blessings, and curses, all of these with the depth of a philosopher and believer for whom Greek ethics and the Law of Moses combine and enlighten one another for the best understanding of the service of God. But the most remarkable is the use he makes of the theme of the Fathers in his meditation on the Patriarchs, who represent the three ways to perfection, and on the other great figures of the history of Israel found in the Law of Moses.

The same names of Ancestors celebrated in Ecclesiasticus and Wisdom of Solomon, or, more exactly, those belonging to the Law, reappear in Philo, often with the same remarks. For instance, both Adam and Cain are examples of sin, but the former also of repentance, and the latter of perseverance in sin (Wisd. of Sol. 10:1–3, in Philo, *Post.* 10). Ecclus. 49:14–16 praises Seth, Enoch, Shem, and (44:17) Noah. We read (Ecclus. 44:16), "Enoch pleased the Lord, and was taken up; he was an example of repentance to all generations." Philo develops this idea, and introduces Enoch as the type of the repenting man who, because of his change for the better, is "translated" by God to a higher rank (*Abr.* 17–26). Philo distinguishes a

first triad consisting of Enos, Enoch, and Noah, the figures
respectively of hope, repentance, and justice (*Abr.* 7–48;
Praem. 10–23), and a second triad with the three patriarchs Abraham, Isaac, and Jacob, who figure the three
ways to perfection: through learning, through the gift of a
good nature, and through practice or asceticism (*Abr.*
48–56).[55] *Jos.* 1 adds a fourth type, Joseph, as the political man. Wisd. of Sol. 10:10–12, like Philo, introduces
Jacob as the Ascetic, the man of effort (*ponos*).

With Moses, Philo opens another series of symbols,
especially Pharaoh, Aaron, and Phinehas, who are praised
in Ecclesiasticus, chapter 45. As compared to Pharaoh,
Moses is a "man of God," or the wise man who opposes
the fool, and whom the latter should consider as his master
or even his god (*Mut.* 128). According to the same symbolism, Moses represents the mind inspired by God, which
is godlike in comparison to the body and the irrational
part of man (*Leg. Al.* 1.39–40; *Q.G.* 2.76). We explained
the pair Moses-Bezaleel above. The pair Moses-Aaron is
related to wisdom, since Moses is often called "the wise
man," for instance in *Prob.* 29. The *logeion* (Exod. 28:30)
upon the breast of Aaron represents clarity of thought and
of expression, and also reason analyzing and resolving the
disorder of passion (*Leg. Al.* 3.116–126). However even
with the possession of reason, Aaron is inferior to Moses,
according to the symbolism of Lev. 8:29 and 7:34: Moses
removes the breast of the ram of consecration, whereas
Aaron is given the breast and shoulder from the sacrifices
of salvation. Philo derives from this symbolism that Moses
figures the ideals of *apatheia* (the Stoic notion of the total
uprooting of the passions), and Aaron, that of *metriopatheia* (the Peripatetic and Middle-Platonic notion of a
compromise between reason and the passions, or of a
positive and sound evaluation of the lower goods, i.e., of
bodily and material goods). Phinehas figures the fight
against sensual pleasure which enslaves the mind and leads
it away from God. Just as the fight of Phinehas led him to
the priesthood, the fight against the passions is connected

with dedication to God, which is the characteristic of the priesthood (*Post.* 182–183).

Eden

Although Proverbs and Wisdom of Solomon contain allusions to Eden, for instance the tree of life[56] and the tree of the knowledge of good and evil, or the entry of death into the world by the jealousy of the devil (Wisd. of Sol. 2:23), and although Ecclus. 16:26–17:14 is a meditation on the narrative of the creation, the great text, and the only one which we must consider in the present context, is Ecclus. 24:25–34, the chapter also referring to the Tabernacle and the Law. Wisdom is compared to the rivers of Eden, but an Eden enlarged according to the dimensions of the Land promised to Abraham in Gen. 15:18–21, since, with the addition of the Nile and the Jordan, there are six rivers instead of four, and the limits are the river of Egypt and the Euphrates. These rivers water the garden, but "the canal of wisdom became a river, and her river became a sea." Perhaps the instruction of wisdom shining forth like the dawn and reaching all future generations points to the image of the East, where God planted the garden.

In Philo, the image of Eden is very important for his notion of wisdom. The three books of *Legum Allegoriae* comment on Genesis, chapters 2 and 3, and similarly *Q.G.* 1.1–57. For instance, *Leg. Al.* 1.63–87 deals with the four rivers of Eden: the river going forth from Eden to water the garden and dividing into four "heads of rivers" (Gen. 2:10) is "generic virtue, taking its start from Eden, the wisdom of God, which is full of joy, and brightness, and exultation, glorying and priding itself only upon God its Father; but the specific virtues, four in number, are derived from generic virtue, which like a river waters the perfect achievements of each of them with an abundant flow of noble doings." The general idea is that Divine Wisdom is the source of the cardinal virtues and of all other virtues in man, and that *sophia,* the *Logos,* generic virtue, Goodness, and the Spirit of God, all are associated in this achievement.[57] Eden is the symbol of "delicacies," or "luxury", which means excellence and happiness, and thereby it is the copy of the heavenly wisdom.[58] Eden is also the symbol of the soul as the garden of virtue, "The bountiful God plants in the soul as it were a garden of virtues and of the modes of conduct corresponding to each of them, a garden that brings the soul to perfect happiness," a happiness suggested by the name "Eden" and culminating in the worship of the Only Wise (*Plant.* 7–39). Paradise is also a symbol of wisdom in the sense of philosophy, i.e., the knowledge of the divine and human and of their causes, for the purpose of praise (*Q.G.* 1.6). The tree of life in Philo is a figure of wisdom or goodness and is distinguished from the tree of the knowledge of good and evil.[59] The gold and gems also figure wisdom (*Leg. Al.* 1.77–84) and remind us of Gen. 2:12. And Philo develops the image of wisdom shining like dawn in the East (*Leg. Al.* 1.46; *Plant.* 40).

The three images studied in the present section, the Tabernacle, Law, and Eden, are unquestionably Jewish and biblical. It would be fruitless to try to prove that Philo interprets them with reference to Ecclesiasticus, chapter 24 for many reasons, the first being that these images are scattered throughout his works. But we can see that both Philo and Judaism hold them as preexisting entities, identified with Wisdom, and created by God before the world,[60] and therefore as an extension of preexisting Wisdom. In this sense, Philo is Jewish. However, can we say that the contents of his developments, or the ideas, are Greek? We certainly can, and they are very Greek indeed, since the Tabernacle figures the universe and its archetypes according to the Platonic theory of exemplarism; the Law is understood in the sense of the Stoics as the Natural Law; and the Patriarchs are the symbols of the three ways to perfection (*Jos.* 1), classical from the time of Plato and Aristotle.[61] Moses and Aaron respectively figure *apatheia* and *metriopatheia,* thus echoing a discussion between Stoics, Peripatetics, and Middle-Platonists concerning the value of the several kinds of goods: spiritual, bodily, and material.[62] Joseph figures the political man and thus recalls a controversy on temporal values, considered pejoratively in the Allegorical Commentary;[63] but Joseph, in the treatise named after him, *De Josepho,* becomes the image—more comforting—of the Hellenistic ideal of kingship such as we find in the Neo-Pythagorean treatises on Kingship.[64]

Exodus and Liturgical Symbols

The books of wisdom contain reflections concerning the events of Exodus and liturgical matters, both interpreted as symbols. The liturgy of ancient Israel in Exodus and Leviticus is also closely connected with these events which provide its historical setting of interpretation: the Redemption of Israel and the Covenant. The books of wisdom are aware of the importance of Exodus, and, for instance, Wisdom of Solomon, chapters 10–15 is a kind of homily on Exodus presented as the achievement of divine Wisdom. In Philo also the Exodus as a whole and in its detail appears as the work of God,[65] and, according to the allegorical meaning, figures the progress of man towards perfection.[66] The pentecostal vigils of the Therapeutae seem to refer to the mystery of salvation based on Exodus, including the liturgical dance of thanksgiving on the seashore and perhaps at the well (*Cont.* 68ff.). The Crossing-festival (*Spec. Leg.* 2.147) with all its detail suggests the purification of the soul according to interpreters whom Philo does not name *Q.G.* 1.4 interprets the crossing allegorically as a change from ignorance and stupidity to science and wisdom, and from vice to virtue. In the Passover meal, in the same sense, the herbs signify repentance leading to conversion and to the contemplation of wisdom (*Q.E.* 1.15).

The inhospitality of Egypt is emphasized in both Wisd. of Sol. 19:1–4, cf. 10:7, and in Philo (*Mos.* 1.140–142), and both also interpret the plagues similarly as punishing the Egyptians and rewarding the Israelites (Wisd. of Sol. 11:59, cf. Philo, *Mos.* 1.143–146). Both explain the miraculous aspect of the plagues as resulting from a change in the properties of the elements by divine will, not in their nature (Wisd. of Sol. 19:18, cf. Philo, *Mos.* 1.143–146). But Egypt is not yet in Wisdom of Solomon, as it is in Philo, an allegorical figure of the body or of materialistic atheism, although we find the cartoon of Egyptian idolatry in Wisd. of Sol. 15:14–19.

The Rock is mentioned in Wisd. of Sol. 11:4 in the literal meaning only. Philo develops the allegorical meaning. In *Det.* 115–117: the Rock and the field of Deut. 32:13 figure God's wisdom and the modest virtues of men respectively, and the manna is mentioned in the same context interpreted as the divine word,

> He [Moses] uses the word "Rock" to express the solid and indestructible wisdom of God, which feeds and nurses and rears to sturdiness all who yearn after imperishable sustenance. For this divine wisdom has appeared as mother of all that are in the world, affording to her offspring, as soon as they are born, the nourishment which they require from her own breasts. But not all her offspring are worthy to eat divine food, but only such as are found worthy of their parents; for many of them fall victims to the famine of virtue, a famine more cruel than that of edible things. The fountain of the divine wisdom runs sometimes with a gentler and more quiet stream, at other times more swiftly and with a fuller and stronger current. When it runs down gently, it sweetens much as honey does; when it runs swiftly down, it comes in full volume as material for lighting up the soul, even as oil does a lamp. In another place he uses a synonym for this rock, and calls it "manna." Manna is the divine word, eldest of all existences, which bears the most comprehensive name of "Somewhat."

Usually, the symbolism of water refers to wisdom, and for this reason a well is a symbol of wisdom.[67] Already Deut. 32:2–4 associated rain or dew with the word of God.

Wisd. of Sol. 16:25–29 interprets the manna as the food of the word of God. Philo offers a long discussion (*Leg. Al.* 3.162–181) concerning the manna, which he interprets similarly as the heavenly bread of the word of God, as the food of light which should be taken daily for the sake of Light and of Beauty, as the seed which can be compared to the apple of the eye because it sees things above, and as the frost which can freeze the passions. This food is that with which Jacob was nourished by God from his youth (Gen. 48:15ff), and this seed opens the wombs of virtue and closes those of the love for bodily goods. According to *Fug.* 137–139, this food is the Divine Word from which all kinds of instructions and wisdom flow in perpetual stream, and the ethereal wisdom which God drops from above upon minds which are by nature apt and take delight in contemplation (*Mut.* 259; *Her.* 191).

These symbols are not properly liturgical, although they became the symbols of Christian sacraments; but those related to the high priest and his offerings, according to Philo, confer on the wise man and on wisdom or virtue a priestly and sacrificial character. We can say that Ecclesiasticus and Wisdom of Solomon do present developments on the liturgy of the high priest, and the latter on the cosmic symbolism of his robe.[68] We read in Wisd. of Sol. 18:24, "For upon his long robe the whole world was depicted, and the glories of the fathers were engraved on the four rows of stones, and thy majesty on the diadem upon his head."

In Philo, the wise man, like the high priest coming into and out of the holy of holies, stands on the borderline between men and God, being superior to men but less than God (*Som.* 2.228–236, about Lev. 16:17). The robe of the high priest is the symbol of the universe, which is the fellow-ministrant of the high priest and the son of the Father of all, according to *Spec. Leg.* 1.93–97,

At the very lowest part of the skirt there are appended
golden pomegranates and bells and flower-work, symbols of earth and water: the flower patterns of earth
because they grow and flower out of it, the pomegranates of flowing fruit, of water, the name preserving
its derivation from "flowing," while the bells shew forth
the harmony and concord and unison of the parts of the
universe. The order in which the parts are arranged is
also admirable. At the very top is what he calls the
breastpiece in which are placed the stones, a copy of
heaven because heaven also is at the top. Then under it
the full-length skirt, dark blue right through because the
air also is black and occupies the second position below
the heaven, and the flower-work and pomegranates at
the extremities because to earth and water is alloted the
lowest place in the universe. Such is the form in which
the sacred vesture was designed, a copy of the universe,
a piece of work of marvellous beauty to the eye and the
mind. . . . It expresses the wish first that the high-priest
should have in evidence upon him an image of the All,
that so by constantly contemplating it he should render
his own life worthy of the sum of things, secondly that
in performing his holy office he should have the whole
universe as his fellow-ministrant. . . . The high-priest of
the Jews makes prayers and gives thanks not only on
behalf of the whole human race, but also for the parts
of nature, earth, water, air, fire. For he holds the world
to be, as in very truth it is, his country, and in its behalf
he is wont to propitiate the Ruler with supplication
and intercession, beseeching Him to make His creature a
partaker of His own kindly and merciful nature.

As we see, the relations between the high priest, the
Logos, and the wise, and between the cosmic cult and the
priestly consecration of the wise to God, strengthen the
character of adoration and of mediation of the wise
man.[69]

The offering of the high priest also represents the offering of the cosmic praise and that of virtue in the soul by
the wise. The wine offered by the heavenly or by the
earthly high-priest as a "libation of himself" is contrasted

with the wine of folly from the vine of Sodom (*Som.* 2.183, 190–192). The composition of incense represents the universe wrought by wisdom and the thanks given for the cosmos (*Her.* 196–200). But the altar of incense represents the thankful soul of the wise who offers up to God the incense of virtue. Finally, the sacred light ever burning on the altar is a symbol of wisdom (*Spec. Leg.* 2.287).

The abundance of symbolism in relation to wisdom shows how intensely interested Philo was in the investigation of every aspect of wisdom. However, the content of his developments is biblical in expression and in most of the ideas, and the cosmological and anthropological speculations elaborated on the basis of this symbolism fit into the frame of his religious faith and of his praise of the Creator.[70]

Similarities of Method between Philo and the Books of Wisdom

The reader is certainly struck and perhaps wearied by the abuse of symbolism and of allegory in Philo. Philo, indeed, does abuse this method, but we must also understand that biblical symbolism is his most characteristic and favorite mode of expression, what today we would call his philosophical language. This language is common to him and to the allegorists of his time. He is not content to express the data of philosophy in classical terms, but he also uses symbolism based on the etymologies of biblical names, on the lives of the most famous men and women of the Law, on the peculiarites of the conjugal life of the Patriarchs, on the events and materials from Scripture and from Jewish worship, on laws. This biblical language enables him to develop what he calls the philosophy of Moses, a philosophy stuffed, indeed, with Greek dressing, but purified by the language and the theology of Scripture. The books of wisdom are more discreet in the use of this method, but we find in them also the presence of allegory and of many images exploited by Philo, as, for example, the allegory of the hostess and the image of the garden. Philo is surely as much indebted to the Bible as he is to Greek philosophy.

A second point is equally important, namely the use of the method of contrast, or of the coupling of opposites. We find it in the books of wisdom. For instance, Proverbs parallels wisdom and folly throughout, and Ecclesiasticus (33:14–15) explains the method of contrast, "Good is the opposite of evil, and life is the opposite of death; so the sinner is the opposite of the godly. Look upon all the works of the Most-High; they likewise are in pairs, one the opposite of the other." The method of the couples of opposites is one of the chief principles of Philo's dialectics. He contrasts moral and philosophical doctrines, and biblical figures, on every page of his writings. In Philo, this method is not merely a device of presentation, but a true dialectic, i.e., a method of reasoning. In *Her.* 207–214, he gives a long series of pairs of opposites, and credits Moses with this method which the Greeks ascribe to Heraclitus, "It was Moses who long ago discovered the truth that opposites are formed from the same whole, to which they stand in the relation of sections or divisions" (*Her.* 48; *Q.G.* 3.5).

Philo does not justify this method of the use of contraries one time only to make a point without further consequences. He not only repeats the principle of this method, but he uses it frequently (*Mut., passim*). For example, he repeats it in *Q.G.* 4.158, "When the soul of the virtuous man (Isaac) becomes filled with the contemplation of wisdom, which, like the day and the sun, illumines the whole reason and the mind, then it begins to give birth to opposites in the separation of distinction and discrimination between holy and profane." Or, to take another example from *Q.G.* 4.206, "Let us say allegorically that the soul of each of us has, as it were, several kinds of man in itself in accordance with the various incidences of similar things. It is as if Esau were in me, an inflexible oak, unbending and hairy, and a type alien to the thoughts of virtue, and confused in his impulses, and yielding to irrational and inscrutable impulses. In me is also Jacob, smooth and not rough. In me are both an old man and a youth, both a ruler and a non-ruler, both a holy person and a profane one."

Like the books of wisdom, Philo not only proclaims the principle of reasoning by the coupling of opposites but puts it into constant practice to such an extent that we can consider this device one of the chief instruments of his thought. Baer was able to write a book concerning the categories male and female in Philo. Let us recall others: the man created after the image and the man fashioned out of the clay, Cain and Abel, the two Enochs, Sarah and Hagar, Esau and Jacob, Leah and Rachel, Moses and Aaron, the speech of the beloved and that of the hated woman, the libation of the high-priest-Logos and the wine of folly, ecstatic and material drunkenness, pure and unclean animals, flesh and spirit, or even two manners of riding on horseback, and of being shaved.[71] Therefore, we can say that Philo makes extensive use of the method of contraries and that he considers it as biblical as well as Greek, since he ascribes it not only to Heraclitus, but also to Moses. Essentially, it is the method of analysis, or of distinction, according to which one who does not distinguish correctly confuses. Philo found it used by the books of wisdom and adopted it in his turn. He applies this method to all the opposites he finds in the Law. No Greek, however, except for the famous and mysterious Heraclitus, has ever made of this method the basic element of his dialectics. Socrates practices analysis and looks for contraries, in order to identify every part of the truth, but is not actually interested in the method of contraries. But he who wants to understand Philo must know that each biblical type has its opposite, and that they coexist in each of us dialectically and, let us add, dynamically. With this method, Philo is creator of a new way of thinking. He extends its use to his favorite areas of interest: cosmology, anthropology, and especially religious psychology or the life of virtue.

Conclusion

Our inquiry has discovered in Philo the presence of many of the motives, images, and themes found in the biblical books of wisdom. Their massive use and assimilation by Philo invites us to treat them as an essential component of his thinking and not merely a superficial "biblicism" appropriate to a Jewish thinker. Of course, he alters whatever he appropriates and mixes it with Greek concepts and images. But he does the same with Greek philosophy. Whatever he receives from his predecessors, be they Jew or Greek, he makes his own. We must recognize that he inherits a tradition about wisdom but he also goes beyond the biblical wisdom books. We must acknowledge that without the contribution of the biblical books of Wisdom and the tradition of thinking associated with these books Philo would not be what he is.

Our investigation has, of course, been preliminary, devoted more to locating widespread use of such material in Philo rather than assessing its full significance or analyzing the manner in which Philo transforms the wisdom tradition. Yet perhaps we might be allowed to conclude that the importance of the wisdom literature does not lie solely or even primarily in the influence of wisdom "ideas" on Philo's work, but that the very similarity in method is equally important. By that I mean that just as Philo uses Greek methods of exegesis—etymologies, number speculation, allegory—these same "methods" are found in the wisdom books alongside characteristic Jewish forms of symbolism, midrash, et al. Philo makes a large, almost excessive, use of methods which are used only moderately in the wisdom books. And he puts these methods to use in ways sometimes foreign to the wisdom literature, as in his preoccupation with cosmology, the spiritual life, anthropology.

The use of biblical figures and images is itself a method of thought. Indeed it might be called a method of exegesis which opens up other sections of the Bible as well. In the hands of a sophisticated thinker such as Philo this preoccupation with biblical images and figures turns out to be a tool for the investigation of the philosophy of religious life which parallels and in fact competes with the concepts and language derived from the Greek philosophical tradition. Philo cannot be understood without reference to the Bible and, among the biblical books after the Pentateuch, the wisdom literature has the greatest attraction for him. In Philo we find a philosophical language in biblical figures, highly developed, coherent, and creative. In this regard he deserves attention from students of philosophical language. But most of all it is time to underscore that without reference to the biblical tradition, and in this case the biblical wisdom tradition, we will never understand Philo and that we will never understand what is most original in his thinking if we repeatedly and tediously wash it away in the common bath of Hellenistic eclecticism.

NOTES

1. The translation used in this chapter is that of F. H. Colson, *Philo,* 10 + 2 vol., in the Loeb Classical Library (Cambridge, 1962–).
2. E. R. Goodenough, *By Light, Light: The Mystic Gospel of Hellenistic Judaism* (New Haven, 1935); H. A. Wolfson, *Philo* (Cambridge Mass., 1968); R. A. Baer, *Philo's Use of the Categories Male and Female* (Leiden, 1970).
3. *Cont.* 25; *Ebr.* 84ff. to Prov. 8:8; 3:4; 4:3; *Congr.* 177 to Prov. 3:11–12; *Ebr.* 31ff. to Prov. 8:22; *Virt.* 62f. to Prov. 8:22; *Hypoth.* 7–8 to Prov. 11:1; 16:11; 17:2; *Hypoth.* 7.6 to Prov. 19:7; *Aet.* 19 to Wisd. of Sol. 11:17.
4. See Loeb edition, vol. IX, p. 197.
5. Ibid., p. 427; 429.

6. Ibid., p. 5.

7. C. Larcher, *Études sur le Livre de la Sagesse* (Paris, 1969), pp. 151–178, investigates the analogies between Philo and Wisdom of Solomon. He acknowledges the existence of a common background of thought and the proximity in time, but denies that the author of Wisdom of Solomon knew Philo, or that Philo is its author. Philo may rely on some texts of Wisdom of Solomon, but we cannot prove it. However, Larcher mentions many analogies and parallels between Wisdom of Solomon and Philo, esp. p. 177.

8. Between the biblical books of wisdom and Philo, there is not a complete blank. Wisdom of Solomon, an Alexandrian writing, represents an important step forward. But the *Letter of Aristeas* and the Allegorists quoted by Philo provide another link. We suggest the following ideas in common between Philo and *Aristeas:* the wisdom of the King (*Aristeas* 188ff., 294); the importance of the principle of piety (200); the praise of the Law (128–172; 178–179) and of the Lawgiver (Moses) (312); the moral value of the particular laws through symbolism (150, 159); meditation on the works of God (159); maxims of moral life stamped with the seal of piety (*passim*, 207); wisdom as a gift of God (*passim*, 240); the imitation of God (254); wisdom for the sake of wisdom (260); the connection between wisdom and philosophy in the field of ethics (285); and, of course, the divine authority and perfect reliability of the LXX (310).

J. Daniélou, *Philon d'Alexandrie* (Paris, 1958), pp. 115–116, mentions some of the allegories given by Philo as coming from exegetes of his time. Let us mention the crossing of the Red Sea (*Spec. Leg.* 2.147); the Cherubim above the ark of the covenant (*Mos.* 1.98), the king of Egypt (*Jos.* 151); the symbolism of man and woman (*Abr.* 99); the tree of life (*Q.G.* 1.10). To these can be added the speculations on numbers, for instance, *Spec. Leg.* 2.56. The method of allegorical interpretation was common in the time of Philo, particularly among the Stoics. In the Alexandrian allegorists, J. Daniélou notices cosmological, moral, and even mystical exegeses. Of course, the emphasis was on cosmological and anthropological exegesis. Philo follows this tradition, but lays the emphasis on the allegories of virtue and spiritual life.

9. The book of Deuteronomy shares some images and ideas with the wisdom books. Although Philo does not offer a running commentary on Deuteronomy, but only of Genesis and Exodus, he does rely on this book, since it belongs to the Law of Moses, and he occasionally develops and comments on its teachings as he does with

Numbers and Leviticus, for which also no running commentary is extant. Therefore, we can suppose that the presence in Philo of an idea or an image common to the books of wisdom and to Deuteronomy suggests an implicit or explicit reference to Deuteronomy, and only indirect to the books of wisdom. For this reason, we shall mention parallels with Deuteronomy.

10. Ecclus. 37:23ff.; Wisd. of Sol. 7:13; in Philo, *Leg. Al.* 3.193; *Sobr.* 59–69.

11. Larcher, *Études*, pp. 201ff.

12. Other lists of disciplines: *Som.* 1.205; *Ebr.* 921–92; *Cher.* 101–105.

13. Wisd. of Sol. 13:1–9; in Philo, *Congr.* 64ff; 121:133.

14. Wisd. of Sol. 13:1–9; Ecclus. 39:12–35; in Philo, *Abr.* 150, 162; *Praem.* 40; *Aet.* (*passim*); *Congr.* 47–50; *Spec. Leg.* 1.13–20; 3.185–194; *Op.* 53–54, 77–78.

15. A. J. Festugière, *La révélation d'Hermes Trismégiste,* II, *Le Dieu cosmique* (Paris, 1949), pp. 152–340; A. H. Chroust, "A Cosmological Proof for the Existence of God in Aristotle's Lost Dialogue 'On Philosophy,' " in *The New Scholasticism*, 40 (1966), 447–462; "The Doctrine of the Soul in Aristotle's Last Dialogue 'On Philosophy,' " ibid. 42 (1968), 364–373.

16. Festugière, *La révélation,* pp. 504–518, concerning *De Mundo.*

17. Wisd. of Sol. 11:17 in Philo, *Aet.* 19; in Plato, *Timaeus* 51a.

18. Physical evil can be explained either as the result of mere natural events or as God's chastisement and trial of men. But the problem of death and of moral evil is far more difficult, and preoccupied the readers of Ecclesiasticus and of Wisdom of Solomon. The author of Ecclesiasticus writes (39:34), "The works of God are all good, and he will supply every need in its hour. And no one can say, 'This is worse than that.' " Wisdom of Solomon (1:13–14; 2:24; chaps. 3 to 5 *passim*) rejects the accusation that God is the author of death, and ascribes it, morally or physically, to the envy of the devil, before enlarging on the ultimate solution which is expected at the last Judgment. Ecclesiasticus also (15:11–20) clears God from the responsibility for our sins, which are committed against his will. Our free will alone is responsible (Ecclus. 17:6–14). Wisdom of Solomon (9:13–18) seems to accuse the flesh, or the weight of the body, which prevents the soul from knowing things on earth and things in the heavens, especially the will of God, which is known through his spirit of wisdom. Philo considers as blasphemous

making God responsible for evil, especially for the sins of men and their consequences (*Q.G.* 1.68, 89). He lays the emphasis on our free will and our full moral responsibility for evil, and adds that God would not submit us to an unequal struggle against too strong an enemy (*Leg. Al.* 3.104–106). Philo distinguishes between "natural" and "spiritual" death. He explains the latter, like Wisd. of Sol. 9:13–18, by the conflict between flesh and spirit, or between the mind and senses (*Q.G.* 1.47; *Op.* 151; *Leg. Al.* 2.49–52; *Her.* 53). He, like Plato (*Timaeus* 41d–42d), also explains evil as a mixture, figured by the tree of the knowledge of good and evil (*Q.G.* 2.11; *Leg. Al.* 2.53; 3.35–36).

19. R. G. Hammerton-Kelly in his review of my book *La doctrine eucharistique chez Philon,* in JBL 92 (1973), 630–631.

20. A. Jaubert, *La notion d'Alliance aux abords de l'ère chrétienne* (Paris, 1963), p. 440. The author deals with the Covenant in Philo in ch. 13, esp. pp. 376–379; 414–442.

21. *Deus* 49–50, referring to Deut. 30:15; *Fug.* 58 referring to Deut. 30:20.

22. Prov. 2:1; 3:1; 4:1; 8:1; Ecclus. 3:11.

23. Ecclus. 31:1; Prov. 1:8; 6:20.

24. Prov. 15:1–2; 20:1; 23:29–35; 24:1–2; Ecclus. 6:2–4; 18:30 to 19:4; 31:12 to 33:13.

25. Of wisdom, *Q.G.* 4.59; *Migr.* 149; *Fug.* 48–51; *Leg Al.* 3.1–3; of folly, *Q.G.* 4.36.

26. Aristotle, *Nicomachean Ethics* 1.9.2 (joy as a companion of virtue); in Philo, *Mut.* 167–169; *Q.G.* 1.56; 4.235; *Virt.* 8. See Wolfson, *Philo* II, pp. 283ff.

27. *Sacr.* 5–8; fragment 10 on Gen. 6:18 Book II; see Wolfson, *Philo* I, chap. VII, pp. 395ff.

28. Functions of the body: *Q.E.* 2.12; *Virt.* 5–10; temporal blessings: *Praem., passim.* Philo spiritualizes these temporal goods, ibid. 104; esteem of neighbor: *Ebr.* 84–92; *Praem.* 81; *Fug.* 36; statesman and citizen of the World: *Jos.* 67ff; *Sobr.* 54; *Jos.* 29; 69; *Op.* 142–150; passion destructive of body and soul: *Leg. Al.* 3.156, 225; *Virt.* 11–14; *Q.G.* 1.49, 50; 2.9; disastrous for neighbor: *Spec. Leg.* 3.11; for the time of Philo, *Legat.* 15–21; *Flac.* 19; wisdom as a remedy: *Cher.* 20; *Post.* 20–21; *Her.* 21; *Sobr.* 54–58; *Prob.* 18, 41.

29. *Virt.* 175–179; *Sacr.* 111.

30. Larcher, *Études,* pp. 289–292, 321–327.

31. *Phaedo* 106 b-e ("unending death"); immortal life in Plato: *Phaedo* 84 a-b; in Philo: *Q.G.* 4.166.

32. *Migr.* 37.

33. *Sacr.* 5–8; fragment 10 on Gen. 6:18, book II.

34. Prov. 8:19–21 and parallels.

35. *The Jerome Biblical Commentary* (Englewood Cliffs, N.J., 1968), p. 562.

36. Larcher, *Études*, pp. 334–336.

37. Cf. *Det.* 115 (*tithēnēs*); for *ektise*, see Colson, *Philo*, III, p. 501.

38. *Q.G.* 1.6; cf. *Q.G.* 3.7, 103; *Q.G.* 4.1, 101, 158.

39. H. Lewy, *Sobria Ebrietas. Untersuchungen zur Geschichte der antiken Mystik* (Giessen, 1929), pp. 42–54; Wolfson, *Philo*, II, chap. IX; concerning the mystical aspect of contemplative life in Philo: *Q.G.* 1.57; 3.43; 4.1, 46.

40. *Congr.* 127–129 (Hagar); *Leg. Al.* 2.47 (Leah); *Cher.* 40–42, 47 (Sipphorah); *Mut.* 143–144 (Hannah); *Cher.* 49 (Jeremiah); *Mut.* 139 (Hosea); *Cher.* 48–49 (Allegorists).

41. J. Laporte, *La Doctrine Eucharistique* (Paris, 1972), pp. 203–213.

42. Goodenough, *By Light, Light,* pp. 1–47, 161; Festugière, *Le Dieu cosmique,* p. 549. Festugière rightly insists on the importance of Greek philosophy, since Philo's *paideia* is definitely Greek, and his Platonism is obvious in his discussion of the problem of knowledge, of inspiration, and of virtue.

43. M. J. Weaver, " '*Pneuma*' in *Philo of Alexandria*" (Ph.D. diss., Univ. of Notre Dame, 1973).

44. Moses, *Mos.* 2.188–192; Abraham, *Migr.*; Isaac, *Mut.* 88; 139; Jacob, *Som.* 1 *passim;* Hannah, *Praem.* 159; Jeremiah, *Cher.* 49; Therapeutae, *Cont.* 10–12; 68; 83–89; concerning the prophecy through ecstasy, see H. Levy, *Sobria Ebrietas,* pp. 3–34; Wolfson, *Philo,* pp. 11–22.

45. See Larcher, *Études,* p. 217 (the terminology of Stoicism in *Wisdom*); negation of Pantheism, Wisd. of Sol. 9:13–18.

46. Weaver, " '*Pneuma*,' " pp. 56–74; G. Verbeke, *L'Evolution de la doctrine du Pneuma du Stoicisme à saint Augustin* (Paris, 1945), pp. 236–260.

47. *Q.G.* 1.90; *Gig.* 22–25; in association with prophecy; *Her.* 257–266; *Q.G.* 3.9; *Gig.* 23–17. Cf. Weaver, p. 80ff.

48. *Det.* 83–85; *Leg. Al.* 1.36–40; *Sacr.* 78–79; *Deus* 3–4; *Migr.* 40; *Q.G.* 1.7, 47; 4.93, 98 for illumination. *Leg. Al.* 1.53–55; *Plant.* 22–31, 39 for energy.

49. *Leg. Al.* 3 *passim;* for the priority of evil in the first age of the individual man, for instance, *Sacr.* 15–16.

50. *Sacr.* 111; *Leg. Al.* 3 *passim.*

51. *Her.* 57, "There are two kinds of men, one that of those who live by reason, the divine inbreathing, the other of those who live by blood and the pleasure of the flesh. This last is a molded cloth of earth, the other is the faithful impress of the divine image."

52. Wolfson, *Philo,* I, pp. 138–154.

53. Prov. 11:1; 16:11; Ecclus. 42–45; cf. Deut. 25:13–16; in Philo, *Hypoth.* 7:8.

54. E. R. Goodenough, *Introduction to Philo Judaeus* (Oxford, 1962), p. 63.

55. *Mos.* 1.76; about Shem, *Q.G.* 2.76; Seth, *Post.* 125; Noah, *Q.G.* 2 *passim; Leg. Al.* 2.60–63; Japhet, *Q.G.* 2.76; Esau, *Q.G.* 4.236–237: cf. Goodenough, *By Light, Light,* chaps. III, V, VI.

56. Prov. 3:18; 11:30; 13:12; 15:4.

57. *Som.* 2.240, 245; *Post.* 125–129; *Q.G.* 1.12.

58. *Leg. Al.* 1.43–47; *Q.G.* 1.7, 8, 56.

59. *Leg. Al.* 1.59–61; 3.52; *Migr.* 36–37; *Plant.* 36–38; *Q.G.* 1.11; 2.12.

60. L. Ginzberg, *The Legends of the Jews* (Philadelphia, 1954), I, p. 3.

61. Philonic archetypes: *Plant.* 26–27; *Her.* 112; cf. Wolfson, *Philo,* I, pp. 240ff.; Natural Law: Wolfson, *Philo,* II, p. 165–200; Goodenough, *Introduction,* pp. 126ff. Concerning the three ways in the Greeks, see W. Völker, *Fortschritt und Vollendung bei Philo von Alexandrien. Eine Studie zur Geschichte der Frömmigkeit,* TU 49, 1 (Leipzig, 1938), pp. 126–137.

62. Philo, *Q.G.* 2.76; 4.182; see Daniélou, *Philon d'Alexandrie,* p. 58.

63. *Leg. Al.* 3.36ff.; *Som.* 2.1–214.

64. The device of the king as the man searching for wisdom is common to the books of wisdom (Prov. 8:15–16; 20; Wisd. of Sol. 6:3–4; 6:20–22; 8:15; 12) and to Philo, who has a Hellenistic philosophy of Kingship. Abraham (*Mut.* 152; *Sobr.* 57; *Som.* 2.244; *Q.G.* 3.44; 4.76) and Moses (*Mos.* 2.1–16) are depicted according to the ideals of the sage as a king. The political man figured by Joseph in *Jos.* 1 also figures this ideal and is an addition to the three types of wisdom represented by the three Patriarchs. He is trained in shepherding, hunting (*Jos.* 2–3; *Agr.* 41), self-mastery (*Jos.* 55), and house-management (*Jos.* 38) before being entrusted with the leader-

ship of men, and, at least according to *De Josepho,* he becomes the type of a good statesman, able to resist the passions of the mob and to become the good interpreter of the dreams of men (*Jos.* 143–144). Philo combines the biblical images of the Patriarchs and of Moses as leaders with the Stoic notion of the Sage as a free man and a king (*Prob.* 1, 25, 41, 117, 154; *Q.G.* 3.29, 30; *Migr.* 197). Concerning the Hellenistic philosophy of kingship, see E. R. Goodenough, *The Political Philosophy of Hellensitic Kingship* (New Haven, 1928) and *The Politics of Philo Judaeus* (New Haven, 1938); Louis Delatte, *Les traités de la royauté d'Ecphante, Diotogène et Sthénidas,* Bibliothèque de la Faculté de Philosophie et Littérature de l'Université de Liege, no. 97 (Liege, 1942).

65. *Mos.* 1, *passim;* in Philo's time, *Legat.* 196; *Flac.* 121–124.

66. *Leg. Al.* 3.94; *Q.E.* 1 *passim,* esp. 4.

67. Concerning water, *Virt.* 79; *Fug.* 195; *Q.G.* 4.94; the well, *Ebr.* 112; *Q.G.* 4.138; the water of Mara softened by the wood of a tree, which is likened to the tree of life (Gen. 2:9), and figures goodness as seen by the wise man in the divine light.

68. Ecclus. 45:6–22; 50; Ecclus. 18:20–25.

69. Laporte, *La doctrine eucharistique,* pp. 149–162.

70. Prov. 21:3, 27 and Ecclus. 34:18ff attack those who pretend to please God with their sacrifices in spite of their injustice (cf. this teaching in the prophets, Amos 5:22; Hos. 6:6; Isa. 1:11; Jer. 7:21–28). Philo repeats the same criticism, for instance, *Spec. Leg.* 1.271.

71. The man created after the image and the man fashioned out of the clay: *Leg. Al.* 2.4; Cain and Abel: *Sacr.* 1–5; 15–16; the two Enochs: *Post.* 41; *Abr.* 17–26; Sarah and Hagar: *Congr.* 80; Esau and Jacob: *Sacr.* 17; Leah and Rachel: *Sacr.* 19; *Her.* 45–48; Moses and Aaron: *Leg. Al.* 3.133–137; the speech of the beloved and that of the hated woman: *Sacr.* 19–44; the libation of the high-priest and the wine of Folly: *Q.G.* 4.59; *Migr.* 149; *Fug.* 48–51; *Leg. Al.* 3.1–3; *Q.G.* 4.36 (of Folly); clean and unclean animals: *Abr.* 131–145; *Post.* 148–152; flesh and spirit: *Leg. Al.* 1.31–42; 2.38–52; *Deus* 140–144; 159–165; two manners of riding: *Leg. Al.* 2.99–104.

6: Wisdom and Philosophy in Early Christianity

Robert L. Wilken

WE ARE ACCUSTOMED TO THINKING THAT PHILOSOPHY HAD a large role in the development of early Christianity. The classical discussions of early Christian thought center on the influence of Greek philosophical ideas on Christian thinkers, and modern handbooks, in their surveys of the background to Christian thought, usually devote a section to the various philosophical options in the Greco-Roman world. Philosophy was central to the intellectual enterprise of Justin Martyr, Origen, Gregory of Nyssa, Augustine. With the rise of the apologetic movement in the middle of the second century a generation of Christian thinkers arose and a style of Christian thought took shape which sought to give expression to the Christian faith within the conceptual framework of Hellenistic philosophy. Not all Christian thinkers were as indebted to philosophy as Origen or Gregory of Nyssa, yet philosophy has proven to be one of the most useful perspectives from which to view early Christian intellectual life. It has provided a key for understanding which continues to bear fruit.

Wisdom is another story altogether. Except for discussions of the personification of wisdom in the development of christology and the debates over the interpretation of Prov. 8:22, "The Lord created me [Wisdom] the beginning of his ways," in the trinitarian controversies, the study of wisdom has been but a minor tributary alongside the great river of patristic thought. Where it has been traversed it has been traversed by specialists with seemingly idiocyncratic interests. Even in cases where the Jewish wisdom books were used extensively (Clement of Alexandria, for example) this aspect has received only passing attention.[1]

What is perhaps even more curious is that the study of ancient wisdom has been carried on quite independently of ancient philosophy. I call this curious for the very obvious reason that the ancients did not make the distinction we do between wisdom and philosophy. Our modern inclination to distinguish wisdom from philosophy stems from the predilection to think of philosophy primarily as an intellectual enterprise. We identify wisdom with character and life style. The wise person is one who has gained understanding through experience, often by suffering or hardship, and by observing the foolishness around him. A modern day philosopher may be considered brilliant, but simply because he is a brilliant thinker does not make him a wise man. Yet in antiquity the terms were often interchangeable. Philosopher could designate a wise man and *sophos* a philosopher. Philosophy was as much concerned with life as it was with ideas. In the following pages, then, I should like first to examine one form of early Christian wisdom, the *Sentences of Sextus,* and then show how wisdom and philosophy are closely interrelated in early Christianity. The study of early Christian wisdom can, I think, help us to appreciate certain aspects of early Christianity which earlier generations have overlooked or ignored.

The Sentences of Sextus

Toward the end of the second century a collection of sayings began to be circulated among Christians in the Eastern part of the Roman Empire. These sentences or maxims, usually known as the *Sentences of Sextus* (Σέξτου γνῶμαι), were written in Greek and closely resembled other collections of sayings known in the Greco-Roman world.[2] In many cases the sayings of Sextus parallel word for word a collection passed on under the name of Pythagoras and a similar collection which goes under the name of Clitarchus. Many of the sayings are also similar to maxims quoted in writers such as Seneca, Musonius Rufus, Maximus of Tyre, Epictetus, and Porphyry. The sayings of Sextus are clearly a reworking of an earlier collection and for this reason some have held that the present form of the sayings does not come from a Christian author or redactor. Familiar Christian ideas and language are veiled and the content seems uncharacteristic of Christianity. Yet in recent years, after close examination, a number of scholars have concluded that they are the product of a Christian redactor. Henry Chadwick, for example, in his edition of the sayings calls attention to the hand of a Christian editor and shows that Origen knew the work as a Christian collection. In a sermon on the prophet Ezekiel Origen quotes a saying from Sextus, "It is dangerous to speak even the truth about God" (352), and attributes it to a "wise and believing" man, i.e., to a Christian.[3]

The *Sentences of Sextus,* as they were known to Origen in the third century and to other Christians in the later part of the second century, is a collection of over four hundred proverbial type maxims setting forth the ideal life to which faithful Christians should aspire. It is a book designed to show the way to achieve moral and spiritual perfection. The organization is apparently haphazard, reflecting a tradition which had been a long time in the making and which grew simply by the addition of new maxims. At times the maxims seemed grouped together around a common theme (sometimes three to five maxims are related), but in most cases they are loosely strung together with no transitions from one to another. They touch on one subject, go on to another, and sometimes return to the same or a similar topic a hundred or two hundred sentences later. The range of topics is large, though the maxims for the most part shun metaphysical considerations and are concerned with practical aspects of the moral and religious life: gluttony, drunkenness, loquacity, marriage, begetting of children, pleasure, the body, sex, death, sleep, wealth and money, possessions, poverty, pride, love, knowledge and self-knowledge, freedom, the soul, prayer, desire, happiness, fate, providence, hypocrisy, ambition, self-love, the use of time, laughter, self-control, wisdom, fame, *et al.*

Some examples illustrate the character of the collection:

1. A faithful man is an elect man.
2. An elect man is a man of God.
3. A man of God is one who is worthy of God.
4. One who is worthy of God does not do anything unworthy of God.
13. Every member of the body which encourages intemperance cut off; for it is better to live chastely without the limb than to live with it while heading for destruction.
18. The wise man who is poor is like God (ὅμοιος Θεῷ).
53. When a wise man is alive his fame among men is small, but when he dies, men sing his glory.
78. Say goodbye to the things of the body insofar as you are able.
86a. Self control is the foundation of piety.
110. It is not food and drink entering through his mouth which defile a man, but those things which proceed from a bad character.
155. Loquacity does not escape sin.
167. Wisdom leads the soul to God.
230a. May it be given to you to refrain from marriage that you might live close to God.
230b. You know that both marriage and childbearing are difficult; but if you know this as one knows the fight will be hard and yet would be brave, marry and have children.
317. Don't seek the good in the flesh.
391. No wise man looks to things below such as the earth or tables.

406. Divine wisdom is the gnosis of God.
425. The soul of the wise is tested through the body by God.
446. Seeing God you will see yourself.

These few maxims indicate that the sayings of Sextus are similar in content to sayings from the Jewish wisdom books, e.g. Proverbs or Ecclesiasticus. Yet is also apparent that there are significant differences. Let us look first more closely at some of the sayings which resemble sayings from Proverbs and Ecclesiasticus and to a lesser extent the Wisdom of Solomon.

74. Let your reasoning (*logos*) precede your impulses.
Ecclus. 37:16. The beginning of every deed is reason, and consultation precedes every action.
152. It is preferable to cast a stone without thinking than to say a word [without thinking].
Ecclus. 28:17. The lash of a whip raises weal, but the lash of a tongue breaks bones. Many have been killed by the sword, but not so many as by the tongue.
163a. A word at the wrong time is proof of an evil mind.
Ecclus. 20:7. The wise man is silent until the right moment, but a swaggering fool is always speaking out of turn.

In these cases the saying from Sextus and the text from Ecclesiasticus share a common idea or truth, though the terminology and in one case the image differs. The three texts from Ecclesiasticus employ the familiar parallelism of Hebrew verse, but such parallelism is not present in the sayings of Sextus. Of course parallelism is not a necessary characteristic of Hebrew Wisdom, as can be seen for example, in the later sections of the Wisdom of Solomon.[4] The sentences of Sextus employ the familiar Greek gnomic style.[5] They take the form of a simple declarative sentence, or an imperative, or sometimes a rhetorical question.

In some instances the parallel between maxims from the

wisdom books and Sextus extends beyond the idea to the terminology.

155. Much talk does not escape sin.
Proverbs 10:19. When men talk too much, sin is never far away.
155. πολυλογία οὐκ ἐκφεύγει ἁμαρτίαν.
Proverbs 10:19. ἐκ πολυλογίας οὐκ ἐκφεύξῃ ἁμαρτίαν.

Here the saying from Sextus differs from the Greek text of Proverbs only in grammatical structure. The words are the same. In another case Sextus and Ecclesiasticus share a similar idea as well the key terms "laughter" and "smile."

280a-b. Loud laughter (ἄμετρος γέλως) is a sign of being ignored; don't allow yourself to let go with anything more than a smile (μειδιᾶν).
Ecclus. 21:20. A fool laughs (ἐν γέλωτι) out loud, a clever man smiles (μειδιάσει) quietly, if at all.

In several instances sayings from Sextus are reminiscent of passages from Ecclesiasticus, though the similarity is not as striking as in the passages already cited.

247. The faithful man wants especially not to sin, but if he does, he does not do the same sin twice.
Ecclus. 7:8. Do not pile sin upon sin, for even one is enough to make you guilty.
285. Consider it great wisdom that you are able to bear the lack of learning of the ignorant.
Ecclus. 22:15. Sand, salt, and a lump of iron are less of a burden than a stupid man.

In this category we might include the following sayings as well.

340. One who cares for orphans will be a father, loved by God, of many children.
Ecclus. 4:10. Be a father to orphans and as a husband to their mother; then the Most High will call you his son. . . .
161. Speak when silence is not appropriate.

Ecclus. 4:23. Never remain silent when a word might
   put things right, for wisdom shows itself by speech,
   and a man's education must find expression in
   words.

Finally, one saying is reminiscent of a passage from the
Wisdom of Solomon.

419. The heart of one who loves God is secure in the
   hand of God.
Wisd. of Sol. 3:1. The souls of the just are in God's
   hands.

Now there is no reason to make more out of these
parallels than they allow. I wish simply to call attention to
the similarity of subject matter. Except for 155 where
there is a clear verbal parallel, the similarities need not be
traced to the influence of the biblical books of wisdom.
One does not have to turn to the books of Proverbs or
Ecclesiasticus to obtain such advice as that offered in these
sayings. Pithy and pointed sayings about fame or loquacity
are as old as the human race. *Gnomes* (Latin, *sententia*),
which have as their themes common human experiences
and which embody common sense and convey insight into
human behavior, often with a moral overtone, and whose
point is universal and immediately obvious, are familiar in
most cultures and are amply attested from Greek and
Latin antiquity.[6] Although there may be some slight influence of the biblical wisdom literature on the *Sentences of
Sextus,* these sayings clearly originate in non-Jewish Greek
tradition. The existence of independent collections closely
parallel to Sextus make this obvious. Conceivably the
redactor, in refashioning the sayings for Christian use, may
have introduced some material from the biblical wisdom
books, but if so he did so with a light hand. However, like
many historical questions the matter of origins may not be
the most interesting or significant. The more important
question is what the redactor thought he was doing with
the material he received. To this question we will return.

The Wisdom of Sextus

The term wise (σοφός) occurs often in the sentences, some forty times, and it (and to a lesser degree, "philosopher") is the regular term used to describe the ideal person. In itself this terminology is interesting in a Christian document, because sage or wise man is not the most characteristic expression used by Christians for the ideal person.[7] But in popular philosophy especially in Stocism, and in Neo-Platonic writers such as Porphyry, the term *sophos* is a frequent term used for the ideal to which the philosophical life aspires.[8] The *Sentences of Sextus* express this ideal in many different ways.

53. When a *sophos* (wise, sage) is alive his fame among men is small, but when he dies, men sing his glory.

143-5. The mind of the *sophos* is always with God. God dwells in the mind of the *sophos*.
The *sophos* is known by a few words.

190. Honor the wise person as the image of the living God.

191. The wise person, even though he is naked, will show you that he is wise.

199. You will never become wise if you think you are wise before you are.

214. A wise person appears valueless to evil men.

226. Whoever does not love a wise person does not love himself.

246. Whoever is not able to bear a wise person is not able to bear good.

252. Whoever knows those things worthy of God is wise.

301. Whatever you work hard at for the sake of the body, if you work as hard for the sake of the soul, you will be wise.

309. No one is as free, except for God, as the wise person.

310. Whatever things are God's possessions, they are also the possessions of the wise.

311. The wise person shares in the kingdom of God.

415b-418. The soul of the wise hears God.
The soul of the wise adapts himself to God by means of God.
The soul of the wise always sees God.
The soul of the wise is always with God.
421. The wise person follows God and God the soul of the wise.
422. The ruler rejoices with the one who is ruled, and God rejoices with the wise.
423. The ruler is inseparable from the one who is ruled, and God watches over and governs the wise.
424. God is the guardian of the wise, and for this reason he is blessed.
427. The wise person honors God even when he is silent.
441. The faithful soul is pure and wise and a prophet of the truth of God.

If we look at these sayings closely it is apparent that they are suggesting an ideal for life which, though similar in some respects to that provided by the Hebrew wisdom books, differs in significant respects. Some of these sayings reflect wisdom gained from experience, e.g. 199, "You will never become wise if you think you are wise before you are," and are proverbial expressions of universally accepted truths. Others, however, reflect a particular view of man and of man's relationship to God. Sextus pictures the sage as the "image of the living God," as one who always "sees God" and is "with God, and in whose mind God dwells." To be like God is to possess freedom which is to be liberated from the things of the body. Such a goal is achieved through the process of self-knowledge, "know yourself" (398) but also by discipline and training, askesis ($\check{\alpha}\sigma\kappa\eta\sigma\iota\varsigma$). (98). If the soul is to "ascend from the earth to God" (402) it must free itself from worldly distractions, because only spiritual realities, those things which belong properly to the soul, are sure and stable (77). Whatever contributes to bodily pleasure is to be avoided (139) because insofar as the soul pursues

bodily desires it is ignorant of God (136). "Whoever loves
what is not necessary does not love what is necessary"
(141). Money, wealth, possessions, and other temptations
stand in the way of realizing the goal of likeness to God,
and even meat and wine should be avoided or used only in
small amounts (109, 268). While it is not forbidden to
marry and have children, Sextus reminds men of the dangers inherent in marriage and urges a higher way, namely
to live as a consort of God (230a). In Sextus' view the
highest form of piety is inward and the most holy temple
to God is the "mind of a pious person" (46b).

Most of the sayings are an elaboration of these basic
ideas. Pleasure and desire, gluttony and drunkenness, sex,
and even diet are severely limited for the purpose of
achieving a likeness to God. In the fashion of other religious teachers in his age Sextus recommends abstention
from flesh as conducive to piety. The sage should avoid
too much contact with the mass of men, the mob, for they
will not understand nor will they value his wisdom. The
sage should shun fame as much as he shuns wealth. He
should not set his heart on anything which does not
endure. "The goal of all this striving," writes Chadwick, "is
sinless perfection (8–11, 60, 234, 247, 282), which is the
divine likeness. By making a habit (129, 412, 414, 445) of
withdrawal from the external world of sense, the soul
ascends to God by faith (402) through his word (420), is
illuminated by the light of God (97, cf. 95b), and at all
times and in all places practices the presence of God (288,
289, 445). All time not actually spent in meditating on
God is so much time wasted (54, 55, cf. 442–448, 450)."[9]

These sayings, then, reflect popular moral and religious
ideas widespread in the Greco-Roman world. Porphyry, in
his little philosophical letter written to his wife Marcella
and in his treatise *On Abstinence From Animal Food*,
elaborates a view of life and of man and his relation to
God similar to that of Sextus. And he does so with the
help of many of the same sayings that appear in Sextus,
though he knows them through their pagan form. The

letter to Marcella itself is an *apologia* for his marriage, an apology that was necessary because marriage, even in old age, hardly seemed appropriate to the life of the sage. In this letter Porphyry urges Marcella to set her mind on those things which are sure and stable, to turn away from externals, and to discipline the passions and emotions. The sage needs only God, and he knows that whoever desires bodily things is ignorant of God. If one loves the body he is impious. Therefore the proper worship of God is spiritual and intellectual.[10]

But even though the sentences reflect ideas which were current in the Greco-Roman world in the second and third centuries, they also show the hand of the Christian redactor. In some sayings Sextus has substituted the term "faithful" for "wise," a term more comfortable to Christians. The effect is to give the sayings a more distinctly Christian ring. For example 49 reads, "God needs no one, the *faithful person* (needs) only God." In the Pythagorean collection the same maxim reads, "God needs no one; the *wise person* needs only God."[11] Whereas the idea is the same the Sextine formula is more congenial to a Christian reader. Sextus also uses phrases such as "elect" (1, 2, 35, 433), the "image of God" (190), as well as "kingdom of God" (311), "the blessed life" (326b), "love the Lord your God" (442), and others.[12]

On the other hand, if one compares these sayings to earlier Christian comments on wisdom, it is noteworthy that wisdom almost always appears here in a concrete sense. As we have already observed, there are some forty occurrences of the term sophos, either as a noun to designate the sage or as an adjective. Yet there are less than half a dozen uses of *sophia*. In the New Testament the situation is almost the reverse. *Sophia* is used much more frequently than *sophos*. There are some earlier Christian texts where *sophos* has this concrete moral and religious sense, in the epistle of James for example, but the earliest Christian writings are more interested in the *sophia* of God than in the sage.[13] And in Sextus, even where *sophia* is used, the

term has a concrete reference. "Wisdom follows hard on
brevity of speech" (156). "Nothing belongs more to wisdom than truth" (168). (See also 167.) Only in one case
could it have a different meaning, but even this one is
ambiguous. "Divine wisdom is the gnosis of God" (406).
These sayings indicate that the collection is more concerned with wisdom as a moral and religious category to
describe man, i.e. the sage, than it is in speaking of wisdom
as a characteristic of God.[14]

Sextus and Jesus

There are approximately a dozen sayings which closely
resemble sayings from the gospel tradition or the non-
canonical collections of sayings of Jesus such as the Gospel
of Thomas and the Oxyrhynchus papyri.[15] In cases where
the saying in Sextus parallels a saying from the gospel
tradition there is often no parallel with the other collections of Greek sayings, though this is not always the case.
Here I wish to take note of some of the similarities
between sayings of Sextus and the sayings of Jesus preserved in the gospel tradition. How significant these parallels are can be determined only on the basis of a much
more comprehensive examination.

> Sextus 110. It is not the food and drink which goes
> into man through his mouth which defiles him, but
> the things which go out through evil habit.
> Matt. 15:17–18. Do you not see that whatever goes in
> by the mouth passes into the stomach and so is
> discharged into the drain? But what comes out of the
> mouth has its origins in the heart; and that is what
> defiles a man.
> Gospel of Thomas 14b. For that which goes into your
> mouth will not defile you, but that which comes
> forth from your mouth, that is what will defile
> you.[16]

The wording here is close to that of Matthew, except for the non-Matthean term habit (ἦθος) which is used in the Sextine collection and in the Pythagorean collection and Porphyry. Interestingly, this maxim occurs in a context where it seems out of place. Maxim 109 says that the eating of any living thing is a matter of judgment, but it is "more reasonable to abstain." The accent there is on *abstention* from certain foods, whereas number 110, which is parallel to a saying of Jesus, suggests that what one eats and drinks is of little consequence. The two sayings seem to be making quite different points.

Another saying similar in content but somewhat different in context is Matt. 5:29 (par. Mark 9:43 and Matt. 18:8–9):

> If your right eye is your undoing, tear it out and fling it away; it is better for you to lose one part of your body than for the whole of it to be thrown into hell. And if your right hand is your undoing, cut it off and fling it away; it is better for you to lose one part of your body than for the whole of it to go to hell.
> 13. Every member of your body which encourages intemperance [σωφρονεῖν] cut it off; for it is better live temperately without the member than to live with it while heading for destruction. [See also 273.]

In the Matthean version the saying occurs in the context of the Sermon on the Mount with its emphasis on the Kingdom of God, whereas in Sextus it is not the Kingdom but temperance (σωφροσύνη) which interests the author. The Markan version reads: "And if it is your eye, tear it out; it is better to enter into the kingdom of God with one eye than to keep both eyes and be thrown into hell, where the devouring worm never dies and the fire is not quenched."

Another saying reflects a similar shift in terminology.

> 41. Whatever you treasure above all things, that will rule you.
> Luke 12:34 (Matt. 6:21). Wherever your treasure is, there also will your heart be.

> Gospel of Thomas 76. The kingdom of the Father is like a merchant who has a load (of goods) and found a pearl. That merchant was wise. He sold the load, and bought for himself the pearl alone. You, also, seek after his treasure which does not perish but endures, where moth does not enter to devour, nor does worm destroy.

The terminology of Sextus differs from that of Q (Sextus uses ὃ ἂν τιμήσῃς and Q uses ὁ θησαυρὸς ὑμῶν) but the idea is similar. Justin Martyr also cites the passage from Q in connection with a number of other similar sayings of Jesus, some of which are also parallel to sayings in Sextus.[17] Justin, however, is clearly citing sayings which he identifies as the teaching of Jesus.

Two other sayings which closely parallel passages from the gospels are 183, "Whoever judges a man will be judged by God," which is similar to Matt. 7:1, "Do not judge and you will not be judged;" and 193, "It is hard to save someone who is rich," which parallels Mark 10:23, "How hard it will be for the wealthy to enter the kingdom of God." Besides these parallels there are several other sayings which resemble words of Jesus. For example, 213, "Pray that you may be able to do good to your enemies," can be compared to "Love your enemies and pray for your persecutors" (Matt. 5:44), and 89, "As you wish to be treated by your neighbors, treat them in the same way," and "Always treat others as you would like them to treat you" (Matt. 7:12).[18]

It is clear from these passages that a number of the sayings of Sextus resemble sayings of Jesus.[19] In some cases the parallel is quite close, extending to terminology, and in others the similarity lies in a common idea or thought. Once again, however, we should not make too much out of these parallels, at least not without extensive analysis of all of the sayings of Sextus and other "sayings" traditions in early Christianity. It does appear, however, that the editor of the *Sentences of Sextus* knew the gospels or traditions of sayings similar to those in our gospels. If he was a Christian there is no doubt that he was familiar with the sayings of Jesus and it appears that he used these sayings in his redaction of the Greek sentences.

If the editor of the sayings of Sextus knew the sayings of Jesus, he does not mention Jesus, and even when he seems to be using material passed on as words of Jesus he does not attribute these sayings to Jesus. It is possible that Sextus intentionally presented his wisdom in a form which would not be associated directly with Jesus, as he veils other references to Christianity, because of the use he intended to make of the collection. If he was an apologist for Christianity, for example, he may have found his work more effective if he did not identify Jesus as the source of his teaching. Origen mentioned that in conversations with hostile pagans he sometimes found it helpful not to mention he was a Christian until he had time to develop his arguments further.[20] And the apologist Athenagoras, who may have been a closer contemporary to Sextus than Origen, also did not attribute his teaching directly to Jesus, even though he cites sayings taken from the gospel tradition. "What then are the teachings on which we are brought up? 'I say to you, love your enemies, bless them who curse you, pray for them who persecute you, that you may be sons of your Father in heaven.' ..."[21] In fact Athenagoras does not mention Jesus anywhere in his apology.

Another interesting aspect of the collection is that the moral teaching of Jesus as presented by apologists such as Justin and Athenagoras is similar to that presented by Sextus. In the case of Justin a significant number of the sayings he chooses to cite from Jesus are precisely those sayings in the gospels which resemble those in the sayings of Sextus. We have already noted that Justin cites the sayings about laying up treasures, praying for one's enemies, and several others. He also cites Jesus' word about committing adultery in one's heart (Matt. 5:28), a saying which has a parallel in Sextus, and the saying that "it is better for you to enter the kingdom of heaven with one

eye than with two to be sent into eternal fire," a saying
which also has a parallel in Sextus.[22] To a lesser extent the
same situation exists for Athenagoras. What these comparisons suggest is that Justin as an apologist was attracted to
those aspects of the teaching of Jesus, e.g. stress on continence, inward purity, concern for one's neighbor, which
are similar to the moral and religious ideal set forth in
Sextus. Or, to put the matter in another way, Justin, as an
early Christian apologist, inhabits a similar spiritual milieu
as the redactor of the *Sentences of Sextus*. This returns us
to our original question concerning the setting in which
sayings such as these would have their place.

Wisdom and Philosophy

What kind of person would put together such a collection of sayings for Christian use and what did he hope to
accomplish by doing so? What was their function within
the life of the Christian community to which the redactor
belonged? From the study of ancient wisdom in other
cultures we know that wisdom was often cultivated by
certain classes within society. In the ancient near East
wisdom was cultivated and transmitted in schools or academies for court officials and scribes.[23] But in the Greco-
Roman world of the second and third centuries we have to
look elsewhere, and the best place to begin is with the
identification Sextus makes with the term "wise person"
(*sophos*) and "philosopher." Though the term philosopher
does not occur as often as the term *sophos,* it does occur
frequently. The ideal person can be described as either a
philosopher or a sage. "Honor the philosophical man as
servant of God after God" (319). "Honor the sage after
God" (244). In some cases philosopher occurs where sage
could serve equally well. "Let the philosopher not consider
any possessions his own" (227). "Do not judge anyone to
be a philosopher unless you believe everything he says"
(258). "Someone is not a philosopher who takes away

freedom" (275). The term faithful (*pistos*) is also often used as an equivalent for sage or philosopher. "God needs no one, the faithful needs only God" (49). "The faithful does evil to no one" (212). "The faithful is nurtured in continence" (438).

The use of the term philosopher and sage reflects usage common to the philosophical schools of the Greco-Roman world. As we have already observed, among the Stoics *sophos* is the most frequent term used to describe the ideal toward which men should strive.[24] The wise man is not affected by the evils that surround him, he is not deceived by others and does not deceive, he is free and blessed, he alone is holy and pious and skilled in divine matters. Seneca disclaims that he is a wise man because he has not attained to such a height of perfection. "Do I say I am a wise man? By no means, for if I could make that claim, I should also declare that I am the most fortunate of all men and had been brought into nearness with God. As it is, fleeing to that which is able to lighten all sorrows, I have surrendered myself to wise men."[25] Several generations later Marcus Aurelius speaks much the same way about philosophy as an ideal. "This too can make you despise vain glory, the fact that you can no longer achieve the aim of having lived your whole life, or at least your life from manhood as a philosopher. To many people as well as to yourself you have plainly fallen short of philosophy. So you are tainted and it is no longer easy for you to gain the reputation of a philosopher."[26]

We know that in this period philosophers had moved out of their classrooms into the streets to preach a popular moral and religious ideal.[27] Their diatribes were often directed at a popular audience and they spoke about pain and suffering, death, freedom, the dangers of wealth, sex and desire, passions, ambition, pride, friendship, old age, wealth; in short, about the concrete realities of everyday life. Even sarcophagi pictured the philosopher as the representation of one who strove to live a life of philanthropy to his fellows and piety toward the gods.[28] One term used for philosophy was *bios,* life, or perhaps better, way of life. In his humorous dialogue "Philosophies (βίοι) for Sale." Lucian portrays a slave auction in a marketplace. What are to be sold, however, are not slaves, but "ways of life," such as the Pythagorean, the Cynic, the Platonic, the Stoic, and others. Hermes is the auctioneer and Zeus comments on the proceedings.

> Zeus: Many are gathering, so we must avoid wasting time and delaying them. Let us begin the sale, then. Hermes: Which do you want us to bring on first? Zeus: This fellow with the long hair, the Ionian, for he seems to be someone of distinction. Heremes: You Pythagorean, come forward and let yourself be looked over by the company. Zeus: Hawk him now. Hermes: The noblest of philosophies (τὸν ἄριστον βίον) for sale, the most distinguished; who'll buy? Who wants to be more than man? Who wants to apprehend the music of the spheres and to be born again? Buyer: For looks, he is not bad, but what does he know best? Hermes: Arithmetic, astronomy, charlatany, geometry, music and quackery; you see in him a first-class soothsayer.[29]

Sometime in the 150s or 160s a few Christians began to claim that Christianity offered men a philosophical way of life. From the perspective of earlier Christianity, this claim was novel and unexpected, and some Christians resented the identification. At an earlier stage most Christians had only criticism for philosophy.[30] Those who wished to make this new claim, and thereby to offer a reinterpretation of the Christian tradition, were aided by the philosopher-physician Galen who began to call Christianity a philosophical school. Actually Galen did not think a great deal of the Christian "philosophical school," because he thought Christians refused sound reasoning and demonstration in the development of their teachings, but Galen did not have much use for the other schools either—and for much the same reason. Nevertheless, for Christianity to be considered even a third-rate philosophical school was a step upward in social acceptance from the time Pliny and Tacitus thought Christianity a first-rate superstition.[31]

Galen, however, was impressed with the Christian way of life, a way of life he thought remarkably similar to that of genuine philosophers.

> Most people are unable to follow any demonstrative argument consecutively; hence they need parables, and benefit from them . . . just as now we see the people called Christians drawing their faith from parables . . . , and yet sometimes acting in the same way as those who philosophize. For their contempt of death . . . is patent to us every day, and likewise their restraint in cohabition. For they include not only men but also women who refrain from cohabiting all through their lives; and they also number individuals who, in self-discipline and self-control in matters of food and drink, and in their keen pursuit of justice, have attained a pitch not inferior to that of genuine philosophers.[32]

Christians were quick to seize on the idea that Christianity could be portrayed as a philosophy.[33] About the time of Galen, and even somewhat earlier, Christian apologists began to present their defense of Christianity as a defense of the Christian philosophy. Justin, for example, describes his conversion to Christianity as a conversion to philosophy. He says that he studied with a Stoic, with an Epicurean, with a Platonist, and with others, but in the end he met an old man who showed him the Hebrew prophets. After listening to the old man, Justin writes, "A flame was kindled in my soul; and a love of the prophets, and of those men who are friends of Christ, possessed me; and while turning these words over in my mind, I found this philosophy alone to be safe and profitable. Thus, and for this reason, I am a philosopher."[34] In his *Apology* he presents Christianity as a philosophy, and Athenagoras writing a few years later does the same. Even Tatian, perhaps the most bitterly anti-Greek of the Greek apologists, speaks of Christianity as a philosophy. He even urges the Greeks not to "treat with scorn the women among us who practice philosophy." Our "maidens philosophize" and "the poor no less than the well to do philosophize with us."[35]

Such philosophy was not primarily a matter of head knowledge. It required discipline, the forming of habits, the slow, gradual transformation of one's life. In short it required wisdom. To achieve this goal some disciples went to live with their teachers and in these conventicles the students were introduced to various exercises which could help them in living philosophically. These exercises included mental rehearsals of things that happened in one's past, concentration on one's weaknesses and faults, reading of appropriate philosophical works, memorizing sentences and maxims from the great teachers of the past, contemplation of the fate of great men who died in war or suffered some catastrophe, and other similar exercises.[36] For those who could not join such a conventicle other means were used. Seneca, for example, "trained" his disciple Lucilius by writing him letters. These letters read like "spiritual exercises."[37] For others who had to live in the world other means were devised. One of the most popular means was the use of sentences or maxims designed to remind the student of the philosophical ideal and to inculcate in him sensibilities appropriate to this ideal. The memorization of such sentences helped to bring thought and action into greater unity.

As evidence of the popular use of these sentences let me cite several examples from the period. In a work written to the newly married couple Eurydice and Pollianus, Plutarch urges them, jointly, to strive to live a philosophical life. To Pollianus he says (after urging Eurydice not to be extravagant or to show off with gilded drinking-cups or showy neckbands for horses), "You already possess sufficient maturity to philosophize, and I beg that you will beautify your character with the aid of discourses which are attended by logical demonstration and mature demonstration, seeking the company and instruction of teachers who will help you. And for your wife you must collect from every source what is useful, as do the bees, and carrying it within your self impart it to her, and then discuss it with her, and make the best of these doctrines her favorite and

familiar themes. . . ." For if women "do not receive the
seed of good doctrines and share with their husbands in
intellectual advancement, they, left to themselves, conceive many untoward ideas and low designs and emotions." And to Eurydice he says, "As for you, Eurydice, I
beg that you will try to be conversant with the *sayings of
the wise and good* (τοῖς τῶν σοφῶν καὶ ἀγαθῶν ἀποφθέγ-
μασιν) and always have at your tongue's tip those sentiments which you used to cull in your girlhood's days when
you were with us, so that you may give joy to your
husband, and may be admired by other women, adorned,
as you will be, without price, with rare and precious
jewels." He concludes, "If Sappho thought that her beauti-
ful compositions in verse justified her in writing to a
certain rich woman,

> Dead in the tomb you shall lie
> Nor shall there be thought of you there,
> For in the roses of Pierian fields
> You have no share,

why shall it not be even more allowable for you to enter-
tain high and splendid thoughts of yourself, if you have a
share not only in the roses but also in the fruits which the
Muses bring and graciously bestow upon those who admire
education and philosophy?"[38]

The second example comes from Galen's book *On the
Passions of the Soul,* a work concerned chiefly with how
to train and discipline oneself for the philosophical life. In
the book Galen cites at various places maxims he uses to
guide his life, and in one place he reveals his own daily
practice. "You may be sure that I have grown accustomed
to ponder twice a day the exhortations attributed to
Pythagoras—first I read them over, then I recite them
aloud." Immediately following this passage he goes on to
speak of the vices he tries to control. It is "not enough for
us to practice self-control over our anger; we must also
cleanse ourselves of voluptuous eating, carnal lust, drunkenness, excessive curiosity, and envy."[39] Apparently he

believed that the memorizing of the maxims of Pythagoras helped him achieve this goal. That is, these sentences functioned not simply as nuggets of wisdom on the nature of man and his relation to God nor on the ideal life; they were instruments by which one hoped to realize the ideal in one's life, to inculcate habits and sentiments which would give new shape to one's life. The sentences were used to change one's life, not simply to learn about what is good and evil.

A passage from Seneca's *Epistulae Morales* can serve as illustration. He urges Lucilius not to read too many books, but to stick to the standard authors. Return again and again to the familiar. "Each day acquire something that will fortify you against poverty, against death, indeed against other misfortunes as well; and after you have run over many thoughts, select one to be thoroughly digested that day. This is my own custom; from the many things which I have read, I claim some part for myself. The thought for today is one which I discovered in Epicurus; for I am wont to cross over even into the enemy's camp—not as a deserter, but as a scout. He says: 'Contented poverty is an honorable estate.' "[40]

Conclusion

The *Sentences of Sextus* are an attempt on the part of a Christian intellectual to provide a collection of sayings for Christians which could be used for leading men and women into the philosophical life, that is for training in moral perfection. Sextus shares the outlook of men such as Justin and Athenagoras that Christianity is a philosophy, but he chose a different vehicle for giving expression to this view. He is not less philosophical than Justin or Athenagoras, but instead of offering an intellectual argument that Christianity should be taken seriously as a philosophy, he attempts to show that Christianity has the resources to help men achieve the philosophical life. It is conceivable that his sentences are intended for men and women on the way to becoming Christians; his maxims offered converts a collection of sayings not too different from what they knew previously, but which began, if only in a small way, to introduce them to the Christian vocabulary and Christian ideas. This may account for the similarity in content between some sayings of Sextus and the sayings of Jesus, even though the language is different. Later these converts could be introduced to the sayings of Jesus in their "original" form and with the preface "Jesus said."

Sextus' accomplishment was to bring the work of the apologists into much more intimate relationship with the philosophical traditions of the Greco-Roman world. Sextus' wisdom is philosophical wisdom which has its roots deep within the moral and ethical concerns of Hellenistic philosophy. His wisdom is characteristically Hellenistic, yet is not wholly Hellenistic. It has begun to draw on resources from biblical wisdom and the sayings of Jesus. In preparing the collection of sayings for Christian use the editor took a first step in the appropriation of wisdom tradition within Christianity. Though his way of doing so is somewhat different (though not wholly) from the teachings of Silvanus, discussed by Schoedel in chapter seven, both Silvanus and Sextus point to the more fully developed synthesis of Clement of Alexandria.[41] The sayings of Sextus are a noteworthy moment in the appropriation of wisdom as a vehicle for understanding the Christian tradition.

NOTES

1. There is no monograph on wisdom in the early church, but the following studies are helpful in locating some material: G.W.H. Lampe, *A Patristic Greek Lexicon* (Oxford, 1961), pp. 1244–47; H. Jaeger, "The Patristic Conception of Wisdom in the Light of Biblical

and Rabbinical Research," *Studia Patristica* IV, TU 79 (Berlin, 1961), pp. 90–106; W. Völker, "Die Verwertung der Weisheits-Literatur bei den christlichen Alexandrinern," *ZKG* 64 (1952–53), 1–33; Henri Crouzel, *Origène et la 'Conaissance Mystique'* (Paris, 1961), pp. 451ff.

2. Text and discussion of the sayings by Henry Chadwick, *The Sentences of Sextus.* Texts and Studies, no. 5 (Cambridge, Eng., 1959). Also G. Delling, "Zur Hellenisierung des Christentums in den 'Sprüchen des Sextus,' " in *Studien zum Neuen Testament und zur Patristik. Festschrift für Erich Klostermann,* (TU 77 (Berlin, 1961), pp. 208–241. There is to my knowledge no English translation of the sentences; when Chadwick translates a saying in the course of his discussion I use his translation, otherwise the translations are my own.

3. Origen, *Homilia in Ezech.* 1.11 (Chadwick, p. 114).

4. James M. Reese, *Hellenistic Influence on the Book of Wisdom and Its Consequences,* AB, no. 41 (Rome, 1970), pp. 25–26.

5. W. Schmid and O. Staehlin, *Geschichte der griechischen Literatur* (Munich, 1929), I,1, p. 372; I,1, p. 378.

6. W. Spoerri, "Gnome," *Der Kleine Pauly* II, 822–829, with bibliography.

7. More common terms would be *pistos, gnostikos,* or *hagios;* see Lampe, *sub voce.*

8. Extensive material on the Stoic wise man collected in H. von Arnim, *SVF* III, 146–171.

9. Chadwick, p. 106.

10. See for example *Ad Marcellam* 11–16; also *De Abstinentia* 2.52: "The philosopher is separated from externals. . . . He approaches through himself the God who is established in the true inward parts and receives the precepts of eternal life."

11. Porphyry cites the maxim in this form in *Ad Marcellam* 11.

12. See Chadwick, pp. 154–155.

13. See U. Wilckens, "*Sophia,*" *TDNT* VII, 514–528.

14. As far as I can see there is no mythological conception or hypostasization of sophia in the *Sentences.*

15. On parallels between the *Sentences* and the sayings of Jesus see Delling, "Hellenisierung," pp. 219ff., and Chadwick's notes.

16. I have noted a parallel here with the Gospel of Thomas and also in the case of 41, but I have not attempted systematically to compare the *Sentences of Sextus* with the Gospel of Thomas. In light of Robinson's comments on the role of collections of sayings in

early Christianity (*Trajectories through Early Christianity* [Philadelphia, 1971], pp. 71–113), the relation between the *Sentences of Sextus* and other collections closer to Q is worth closer examination. A Coptic version of the *Sentences* was found at Nag Hammadi (Robinson, *Trajectories*, p. 100, n. 65).

17. Justin Martyr, I *Apology* 15. On the similarity of sayings of Jesus (e.g. Matt. 5:29) with other *gnomes* from antiquity see Hildebrecht Hommel, "Herrenworte im Lichte sokratischer Überlieferung," *ZNW* 57 (1966), 1–22; discussion of Matt. 5:29, Sextus 13 and 273 on pp. 8, 16–20.

18. For the currency of sayings such as these, i.e. expressing the "golden rule," in the various religious and ethical traditions of the ancient world, see Albrecht Dihle, *Die goldene Regel. Eine Einführung in die Geschichte der antiken und frühchristlichen Vulgarethik* (Göttingen, 1962).

19. Other parallels are 13, Matt. 5:30; 20, Matt. 22:21; 442, Matt. 22:37; 233, Matt. 5:28; 242, Matt. 10:8.

20. *Hom. in Jerem.* 20.5 (Klostermann, ed., pp. 184–185).

21. Athenagoras, *Legatio* 11.2 (Schoedel, trans., p. 23).

22. See especially I *Apology* 13–17. Unfortunately A.J. Bellinzoni, *The Sayings of Jesus in the Writings of Justin Martyr*, NT Supp., no. 17 (Leiden, 1967), who analyzes the sayings of Jesus in these chapters, seems unaware of the *Sentences of Sextus* (pp. 49ff.).

23. For Israel see Hans Juergen Hermisson, *Studien zur israelitischen Spruchweisheit*, WMANT 28 (Neukirchen, 1968), pp. 113ff.; for the ancient near East in general see W.G. Lambert, *Babylonian Wisdom Literature* (Oxford, 1960).

24. See note 8.

25. *Ad Helviam de consolatione* 5. See also Dio of Prusa 8.5; Philostratus, *Life of Apollonius* 1.2; Cicero, *Paradoxa Stoicorum* 4; *Academics* 2.136. In this connection see Kurt Deissner, *Das Idealbild des stoischen Weisen* (Greifswald, 1930), and the comments of David L. Tiede, *The Charismatic Figure as Miracle Worker*, SBL Dissertation Series, no. 1 (Missoula, Mont., 1972), pp. 54ff.

26. Marcus Aurelius, *Meditations* 8.1. See also Alexander Aphrodisiac, *de fato* 6, and Epictetus, *Discourses* 3.13.23, for the ideal of philosophy.

27. See A.D. Nock, *Conversion* (London, 1933), pp. 164ff.; W. Capelle and H.I. Marrou, "Diatribe," in *RAC* III, 990–1009.

28. Theodor Klauser, "Studien zur Entstehungsgeschichte der

christlichen Kunst," in *Jahrbuch für Antike und Christentum* 2 (1959), 115ff.; 3 (1960), 112ff.

29. Lucian, *Philosophies for Sale* 1—2 (Harmon, trans., pp. 450—453).

30. See Gustave Bardy, "Philosophie et 'philosophe' dans le vocabulaire chrétien des premiers siècles," *Revue d'Ascetique et de Mystique* 25 (1949), 97—108; Anne-Marie Malingrey, *'Philosophia': Etude d'un groupe de mots dans la littérature grecque des Présocratiques au IVᵉ siècle après J.-C.* (Paris, 1961).

31. Pliny, *Ep.* 10.96; Tacitus, *Annales* 15.44.

32. Galen, *de pulsuum differentiis* 3.31 (see R. Walzer, *Galen on Jews and Christians* [London, 1949], pp. 38, 45).

33. On the significance of presenting Christianity as a philosophical school in early Christian apologetics, see Robert L. Wilken, "Towards a Social Interpretation of Early Christian Apologetics," *Church History* 39 (1970), 437—458.

34. Justin, *Dialogue with Trypho* 8.1—2.

35. Tatian, *Oratio,* 32—33.

36. See Paul Rabbow, *Seelenführung. Methodik der Exerzitien in der Antike* (Munich, 1954), pp. 215ff.

37. Seneca, *Epistulae Morales,* ed. Richard M. Gummere, 3 vols. (Cambridge, 1917).

38. Plutarch, *Advice to Bride and Groom,* 145b—146 (Babbit, trans., pp. 337—343).

39. Galen, *On the Passions of the Soul* 6 (Harkins, trans., p. 49).

40. Seneca, *Ep.* 2.5—6.

41. Clement uses citations from Proverbs and Ecclesiasticus to set forth his ethical views on topics such as conversation, laughter, gluttony, drunkenness, sleep, behavior at banquets, use of cosmetics, *et al.*, and in the first book of his *Stromateis* he appeals to Proverbs for his understanding of the relation of philosophy and theology (see introduction to this volume). On Clement and Sextus see the interesting remarks of P. Wendland in *Theologische Literaturzeitung* 20 (1893), 492—494.

7: Jewish Wisdom and the Formation of the Christian Ascetic

William R. Schoedel

THE STUDY OF WISDOM LITERATURE IN JEWISH AND CHRIStian scholarship regularly moves from Near Eastern backgrounds through the classical expressions of Jewish wisdom in the books of Proverbs and Ecclesiasticus to the less typical reflections of wisdom in Ecclesiastes and Job or the hellenized form of wisdom contained in the Wisdom of Solomon. There is also a recognition that forms of Rabbinic utterance owe something to Israel's ancient heritage of wisdom and that this heritage appears fragmentarily in other Jewish books (such as Tobit and the collection of sayings known as Pseudo-Phocylides).[1] The student of the New Testament also knows that Jewish wisdom left its mark particularly on the sayings of Jesus[2] and in the book of James.[3] The history of early Christian thought shows that to some extent christology proceeded along a path marked out by the personification and hypostatization of wisdom in Jewish wisdom literature.[4]

The relation between Jewish wisdom and early Christian thought, however, has not been intensively studied. Wisdom, it is generally thought, soon died out as a living religious tradition and exerted influence only as a minor strand in the history of biblical interpretation. The most vital theological movements in the modern period have exalted the prophet over the sage, and New Testament scholarship has made apocalyptic thinking the bearer of the most powerful impulses in primitive Christianity.

Recently, however, there has been a renewal of interest in the problem of wisdom in the early church. The awareness has grown that the importance of wisdom in the gospels has been too quickly belittled,[5] and links between collections of "words of the wise" and Gnosticizing theology have suggested a trajectory of influence worth further exploration.[6] Apocalyptic and wisdom are more and more seen as having been intertwined before New Testament times,[7] and a beginning has been made of the study of this interrelation in the gospels.[8] Paul too is seen as strongly influenced by the Jewish wisdom movement.[9] In Patristic study the area of the influence of wisdom ideas has also been expanding beyond that of christological development.[10] And eventually we may be able to find more than the imitation of biblical forms of wisdom in the sentences that were prepared for monks and nuns beginning with Evagrius of Pontus.[11]

By good fortune the current reevaluation of the wisdom tradition can draw on a new document from Nag Hammadi—*The Teachings of Silvanus.*[12] For our purposes, the importance of Silvanus is that it is written in the style of wisdom literature and witnesses to the vitality of that tradition in one stream of early Christian thought. Unlike most of the treatises found at Nag Hammadi, Silvanus is not Gnostic. The writing freely associates the highest divinity with creation and betrays no docetism in its christology. Gnosticizing tendencies are not fully absent—notably in the tripartite anthropology which has to do with the "three races" from which man originated (92.10ff.). Yet there is little or nothing here that could not have been said by a bold theologian of the stamp of a Clement of Alexandria or an Origen. Silvanus' discussion of the God who "contains" all and is "contained" by none (99.21ff.; cf. 115.36ff.) has close affinities with Philo and, among early Christian writers, especially Theophilus and Irenaeus.[13] The boldness with which such monism is linked with

Gnosticizing motifs suggests a milieu like that of third century Alexandrian Christianity.

A review of the contents of Silvanus already indicates affinities between Silvanus and Jewish wisdom. The treatise occupies about thirty–four pages (84.15–118.9) of Codex VII of the "Coptic Gnostic Library" from Nag Hammadi. (There are thirty-one to thirty-five lines per page.) The following tentative outline may serve as a rough guide to the contents:

(1) The warfare of the soul (84.15–87.4)
(2) "Discipline (*paideia*) and teaching" (87.4–88.35)
(3) Wisdom (88.35–92.10)
   (a) Wisdom and foolishness (88.35–90.28)
   (b) "Return to your divinity" (90.29–91.20)
   (c) "Care for the divine which is within you" (91.20–92.10)
(4) The "three races" (92.10–94.32)
(5) "The Adversary" (94.33–96.19)
(6) Christ "who is able to set you free" (96.19–97.3)
(7) Discriminating speech and friends and counsellors (97.3–99.20)
   (a) Discriminating speech (97.3–97.17)
   (b) Friends and counsellors (97.18–98.8)
   (c) God as father and friend (98.8–98.20)
   (d) Christ the true light (98.20–99.20)
(8) The "place" of the mind, God, and Christ (99.21–102.7)
   (a) The mind (99.21–28)
   (b) God (99.29–101.12)
   (c) Christ (101.13–102.7)
(9) The knowledge of God difficult (102.7–103.11)
(10) The way of Christ (103.11–105.25)
   (a) The narrow way (103.11–28)
   (b) Redemption brought by Christ (103.28–104.14)
   (c) Freedom from carnality (104.15–105.25)
(11) Moral exhortation (105.26–110.14)
   (a) Images of the evils in man: wild beasts, dead things, a tomb (105.26–106.20)

(b) Renewal through Christ, the self, wisdom
     (106.20–107.17)
(c) Surrender to the Logos and the avoidance of
     "animalism" (107.17–110.14)
(12) "Know who Christ is" (110.14–113.31)
    (a) Exhortation to "know who Christ is" and a hymn
         in praise of him (110.14–111.6)
    (b) Humility and pride: divine goodness and wisdom
         vs. human presumption (111.7–112.27)
    (c) The greatness of God and a hymn of praise of his
         Word and wisdom (112.27–113.31)
(13) Various exhortations to awake, be alert, contend
     (113.31–114.26)
(14) The patience and power of God (114.26–115.10)
(15) Things that one should know about God Almighty
     (115.11–117.13)
    (a) "All dwelt in God" (115.11–19)
    (b) The "divine boundary" (115.20–35)
    (c) God knows all things (115.36–117.13)
(16) Final exhortations (117.13–118.7)

This outline suggests greater order than actually obtains in
Silvanus. It is characteristic of the treatise that many
themes reappear throughout. Nor is it always easy to see
where one theme is dropped and another taken up. It is
perhaps safe to say that more and more specifically Christian motifs—including biblical allusions—are to be found
toward the end of the treatise.

A few of the topics—*paideia,* wisdom, discriminating
speech and friends and counsellors—are immediately reminiscent of classical Jewish wisdom. Others go far beyond
traditional themes. A basic question is why wisdom proved
an attractive medium at all for such speculation; for wisdom is not a particularly flexible literary instrument.
Sirach himself, however, expands the range of materials
thought appropriate in the setting of wisdom—hymns,
thanksgiving songs, complaints, prophetic speech, and so
forth.[14] The Wisdom of Solomon, though still in the
tradition of Jewish wisdom, goes beyond this and intro-

duces literary features derived from Hellenism—rhetorical prose, elements of the diatribe, Hellenistic hymns, and so forth.[15] We may conjecture that in Judaism the ideal of wisdom formed a natural point of contact with Greek philosophical themes and that the existence of treatises like the Wisdom of Solomon attest to a Hellenistic form of Jewish wisdom which lies in the background of writers like Philo. Wisdom had the additional advantage of addressing advice and admonition directly to its listeners in harmony with tendencies in popular philosophy in the Greco-Roman world. In Christianity, moreover, the christological patterns perceived in the figure of wisdom guaranteed a continued interest in the wisdom tradition. But long ago Norden pointed to traces of a more vital continuity between wisdom and Christian theology. By a comparison of Ecclesiasticus 51, Matt. 11:25–30 (Luke 10:21–22), and "mystic-theosophical" materials (particularly the Poimandres) he tried to show that the authority of the Jewish wise man expressed itself in a literary pattern closely related to that which also serves as the vehicle for revelatory utterances in Christian and Hellenistic religious texts.[16]

Norden's thesis is no longer tenable in the form in which he presented it. Suggs, for example, has shown that the pattern is difficult to establish: Ecclesiasticus 51 (as discoveries in cave 11 at Qumran show) was a late addition to Ecclesiasticus, Matt. 11:25–30 is not a literary unit, and the parallels in the Poimandres are vague. As a New Testament scholar Suggs is concerned about putting Matt. 11:25–30 in its proper setting. Criticism of Norden's thesis does not involve the denial of the influence of Jewish wisdom in the passage. Suggs cites the Wisdom of Solomon as background for Matt. 11:28–30. Nor does he deny that there is Gnosticizing tendency in the passage.[17] The more careful analysis of the growth of the tradition, then, calls into question the fixed character of the literary pattern that appears in Matt. 11:25–30. Yet the major themes of the passage reflect wisdom material and fall naturally together. As we shall see, similar themes reappear in Silvanus and point to similar preoccupations. In particular, whatever it is in Matt. 11:27 that has led scholars to speak of a Gnosticizing tendency prepares us for the further Gnosticizing of such themes in Silvanus including the appearance of one formula very close to a passage from the Poimandres which was brought into the discussion by Norden. Norden, then, had correctly identified an impulse at work in these materials even though his understanding of the literary pattern involved was faulty.

To a certain extent Silvanus gives the appearance of being no more than an imitation of classical Jewish wisdom (Proverbs, Ecclesiasticus), and one passage shows the typical Christian interest in the hypostatized figure of wisdom in the Wisdom of Solomon. Yet there is reason to believe that imitation alone does not account for the literary form of the treatise. As we shall see, Silvanus is dependent on three main literary genres—classical Jewish wisdom, the Stoic-Cynic diatribe, and the Hellenistic hymn. The same three literary strands stand out with special prominence in Reese's analysis of the literary features of the Wisdom of Solomon. Yet they are blended in such distinctive ways in the two treatises that there is no question of a slavish dependence of the one on the other. This suggests a common theological atmosphere and a still living religious tradition rather than mere imitation or a simple exegetical concern. Silvanus may represent a form of Christian wisdom based on Jewish precursors which paved the way for the activities of Christian theologians like Clement and Origen. It is the purpose of this chapter to present some of the considerations which suggest such a setting for Silvanus.

Silvanus and Classical Jewish Wisdom

Certain themes and images, a tendency to have lines fall into parallelism, and the address to the reader as "my son" all point to the influence of classical Jewish wisdom in

Silvanus. The following passage from the section on "discipline" (*paideia*) may serve to illustrate these points (87.4–88.6):

> My son, receive the discipline and the teaching;
> do not flee the discipline and the teaching;
> > but when you are taught, receive it with joy.
> And if you are disciplined in anything, do what is good,
> > and you will plait a crown of discipline by your governing self. [18]
> Clothe yourself with the holy teaching as a robe,
> ennoble yourself by good conduct,
> gain austerity by good order,
> judge yourself like a wise judge.
> Go not astray from my teaching and do not acquire stupidity,
> > lest you lead astray your people.
> Do not flee the divine and the teaching which is within you;
> > for he who teaches you loves you greatly;
> > for you will gain a worthy austerity.
> Cast out the nature of the animal within you;
> > and do not admit base thought;
> > for the time has come for you to know how I teach you.
> If it is good to rule [visible] things as you see it,
> > [how] much preferable for you to rule everything,
> since you are great over every congregation and every people,
> > and exalted in every way with divine reason,
> since you have become master over every power.

The effort at *parallelismus membrorum* is obvious. The address "my son" corresponds to the practice of Proverbs and Ecclesiasticus but not the Wisdom of Solomon. Whereas the LXX of Proverbs and Ecclesiasticus simply says "son" (*huie* regularly in Proverbs, *teknon* in Ecclesiasticus), Silvanus spells out what is implied ("my son") and what the Hebrew explicitly says. Clement of Alexandria[19] for one also uses the full form of address "my son," and it was common in the Christian catechetical tradition as is clear from the Didache (3.1–6; 4.1; 5.2). The opening exhortation is reminiscent of Prov. 1:8 ("hear, son, the discipline of your father, / and reject not the counsels of your mother") and other passages. A similar call to obedience—"Listen, my son, to my advice (*symboulia*)"—occurs a number of times (e.g. 85.29–30) and obviously represents a variant of Ecclus. 6:23—"Listen, my child, and accept my judgment; / do not reject my advice (*symboulia*)." The image of the crown is closely connected with the theme of discipline in Prov. 1:8–9 and Ecclus. 6:18–31; the image of the robe also appears in the latter passage (Ecclus. 6:31). Silvanus even gives the appearance of continuing the old appeal to kings—" . . . lest you lead your people astray" (cf. Ecclus. 9:17, 10:1, 3).

At the same time, we are conscious of a new tone throughout. Sage advice rooted in experience gives way to imperatives based on doctrine. The Stoic term "governing self" and the Gnosticizing phrase "the nature of the animal within you" indicate Silvanus' point of departure. The "crown" and the "robe" which in classical Jewish wisdom suggest the success and prestige which accompany wisdom refer in Silvanus to an inner spiritual endowment. Kingship itself apparently serves as an image for the freedom of the wise man who rules all things by his victory over himself and all evil powers (cf. Gospel of Thomas, 2; Clement, *Strom.* 2.45.5; 5.96.3). It is likely that the appeal to kings in the Wisdom of Solomon (6:1ff.) is also a spiritual kingship. The common basis for the imagery is probably the conception of the Stoic-Cynic sage as king and/or the ideals of Hellenistic kingship.[20] Silvanus Gnosticizes the theme.

This underlying difference in tone and spirit naturally expresses itself in important shifts in the literary character of this wisdom. To these problems we shall return in detail presently.

Another theme strikingly reminiscent of classical Jewish wisdom is the call of wisdom (88.365–89.34):

Wisdom summons [you],
    and you desire folly.
Not by your desire do you do these things,
    but it is the nature of the animal within you that does
       them.
Wisdom summons you in her goodness, saying,
"Come unto me, all of you, O foolish ones,
    and receive a gift—the insight which is good and
       excellent.
I give you a high-priestly garment
    which is woven of every kind of wisdom."
What is evil death but ignorance?
    What is evil darkness but the knowledge of forgetful-
       ness?
Cast your care on God alone;
    love not gold and silver which are profitless.
But clothe yourself with wisdom as a robe,
    and put knowledge on you as a crown.
Sit upon a throne of perception since these things are
       yours,
    and you will receive them again above a second time.
For the foolish man clothes himself with folly as a robe,
    and as a garment of grief, since he clothes himself
       with shame.
And he sets a crown upon himself in ignorance,
    and he sits upon a throne of [nescience].

The summons of wisdom and the contrast between wisdom and folly are too characteristic of classical Jewish wisdom to require much comment. The general structure of the summons in Silvanus recalls Prov. 2:20ff. But the words put in the mouth of wisdom are closer to Ecclus. 51:23–26 and, it appears, Matt. 11:28. The allegorical treatment of the high-priestly robe is reminiscent of the Wisd. of Sol. 18:24.[21] Such spiritualization is carried further in Silvanus than in Jewish wisdom as the succeeding lines indicate. First, Jewish wisdom does not use terms like "death" and "darkness" as symbols of spiritual deficiencies. The external form of the lines in which this occurs reflects the new mood; for although questions occur in Jewish wisdom, they are not in the form "what is this but that." Second, the call to cast oneself on God and to despise gold or silver presupposes a connection of ideas foreign to Jewish wisdom. In Proverbs the advice that the happiness and gain derived from wisdom is better than that which comes from gold and silver (cf. Prov. 3:13–14, 8:10–11, 16:16) has none of the otherworldly character that it has in Silvanus. And once again the crown and robe are charged with deep spiritual significance in Silvanus.

The changes involved in the formal character of these materials may be studied more closely in connection with another passage which recalls classical Jewish wisdom (97.3–98.23):

> Speak not evil in your judgment,
>   for every evil man injures his own heart.
> For a foolish man goes of himself to his destruction, but
>   a wise man knows his way.
> For a foolish man guards not himself from speaking a
>   mystery;
>   a wise man does not blurt out every word,
>   but he will examine those who hear.
> Do not blurt out every word
>   when approaching what you do not know.
> Have a multitude of friends,
>   but not of counsellors.
> Examine first your counsellor,
>   for do not honor every man who flatters.
> Their word is sweet as honey,
>   but their heart is full of hellebore.
> For when they think they have become firm friends,
>   then they will turn against you deceitfully,
>   and they will throw you down in the mud.
> Do not trust anyone as a friend,
>   for this whole world has become deceitful,
>   and every [man] who is troubled [is an animal].
> All things [of] the world are useless,
>   but since they are in vain,

> (trust) no one, not even a brother,
> since each seeks his own profit.
> My son, have no man as friend,
> but if you gain him, do not give yourself to him.
> Give yourself to God alone as father and as friend,
> for every man walks deceitfully.
> The whole earth is full of toil and grief,
> and there is no profit in them.
> If you wish to pass your life undisturbed,
> do not walk with anyone.
> And if you do walk with them,
> be as if you did not walk.
> Be pleasing to God and you will need no one;
> live with Christ and he will save you;
> for he is the light of truth
> and the sun of life.

The command to have many friends but not counsellors is close to the advice of Ecclus. 6:6, "Let those that are at peace with you be many, / but let your counsellors be one in a thousand." Ecclesiasticus also goes on (6:7) to show the need for "testing" a friend and not "trusting" him too readily. The theme of the deceit of friends is given attention in the same context (6:8–13) and in two other closely related passages (12:16–18; 37:1ff.). Silvanus' reference to "sweet" words and the "mud" also reflect themes in Ecclesiasticus (12:16): "An enemy will speak sweetly with his lips, / but in his mind he will plan to throw you into a pit." The thought that each man seeks his own advantage is also known to Ecclesiasticus (37:8, 13), but that all toil and grief is profitless reminds one more of Ecclesiastes (2:11).

The description of the fool as one who rashly reveals a "mystery" is probably a reworking of a theme elsewhere in Ecclesiasticus (27:16–21) that the man who betrays "mysteries"—that is, secrets—loses his friend. The comparison helps us see clearly the difference in tone between the old wisdom and the new. Silvanus has evidently related widely separated reflections on friendship in Ecclesiasticus and read deeper meaning into what he has found.

This change in tone and mood brings with it changes in the external literary character of this wisdom which we must now discuss in greater detail.

The section before us contains one of the few sayings in Silvanus which conform to the dominant type of saying in one of the older forms of Jewish wisdom (Proverbs 10ff.):

> For a foolish man goes of himself to his destruction,
>   but a wise man knows his way.

Not only is the antithesis typical, but the clauses have the grammatical form characteristic of Jewish wisdom which Hermisson calls the "Nominalsatz" or (as in the case before us) the "zusammengesetzte Nominalsatz." In such sentences "the predicate makes a statement concerning the subject" in such a way that they may be reduced to the simple form "A is B."[22] Sentences of this type are peculiarly suited to express the conception of order underlying ancient Jewish (and Near Eastern) wisdom—the knowledge which arises especially from the experience of a correspondence between fact and consequences.[23] The proverb conveys such insight and challenges the hearer to see things in the same way.

It has long been held that such "declaratory sentences" are more primitive than proverbs in the form of "exhortations." This can no longer be held.[24] But it is significant, nevertheless, that the declaratory type fades into insignificance in documents like the Wisdom of Solomon and the *Teachings of Silvanus* and that exhortations predominate. In the early period exhortations appear closely related to declaratory sentences. They still give the impression of being distillations of wide and deep experience.[25] It is not that "absolute" values are unknown to the writers of ancient Jewish wisdom but that all values are uncovered by the wise man who grasps the connections between things as he penetrates the surfaces of the natural and social world about him. The disappearance of the declaratory sentences in wisdom or their transformation into direct statements of religious doctrine accompany a disappearance of the ancient understanding of wisdom and the substitution of new foundations for the quest of the wise man. Consequently, exhortations also subtly change their character. Often little difference can be detected on the surface; but sage advice is no longer what we have before us.

We may take the following saying as an example of this change:

> Do not trust anyone as a friend,
>   for this whole world has become deceitful,
>   and every [man] who is troubled [is an animal].

"It is but a slight development of the two-stranded mashal when one part is divided into two synonymous halves"[26] as we have it in the gospels and in the example just quoted. But the character of the clause is quite different from that which is found in classical Jewish wisdom. There, when an exhortation is followed by a reason, the reason is, as Hermisson says, more "elaboration" than "reason."[27] "It is an abomination to kings to do evil, / for the throne is established by righteousness" (Prov. 16:12). In classical wisdom the appeal is based on the connections between things that experience has taught. Later (as in Ecclus. 23:22–23) that begins to change. But it is only in writings like the Wisdom of Solomon and the *Teachings of Silvanus* that reasons regularly support exhortations in a way that goes beyond the older wisdom. In short, the "for" in the statement quoted from Silvanus is a quite different "for" from that which is found in classical Jewish wisdom. Not experience but a metaphysic determines the sentiments.

Another example of this development is the use made of the connective "how much more." This is common in classical Jewish wisdom and occurs also in the sayings of Jesus (Matt. 7:11). But, as Hermisson points out, in classical wisdom the logical character of the connection is not marked; the second element is little more than a variant of

the first: "It is not fitting for a fool to live in luxury, /
much less for a slave to rule over princes" (Prov. 19:10).[28]
Contrast the following statement from Silvanus (98.28ff.):

> For (if) a wicked man in the body (has) an evil death,
> how much more he who has his mind blinded.

Here the logical character of the argument is stronger and
depends for its force on the view that mind is superior to
body. The long discussion of blindness and light which
follows emphasizes the difference. The symbol of light in
particular receives rich elaboration, and the allegorizing
tendency is explicitly marked: "for everything which appears is a type of what is hid" (99.5–7; cf. Mark 4:22). It
is interesting to observe that as the discussion proceeds the
style becomes more prosaic and sustains with difficulty the
suggestion of parallelism of members.

The stringing together of "for" sentences in Silvanus
also calls for comment. The beginning of the passage
quoted above is but one example and by no means the
most impressive of these. Classical Jewish wisdom is regularly satisfied with a single diptych when a "reason" is
given; it does not try to tie together thoughts in this way
at any length. Silvanus is much more closely allied with the
Wisdom of Solomon in this respect. We shall attempt to
deal with the significance of this phenomenon later.

The "intensification" of Jewish wisdom which we have
observed is not to be attributed entirely to the spiritualiz-
ing and allegorizing tendencies noted. The sentiments of a
book like Ecclesiastes, as we have seen, have made their
contribution, and it is interesting to note that the statement beginning "all things of the world are useless" has a
stylistic complexity similar to the more complicated parallelisms in that book. The intensity of other sayings in
Silvanus, however, springs from another source. For example:

> For when they think they have become firm friends,
> then they will turn against you deceitfully,
> and they will throw you down in the mud.

Sayings made up of clauses related by a "when" and "then" are not absent from classical Jewish wisdom (cf. Ecclus. 21:15, 27). But there the sentiment is gnomic, and the future tense which occurs in the second clause refers to what will regularly be the case. Our saying, on the other hand, has the effect of a sharp warning. The future tense underscores the "prophetic" character of the saying. The tense functions this way frequently in the sayings of Jesus (cf. Matt. 5:19, 21–22; 6:14–15), and we may regard this development as perfectly natural in traditions which have absorbed the spirit of the prophet as well as that of the man. This intensification of the exhortations of wisdom provided a stepping stone to the radical demands made by more other-worldly teachers and prophets. The "pessimism" of certain strands of wisdom about man and the world served as a point of departure for a world-denying asceticism. That we should "walk" with others "as if" we did not do so is not without its parallel in Paul (1 Cor. 7:29–31) and has some affinities with the detachment of the Stoic wise man from "externals." But Silvanus' attitude is more radical: it is clearly preferable not to walk at all with anyone.

Silvanus and the Stoic-Cynic Diatribe

The movement from Jewish to Hellenistic wisdom was accomplished partly with the help of the Stoic-Cynic diatribe. Reese has discussed features of diatribe in the Wisdom of Solomon,[29] and we shall show that Silvanus also betrays familiarity with this form of literature. The point of contact was obvious: both wisdom and the diatribe address men and exhort them to reflect upon their behavior and reasons for changing it. It is a mistake to think of the diatribe as a severely fixed form;[30] but some characteristics are sufficiently striking for us to trace its influence on Silvanus.

The dominant characteristic of the diatribe is that of a

dialogue. The technique of introducing objections and questions from an imaginary interlocutor is too well known to be repeated here.[31] The most obvious features of the dialogue thus occasioned cannot be expected to appear within the framework of wisdom literature. But closely related elements do, and they are sufficient to account for important dimensions of the composition of Silvanus.

The address to the reader "man" or "O man" is a well-known mark of the diatribe and appears in a few passages in Silvanus:[32]

> It is better for you, O man, to incline yourself to the human than to incline to the nature of the animal—I mean the fleshly (nature). [93.34–94.3]

> For you appear, O man, as one casting out this one [i.e. Christ] from your temple. [109.27–30]

Equally characteristic of the diatribe is the address "wretched one" or "O wretched one" and related expressions:[33]

> And when all the powers saw him, they fled so that he might bring you, wretched one, up from the Abyss. [104.8–12]

> Do not burn yourself, O wretched one, in the fire of pleasure [108.4–6]

The address "O wretched man," possibly echoing Rom. 7:14, is also found (86.8).

This style of address seems to have affected other formulae. Occasionally the simple sapiential "my son" becomes "O my son" (105.13, 109.34, 118.5). More significant, perhaps, is the address "foolish one" (90.28), "O foolish one" (107.12), or "O foolish ones" (89.8). Jewish wisdom literature knows much of the fool but rarely addresses the fool in this way (Prov. 1:22). The address is more characteristic of the diatribe.[34]

The address "O wretched soul" (85.22) takes us a step further. It forms a bridge between the style of address in the diatribe and the address "O soul" (105.26, 33) or "O soul, enduring one" (94.19, 103.28).[35] This address characterizes neither wisdom nor the diatribe. One passage in particular shows the setting in which it may be understood:

> O soul, enduring one, be sober and cast off drunkenness—that is, the work of ignorance. [94.19–22]

Compare the Poimandres (*Corpus Hermeticum* 1.27):

> O people, who have given yourselves to drunkenness and sleep and to ignorance of God, be sober.

This "mystic-theosophical" address from the Poimandres was connected by Norden with the summons of the wise man in Ecclesiasticus 51.[36] As we have seen, Norden's connections were too facile; yet he correctly identified an impulse at work in the wisdom tradition. In Silvanus we have the final product of this tendency: the call of Wisdom is fused with the call of the Revealer. The address to the soul, then, reflects a more intense, more interiorized spirituality. In view of this, the simple address to "my son" takes on a new color. For in the "mystic-theosophical" literature the address "son" or "O son" is not unknown, and the tradition of the secret teaching is often understood in terms of the relation between a (spiritual) father and his son.[37] In Silvanus, wisdom and the diatribe have become vehicles for revelatory address.

Yet the more sober tone of the diatribe is not fully eclipsed. In addition to the addresses discussed above, there are other familiar marks of the dialogical character of the diatribe: "Do you not know that . . ." (94.33),[38] "but I say that . . ." (93.24),[39] "for I think that . . ." (92.29).[40] These elements together with the direct address that prevails throughout as a feature of the exhortatory style convey much of the atmosphere of the diatribe.

Other features that are common in the diatribe (as well as elsewhere) include the list of vices with which Silvanus begins (84.21–26)[41] —such a list also occurs in the Wisdom

of Solomon (14:25–26)—and exclamations like "O the
patience of God . . ." (114.26–27; cf. 111.13–14).[42] A
common feature of the Greco-Roman rhetoric, the sorites,
occurs both in Silvanus (108.18–24, ending with the Stoic
term "the governing self") and the Wisdom of Solomon
(6:17–20). Especially reminiscent of the diatribe, perhaps,
is one passage which builds its rhetorical effect by heaping
one phrase upon another, each made up of similar grammatical elements and involving the juxtaposition of contraries:[43]

> For he [i.e., the Adversary] casts into your heart evil
>   thoughts
>   as good ones,
> and hypocrisy
>   as firm understanding,
> and love of things
>   as sparing economy,
> and love of glory
>   as that which is fair,
> and boastfulness and pride
>   as great austerity,
> and godlessness
>   as [great] godliness
> (for he who says, "I have many gods," is godless),
> and infirm knowledge he casts into your heart
>   as mysterious doctrines.
> Who will be able to grasp his schemes and his varied
>   turnings
>   since he is a great Mind for those who want to accept
>   him as king? [95.20–96.10]

This example indicates the extent to which parallelism
in Silvanus can depart from the models of wisdom literature and approach that of popular Hellenistic rhetoric.
Parallelism and simplicity of sentence structure characterize both wisdom literature and the diatribe[44] but, as is
obvious, in different ways. Other examples in Silvanus are
equally instructive. One is particularly interesting since we
have a close parallel to it in Theophilus of Antioch.
    In describing the God who contains all, Silvanus says:

> For do not think in your heart that God is in a place;
> if you place the [Lord of] All in a place, then it is
>   fitting for you to say
> that the place is more exalted than he who dwells in the
>   place.
> For that which contains is more exalted than that which
>   is contained. [93.31–100.4]

According to Theophilus (*Ad Aut.* 2.3) we are not to think
that God is

> contained in a place;
> otherwise, the place which contains will be found great-
>   er than he;
> for that which contains is greater than that which is
>   contained;
> for God is not contained,
>   but he himself is the place of all things.

The sentences in these passages are very simply structured.
They may be arranged in loose sense lines; but this has
nothing in common with the parallelism of classical Jewish
wisdom literature. When we note that Theophilus' style is
also marked by features of the diatribe such as the imaginary interlocutor, the address "O man," and many others
(cf. *Ad Autolycum* 1.2), we are encouraged to think that
we have rightly identified the diatribe as an important
source of Silvanus' style.

Another example of parallelism that reflects the style of
simple Greek rhetoric rather than that of classical Jewish
wisdom is the following:

> But before everything else,
>   know your birth,
>   know yourself,
>   that is, from what substance you are,
>   or from what race you are,
>   or from what tribe.
> Understand that you have come forth from three races—
>   from the earth,
>   and from the formation,
>   and from the created.

> The body came into being from the earth
> > from an earthly substance;
> and the formation came into being on account of the
>   soul
> > from the thought of the Divine;
> and the created is the mind which came into being
> > according to the image of God. . . .
> > > [92.10–25]

This is but a part of a long section—it goes on to 94.32—
which includes some of the more obvious features of the
diatribe discussed above. It also displays that delight in
isokolon which, in conjuntion with simple syntax, characterizes the diatribe. The Gnosticizing tendency of the
writer, however, probably has something to do with the
concentration on one aspect of the diatribe—direct exhortation and instruction. (For Gnostic parallels see especially
Excerpta ex Theodoto 78.2; Irenaeus, *Adversus Haereses*
1.7.5; 1.21.5; *First Apocalypse of James* 33, 11ff.) It is
valuable to compare what Epictetus has to say on a similar
topic—"How from the thesis that we are akin to God may
a man proceed to the consequences" (*Discourses* 1.9). At
one point in this discourse, Epictetus indicates what he
himself ought to say when confronted by those who wish
to free themselves from this world by committing suicide:

> Men, wait upon God.
> When he gives the signal
> > and sets you free from his service,
> then you shall depart to Him;
> but for the present endure to abide in this place
> > in which he has stationed you.
> Short indeed is the time of your abiding here,
> > and easy to bear for men of your convictions.
> For what tyrant, or what thief, or what courts are
> > fearful
> > to those who have thus despised the body and its
> > possessions?
> Abide! Depart not in an irrational manner!
> > > [Sections 16–17]

The tone of such a proclamation is, on the surface, not unlike that of the Gnostic revealer. But the proclamation in Epictetus has a different context in which the argumentative and dialogical features of the diatribe are to the fore. The title of the section already suggests the greater emphasis in Epictetus on eliciting the practical implications of a philosophical thesis by reasoned considerations. It is symptomatic that Epictetus put the exhortation in his own mouth. This device emphasizes the distance between the earnest moral appeal of the Stoic wise man and the revelatory speech of the *Teachings of Silvanus.*

Another general feature of Silvanus which may owe something to the diatribe is the frequent repetition of the conjunction "for." It occurs, for example, some twelve times in the section on discriminating speech (97.3–99.20) and some thirteen times in the section on the location of God (99.21–102.7). Within the sections the conjunction tends to accumulate at certain points. We have noted above that this is not characteristic of classical Jewish wisdom but is found throughout the Wisdom of Solomon and contributes to the logical character of the movement of thought. As Reese points out, the Wisdom of Solomon (he is speaking in particular of 1:1–6:11 and 6:17–20) differs from more ancient Jewish wisdom and approaches the ·diatribe in that it represents a "sustained logical appeal for moral uprightness."[45] The repeated use of the conjunction "for" seems to be one way in which at least an appearance of logical progression is maintained in the face of the tendency in Jewish wisdom literature to settle for short independent units. Even in the diatribe, where there are restraints, repetition of the conjunction "for" may be found (cf. Epict. *Diss.* 2.2.1–3).

Finally, we may mention the images and comparisons in Silvanus which go far beyond anything in Jewish wisdom. It seems likely that they may be accounted for by the rich development of similar types of illustration in the diatribe,[46] although the allegorizing tendencies noted above have obviously turned them in a new direction. A more detailed analysis of such elements in Silvanus is not possible here.

It will have been observed that many of the features mentioned in this section are also characteristic of the letters of Paul. Silvanus once explicitly refers to Paul (108.30)—such a reference is itself more in harmony with the diatribe[47] than with wisdom literature—and he sometimes reflects on Paul's letters, particularly the passages on wisdom in 1 Cor. 1:18ff. (107.9–12; 111.22–29). Like many today, Silvanus saw the relevance of these sections in Paul for the problem of wisdom. But the features of the diatribe noted above can hardly be explained alone by dependence on Paul. A different range of phenomena is involved, and the use made of them is distinctive. This is even more clearly the situation when the Wisdom of Solomon is compared with Silvanus.

Silvanus and the Helenistic Hymn

We turn now to a third element which Silvanus shares with the Wisdom of Solomon—what for lack of a better term we may call the Hellenistic hymn. These have a parallelism of lines which made them compatible with wisdom literature. Classical Jewish wisdom had already shown in the case of Ecclesiasticus a marked tendency to develop forms close to the biblical psalms.[48] Both Proverbs 8 and Ecclesiasticus 24 represent hymns of a distinctive cast. And Reese has detected in the praise of wisdom in the Wisdom of Solomon (chapters 7, 8, and 10) the classical Greek "Er-Stil" discussed by Norden[49] and similarities with the aretalogies in praise of Isis which employ that style.[50] One of Silvanus' hymns is very close to that of the Wisdom of Solomon. Another takes a different form and reflects the οὗτός ἐστι style (that is, οὗτός ἐστι or σὺ εἶ followed by participles with the article). This style, in Norden's estimation, has roots in the Jewish world but becomes a "soteriological form of address" used across a wide range of Hellenistic literature.[51] It dominates the following hymn:

> Know who Christ is,
>> and gain himself for yourself as a friend,
>> for he is the friend who is trustworthy.
>
> He is also God and Teacher.
> This one, being God, became man for you.
> This is the one who loosed the iron bars of Hades
>> and the bronze bolts.
>
> This is the one who stretched forth his hand
>> (and) cast down every proud tyrant,
>
> the one who, taking hold of the chains, loosened them
> (and) brought up the poor from the Abyss
>> and the mourners from Hades,
>
> the one who brought low the proud powers,
> the one who put to shame the proud through humiliation,
> the one who cast down the strong,
>> and the boaster through weakness,
>
> the one who contemptuously despised that regarded as
>> an honor
>> so that humility for God's sake might be highly
>> exalted,
>
> the one who put on humanity. . . . [110.14–111.4]

The "Er-Stil" (though blended with the σὺ εἶ and οὗτός ἐστι style) dominates the following hymn.

> Lord almighty, how great glory shall I give you?
> No one has been able to glorify God as he is.
> You are the one who have glorified your Logos
>> who saves everyone, merciful God:
>
> He who came forth from your mouth
>> and from your heart,
>>> the first born,
>>> the wisdom,
>>> the prototype,
>>> the first light.
>
> For he is a light from the power of God,
> and he is an emanation of the holy glory of the almighty
>> [Wisd. of Sol. 7:25b] ,

and he is the holy mirror of the activity of God [Wisd.
    of Sol. 7:26b],
and he is the image of his goodness [Wisd. of Sol.
    7:26c],
and indeed he is the light of the eternal light [Wisd. of
    Sol. 7:26a].
He is the seeing which looks upon the invisible Father,
    ever serving and creating by the will of the Father,
the one who alone was begotten by the Father's good
    pleasure. . . .

[112.27–113.12]

Here the dependence of the middle section on the hymn to
wisdom in the Wisd. of Sol. 7:25–26 is clear. Here too the
"Er-Stil" predominates which characterizes the aretalogies
lying behind the praise of wisdom by Solomon. But Silvanus handles the form with great freedom and more than
mere imitation seems to be at work here.

In another hymnic fragment, biblical elements are reflected which lend themselves easily to the style that our
author naturally adopts:

But no one prevents him [i.e. God] from doing what he
    wills.
For who is stronger than he that may prevent him?
Yea, he is the one who touches the earth,
    causing it to tremble,
    and also causing the mountains to smoke [Ps. 104:
    32],
the one who gathered together great seas as in bags [Ps.
    33:7]
and has measured all the water in his scale [cf. Isa.
    40:12]. . . .

[114.30–115.2]

In yet another hymnic fragment, titles of Christ derived
from or reflected in a variety of sources are set in a new
literary context:

Give them [i.e. the beasts within you] life;
they shall live again.
For Christ is the Tree of Life [cf. Rev. 22:2].

He is Wisdom.[52]
For he is Wisdom [1 Cor. 1:24], he is also the Logos
    [John 1:1].
He is Life [John 1:4] and the Power [1 Cor. 1:24] and
    the Door [John 10:7].
He is the Light [John 1:4] and the Messenger [Justin, 1
    Apology 63.5]
    and the Good Shepherd [John 10:11].
                                                    [106.20–28]

Silvanus' use of hymns and hymnic fragments is not unexpected in light of their appearance also in earlier wisdom literature. Wisdom has obviously been called upon to perform tasks for which gnomic sayings were inadequate. What is notable about Silvanus' hymns is the blend of styles that, whatever their origin, serve as a vehicle of the revelation of the being and activities of the Divine. Their presence here is in harmony with the development of wisdom toward a "mystic-theosophical" religiosity which we have seen throughout this paper.

Conclusions

This study has paid special attention to literary form on the assumption that modes of expression are sometimes a more significant clue to what is expressed than religio-historical parallels. In particular, an effort has been made to identify literary features of Silvanus that would suggest the setting within which the treatise is to be understood. In this connection remarkable similarities with the Wisdom of Solomon have emerged. In both documents the parallelism of Jewish wisdom, Hellenistic rhetoric mediated especially through the diatribe, and Hellenistic hymns have left important marks. Other literary forms may be detected—prayers (111.15–20; cf. Wisdom of Solomon, chapter 9), and so forth. But it is my impression that the three features studied in this chapter are the most decisive from a literary point of view.

In spite of these similarities, the two documents are yet very different from each other. Even the use made of these literary styles is not the same. Either they somewhat fortuitously confronted similar influences or—what I regard as more likely—they represent diverse products of a religious and theological tradition in which these elements were blended in a variety of ways.

Other differences are the result of the fact that Silvanus is not an apologetic Jewish tract directed to the pagan world but an exhortation directed to Christians to receive the true light which shuts out the darkness and displays the uselessness of the things of this world. One likely possibility is that it represents a Christianized form of Jewish wisdom which prepared the way for the thought of the great Alexandrian theologians of the third century. It is in Clement of Alexandria that we find the richest source for a comparison of the use of wisdom. Völker has shown the large place that wisdom—especially Proverbs and Ecclesiasticus—play in Clement's writing.[53] Like Silvanus, he strings together fragments of classical Jewish wisdom to form new mosaics and to suggest fresh applications. Clement, like Silvanus, is impressed by the twin notions of *sophia* and *paideia* in biblical wisdom (*Strom.* 2.4–5; quoting Prov. 3:5, 6, 23; 3:7, 12; Wisd. of Sol. 7:17, 20, 21–22). He quotes Proverbs to show that wisdom is better than gold and silver (*Paed.* 2.129.1–4; quoting Prov. 19:17; 10:4; 3:13–15) and to oppose all luxury (*Paed.* 3.35.3–5; quoting Prov. 8:10, 11, 19; 11:24 and other biblical verses). He bases his whole conception of theological method on wisdom (*Strom.* 1.28.4–10) and finds in the father/son language of wisdom the justification of his literary activity (*Strom.* 1.1.3–1.2.1). It is important to note for our purposes that he interprets the superiority of wisdom over gold and silver in such a way that spiritual realities, are sharply distinguished from material goods. This interpretation, which goes far beyond the intentions of ancient Jewish wisdom, is shared by Silvanus. It is symptomatic of Clement's whole understanding of wisdom.

It is natural to wonder whether it is possible to speak of a wisdom tradition when the original intention of Jewish wisdom has apparently been left so far behind. Could Silvanus be merely imitative? Further research is needed to answer that question fully. We have concentrated our attention on features of the text which suggest that although Silvanus often reflects on biblical materials, he is in a tradition that had been adapting the ways of wisdom to new purposes. A tradition can go only so far in adapting itself before it breaks down and is replaced by something new. We are very close to that point in the *Teachings of Silvanus.*

The question is left as to whether the wisdom tradition as it comes to expression in Silvanus has any connection with other developments in early Christian wisdom. Mention may be made here not only of the collection of sayings in Matthew (and Matt. 11:25–30 in particular) but also other collections such as the Gospel of Thomas and the discussion of wisdom in 1 Corinthians, chapters 1–2. The later creation of sayings in the wisdom style by Evagrius and others may also be relevant to the discussion.

It is clear that anyone who sets out to draw lines connecting such diverse materials must be prepared to emphasize some features and to neglect others. In Silvanus, as we have seen, important elements related by Norden reappear. 1 Corinthians, chapters 1–2 is also reflected. But there is also much more—including the allegorizing of gospel materials (e.g., Matt. 7:7–8: "knock on yourself that the Logos may open to you," 117.7–9; Matt. 21:12–17: "Let him [i.e. Christ] come into the temple within you that he may cast out every merchant," 109.15–17). To what extent are we dealing "merely" with exegetical activity? To what extent did Silvanus "merely" recognize affinities—though perhaps significant ones—in his biblical sources?

Our study of the deeper literary affinities of Silvanus suggests that Silvanus does indeed stand in a living tradition but that it is not one primarily concerned about collecting the words of the wise. Rather the relation is with the sort of thing found in the Wisdom of Solomon. Perhaps there were two major branches of the development of wisdom in the early church (and Judaism), the one retaining an interest in collections of sayings, the other responding to other impulses as well. The tendency in both to move in a Gnosticizing direction may indicate that they sprang up on common soil. It is perhaps significant that Silvanus mirrors a development of ideas which Norden had already discerned however imperfectly on the basis of his analysis of Matt. 11:25–30.

The place of the later inventions of sayings for monks and nuns is even more difficult to assess. Such compositions may have been prompted especially by the prestige of lists of sayings of wise men in the pagan world. The *Sentences of Sextus* witness to a Christianizing of Pythagorean maxims and suggest the power of the pagan literary tradition.[54] The sayings for monks and nuns may have represented an effort to challenge that tradition with more "biblical" forms. Such motives may have been operative earlier as well. Still it does not seem impossible that all such activity in the church also received some inspiration from an older concern for the collection of words of the wise.

In spite of all the uncertainties, Silvanus must be seen as strengthening the case for a significant wisdom tradition in early Christianity. The Jewish image of the sage was rooted deeply enough in human experience that new religious ideas (from Judaism, the Oriental world, Hellenism, or whatever) could crystallize around it or coalesce with it easily and naturally. The personification and hypostatization of wisdom, the sage of Ecclesiasticus, chapter 51, Christ as wisdom incarnate, and the revealer of Gnostic truths represent diverse ways of articulating the ground of the authority of the wise man. The strength of such a tradition may help us understand why, for example, the "delay of the Parousia" was overcome with relative ease— from the beginning possibilities other than apocalyptic were alive in Christianity—and it may also help us see why Alexandrian Christianity developed so distinctive a theology—it relied perhaps on a special tradition of Hellenistic Jewish and Christian wisdom.

NOTES

1. W. Baumgartner, "The Wisdom Literature," in H.H. Rowley, *The Old Testament and Modern Study* (London, 1951), pp. 210–237.

2. Rudolph Bultmann, *The History of the Synoptic Tradition* (Oxford, 1963), pp. 69–108.

3. Hans Windisch, *Die katholischen Briefe,* ed. H. Preisker, 3rd ed. (Tübingen, 1951), pp. 1–36.

4. Harry A. Wolfson, *The Philosophy of the Church Fathers,* vol. I, *Faith, Trinity, Incarnation* (Cambridge, Mass., 1956), pp. 245–247.

5. Norman Perrin, "Wisdom and Apocalyptic in the Message of Jesus," in *SBL Proc.* 2 (1972), 543–572.

6. See chap. 1.

7. Gerhard von Rad, *Old Testament Theology* II (New York, 1965), 306–308.

8. Richard A. Edwards, "An Approach to a Theology of Q," *The Journal of Religion* 51 (1971), 247–269.

9. See chap. 3.

10. Walter H. Wagner, "A Father's Fate: Attitudes Toward and Interpretations of Clement of Alexandria," *Journal of Religious History* 7 (1971), 209–231; Louis Bouyer, *The Spirituality of the New Testament and the Fathers* (London, 1963).

11. Hugo Gressmann, *Nonnenspiegel und Mönchsspiegel des Evagrius Pontikos,* TU 39 (Leipzig, 1913). Cf. Bouyer, *Spirituality,* p. 382.

12. James M. Robinson, "The Coptic Gnostic Library Today," *NTS* 12 (1968), 399. Translations are my own from a text prepared by Jan Zandee and Malcolm L. Peel for the Institute for Antiquity and Christianity at Claremont, California.

13. William R. Schoedel, " 'Topological' Theology and Some Monistic Tendencies in Gnosticism," in *Essays on the Nag Hammadi*

Texts in Honour of Alexander Böhlig, Nag Hammadi Studies, no. 3, (Leiden, 1972), pp. 88–108.

14. W. Baumgartner, "Die literarischen Gattungen in der Weisheit des Jesus Sirach," *ZAW* 34 (1914), 161–198.

15. James M. Reese, *Hellenistic Influence in the Book of Wisdom and Its Consequences,* AB, no. 41 (Rome, 1970), pp. 25–31, 32–62, 90–121.

16. Eduard Norden, *Agnostos Theos* (Stuttgart, r.p. 1956), pp. 277–308.

17. M. Jack Suggs, *Wisdom, Christology, and Law in Matthew's Gospel* (Cambridge, Mass., 1970), pp. 71–97. For the Qumran hymn that corresponds to Ecclesiasticus 51 see J.A. Sanders, *Discoveries in the Judaean Desert,* vol. IV: *The Psalms Scroll of Qumran Cave 11 (11 Q Ps^a)* (Oxford, 1965), pp. 79–85.

18. "Governing self" for the Greek *hegemonikon,* following the translation of the term in A.S.L. Farquharson, *The Meditations of the Emperor Marcus Aurelius* (Oxford, 1944), I, 21. The pursuit of the "governing self" is held up by Epictetus as the first duty of the Stoic wise man (*Discourses* 3.22.9).

19. *Stromateis* 1.29.2.

20. For the gnostic use of the Stoic-Cynic ideal of the wise man see particularly Clement, *Stromateis* 3.30.1 (Prodicus). Reese (*Hellenistic Influence,* pp. 71–87) emphasizes the influence in the Wisdom of Solomon of the Hellenistic tracts on kingship. But this need not rule out influences from other sources. Reese himself sees in the king Solomon of Wisdom "a type of everyman" (p. 76). The Stoic discussion of kingship was not isolated from the political ideal (Martin P. Nilsson, *Geschichte der griechischen Religion,* II [Munich, 1950], p. 127). And Philo, in describing Moses, links the Hellenistic description of the king as "a living law" and the Stoic ideal of living according to nature (*Mos.* 2.4; cf. *Abr.* 5).

21. This allegory is found also in Philo and Josephus. Cf. E.R. Goodenough, *By Light, Light* (New Haven, 1935), p. 276.

22. Hans-Jürgen Hermisson, *Studien zur Israelitischen Spruchweisheit,* WMANT 28, (Neukirchen-Vluyn, 1968), pp. 141–144.

23. Ibid., pp. 137–141.

24. Ibid., pp. 16, 81–88.

25. Ibid., pp. 160–162. Cf. Walther Zimmerli, "Zur Struktur der alttestamentlichen Weisheit," *ZAW* 51 (1933), 184–192.

26. Bultmann, *Synoptic Tradition,* p. 81.

27. Hermisson, *Spruchweisheit,* p. 162.

28. Ibid., p. 160.
29. Reese, *Hellenistic Influence,* pp. 110–113, 115–116.
30. H.I. Marrou, *A History of Education in Antiquity* (New York, 1956), p. 538.
31. Rudolph Bultmann, *Der Stil der paulinischen Predigt und die knyisch-stoische Diatribe* (Göttingen, 1910), pp. 10–19.
32. Ibid., p. 66 (cf. Epictetus, *Diss.* 2.17.33).
33. Ibid., p. 14.
34. Ibid.
35. The phrase "enduring one" is probably to be explained in terms of the immediate context and represents a play on words. After calling to the "enduring" soul to be sober, Silvanus goes on, "If you endure to live in the body . . . you have entered into a bodily birth." The soul is being recalled from such "endurance."
36. Norden, *Agnostos Theos,* p. 295. What follows in Silvanus makes the "mystic-theosophical" character of the address even clearer. The author goes on to say that the enduring soul has gone inside "the bridal chamber" and become "illuminated in mind" (94.27–29). The imagery of the bridal chamber can be traced back at least as far as Valentinian sources (Irenaeus, *Adversus Haereses* 1.21.3; cf. 1.6.4; 1.7.1; Clement, *Excerpta ex Theodoto* 64).
37. Norden, *Agnostos Theos,* pp. 290–293.
38. Bultmann, *Stil,* pp. 13, 65.
39. Ibid., p. 13.
40. Ibid.
41. Ibid., p. 19.
42. Ibid., pp. 33–34.
43. Ibid., pp. 17–19, 25.
44. Ibid., pp. 21–24.
45. Reese, *Hellenistic Influences,* pp. 110–111.
46. Bultmann, *Stil,* pp. 35–42.
47. Ibid., pp. 42–46.
48. Baumgartner, *ZAW* 34 (1914), 169ff.
49. Norden, *Agnostos Theos,* pp. 163–166.
50. Reese, *Hellenistic Influence,* pp. 43, 45, 105.
51. Norden, *Agnostos Theos,* pp. 177–207.
52. This line is probably a dittography.
53. Walther Völker, "Die Verwertung der Weisheits-Literatur bei den christlichen Alexandrinern," *ZKG* 64 (1952), 5–21.
54. See chap. 6.

Bibliography

Abelson, Joshua. *The Immanence of God in Rabbinic Literature.* London, 1912.

Agus, Jacob Bernard. *The Evolution of Jewish Thought.* 2 vols. London, 1959.

Allo, E. B. "Sagesse et pneuma dans la première épître aux Corinthiens." *RB* 43 (1934), 321–46.

von Arnim, H. *Stoicorum Veterum Fragmenta,* vol. III. Stuttgart, 1964. Esp. pp. 146–171.

Baer, R. *Philo's Use of the Categories Male and Female.* Leiden, 1970.

Baer, Yitzkah Fritz. *Yisra'el ba-amnim.* Jerusalem, 1955.

Bauckmann, Ernst Günter. "Die Proverbien und die Sprüche des Jesus Sirach." *ZAW* 72 (160), 33–63.

Baumgartner, Walter. "Die literarischen Gattungen in der Weisheit des Jesus Sirach." *ZAW* 34 (1914), 161–198.

Beardslee, William A. "Proverbs in the Gospel of Thomas." *NTSupp* 33 (1972); 92–103.

_____. "Uses of the Proverb in the Synoptic Gospels." *Interpr* 24 (1970), 61–73.

_____. "The Wisdom Tradition and the Synoptic Gospels." *JAAR* 35 (1967), 231–240.

Ben-Sasson, Haim Hillel, and Ettinger, S. *Jewish Society throughout the Ages.* New York, 1971.

Bialik, Hayyim Nahman, and Ravnitzki, H. *Sefer ha-Agadah.* Tel Aviv, 1956.

Bonnard, Pierre E. *La Sagesse en personne annoncée et venue: Jésus Christ.* Paris, 1966.

Bonsirven, J. "Genres littéraires dans la littérature juive postbiblique." *Bib* 35 (1954), 328–45.

Bousset, Wilhelm. *Judisch-christicher Schulbeitrich in Alexandria.* FRL 23. Göttingen, 1915.

Bouyer, Louis. *The Spirituality of the New Testament and the Fathers.* London, 1963.

Bréhier, Émile. *Les idées philosophiques et religieuses de Philon d'Alexandrie.* Paris, 1908.

Bultmann, Rudolf. "Karl Barth, *The Resurrection of the Dead.*" In his *Faith and Understanding,* trans. Louis Pettibone Smith, vol. I, 66–94. New York, 1969.

_____, "Der religionsgeschichtliche Hintergrund des Prologs zum Johannes-Evangelium." In ΕΥΧΑΡΙΣΤΗΡΙΟΝ, Festchrift H. Gunkel. FRL, n.f. 19, II, 1–26. Göttingen, 1923.

_____. *Der Stil der paulinischen Predigt und die kynisch-stoische Diatribe.* FRL 13. Göttingen, 1910.

_____. "The Stoic Ideal of the Wise Man." In *Primitive Christianity in Its Contemporary Settings,* trans. R. H. Fuller, pp. 135–145. New York, 1956.

Cerfaux, Lucien. *Le Christ dans la theologie de S. Paul.* Lectio Divina, 6. Paris, 1954.

_____. "Vestiges d'un florilège dans 1 Cor. 1:18–3:24?" *Revue d'histoire ecclésiastique* 27 (1931), 521–534.

Chadwick, Henry. *The Sentences of Sextus.* Texts and Studies, no. 5. Cambridge, Eng., 1959.

Christ, Felix. *Jesus Sophia: Die Sophia-Christologie bei den Synoptikern.* ANANT 57. Zurich, 1970.

Cohen, Simon. "Wisdom Literature." *UJEnc* 10 (1943), 538.

Conzelmann, Hans. *Der erste Brief an die Korinther.* Meyer series. Göttingen, 1969.

_____. "The Mother of Wisdom." In *The Future of Our Religious Past,* ed. J. M. Robinson, pp. 230–243.

_____. "Paul und die Weisheit." *NTS* 12 (1965–66), 231–244.

Crouzel, Henri, *Origène et la 'Conaissance Mystique.'* Paris, 1961.

Daube, David. 'Rabbinic Methods of Interpretation and Hellenistic Rhetoric." *HUCA* 22 (1949), 239–264.

_____. *Paul and Rabbinic Judaism.* 2nd ed. London, 1955.

Deichgräber, Reinhard. *Gotteshymnus und Christushymnus in der frühen Christenheit.* SUNT, no. 5. Göttingen, 1967.

Deissner, Kurt. *Das Idealbild des stoischen Weisen.* Griefswald, 1930.

Delatte, A. "Le sage -témoin dans la philosophie stoico-cynique." *Bulletin de l'Academie Royal de Belgique. Classe des Lettres et des Sciences Morales et Politiques,* 5th ser. 39 (Brussels, 1953), pp. 166–186.

Delling, G. "Zur Hellenisierung des Christentums in den 'Sprüchen des Sextus.'" In *Studien zum Neuen Testament und zur Patristik,* TU 77, pp. 208–241. Berlin, 1961.

Dibelius, Martin. *Die Formgeschichte des Evangeliums.* Tübingen, 1959.

Dihle, Albrecht. *Die goldene Regel. Eine Einführung in die Geschichte der antiken und frühchristlichen Vulgarethik.* Göttingen, 1962.

Dillistone, F. W. "Wisdom, Word, and Spirit." *Interpr* 2 (1948), 275–287.

Dörrie, Heinrich. "Emanation. Ein unphilosophisches Wort im spätantiken Denken." In *Parusia. Studien zur Philosophie Platons und zur Problemgeschichte des Platonismus,* Festschrift J. Hirschberger, ed. Kurt Flesh, pp. 119–141. Frankfurt/Main, 1965.

Drubbel, A. "Le conflit entre la Sagesse profane et la Sagesse religieuse." *Bib* 17 (1936), 45–70.

Duesberg, H. *Les scribes inspires.* 2 vols. Paris, 1938–39.

Dupont, J. *Gnosis. La connaissance religieuse dans les Epîtres de S. Paul.* Louvain, 1949.

Efros, Israel I. *Ancient Jewish Philosophy.* Detroit, 1964.

Festugière, A. J. *L'idéal religieuse des Grecs et l'Évangile.* Études bibliques. Paris, 1932.

Feuillet, A. *Le Christ Sagesse de Dieu d'après les épîtres pauliniennes.* Études bibliques. Paris, 1966.

_____. "Jesus et la sagesse divine d'après les evangiles synoptiques. Le 'Logion Johannique' et l'Ancien Testament." *RB* 62 (1955), 161–196.

Fischel, Henry A. "Epicureanism." *EncJ* 6 (1971), 817f.

_____. "Stocism." *EncJ* 15 (1971), 419f.

_____. "Story and History: Observations on Greco-Roman Rhetoric and Pharisaism." In *AOS Middle West Branch Semi-Centennial*

Volume, ed. D. Sinor, Asian Studies Research Institute, Oriental Series, no. 3, pp. 59–88. Bloomington, Ind., 1969.

_____. "Studies in Cynicism and the Ancient Near East: The Transformation of a CHRIA." In *Religions in Antiquity,* ed. Jacob Neusner, Supp. to Numen, no. 14, pp. 372–411. Leiden, 1968.

_____. *Rabbinic Literature and Greco-Roman Philosophy: A Study of Epicurea and Rhetorica in Early Midrashic Writings.* Studia Post-Biblica, no. 21. Leiden, 1973.

_____. "The Uses of Sorites (*climax, gradatio*) in the Tannaitic Period," *HUCA* 44 (1973), 119–151.

Flusser, David. "The Dead Sea Sect and Pre-Pauline Christianity." In *Scripta Hierosolymitana* 4, 215–266. Jerusalem, 1965.

Foerster, Werner. *Von Valentin zu Herakleon. Untersuchungen über die Quellen und die Entwicklung der valentinianischen Gnosis.* BZNW 7. Geissen, 1928.

Foerster, Werner, ed. *Gnosis: A Selection of Gnostic Texts.* Oxford, 1972.

Fohrer, Georg. "σοφία." *TDNT* VII, 476–496.

Francis, Fred. O. "The Baraita of the Four Sons." *SBL Proc.* 1 (1972), 245–283.

Fridrichsen, A. "Gnosis. Et Bidrag till Belvsning av den paulinske Terminologie og Erkjennelsesteori." In *Religionhistoriska Studier Tillägnade Edvard Lehmann,* pp. 85–109. Lund, 1927.

Georgi, Dieter. "Der vorpaulinische Hymnus Phil 2:6–11." In *Zeit und Geschichte,* Dankesgabe an Rudolf Bultmann zum 80. Geburtstag, ed. E. Dinkler, pp. 263–293. Tübingen, 1964.

Gollancz, Hermann. *The Targum to Song of Songs.* London, 1909.

Goodenough, Erwin Ramsdell, *By Light, Light: The Mystic Gospel of Hellenistic Judaism.* New Haven, 1935.

_____. *The Political Philosophy of Hellenistic Kingship.* New Haven, 1928.

Grant, Robert. "The Wisdom of the Corinthians." In *The Joy of Study,* ed. S. Johnson, pp. 51–55. New York, 1951.

Greene, W. C. *Moria.* New York, 1963.

Gressman, Hugo, *Nonnenspiegel und Mönchsspeigel des Evagrius Pontikos.* TU 39. Leipzig, 1913.

Gross, Moses David. *Otsar-ha-Agadah.* 3 vols. Jerusalem, 1954.

Guillaumont, A., Puech, H. Ch., Quispel, G., *et al. The Gospel According to Thomas.* Leiden, 1959.

Guttmann, Alexander. *Rabbinic Judaism in the Making.* Detroit, 1970.

Hadot, Iseltraut. *Seneca und die griechisch-roemisch Tradition der Seelenleitung.* Berlin, 1969.

Hallewi, E. E. *Sha'are ha-Aggadah.* Tel Aviv, 1963.

Harris, J. Rendel. "Athena, Sophia and the Logos." *BJRL* 7 (1922), 56–72.

Hegermann, H. *Die Vorstellungen von Schöpfungsmittler im Hellenistischen Judentum und Urchristentum.* TU 82. Berlin, 1961.

Heinemann, Isaak. *Die griechische Weltanschauungslehre bei Juden und Römern.* Berlin, 1932.

_____. *Philons griechische und jüdische Bildung.* Hildesheim, 1962.

Henricks, A. "Mani and the Babylonian Baptists: A Historical Confrontation." *Harvard Studies in Classical Philology* 77 (1973), 54–55.

Hermisson, Hans-Jürgen. *Studien zur israelitischen Sprüchweisheit.* WMANT 28. Neukirchen-Vluyn, 1968.

Heschel, Abraham Joshua. *Torah Min HaShamayim b-Aspaklaria shel haDorot.* 2 vols. London, 1962–65.

Hoffman, Paul. *Studien zur Theologie der Logienquelle.* Neutestamentliche Abhandlungen, n.f. 8. Munster, 1972.

Holte, Ragner. *Beatitude et sagesse. Saint Augustin et le problème de la fin de l'homme dans la philosophie ancienne.* Paris, 1962.

Hommel, Hildebrecht, "Herrenworte im Lichte sokratischer Überlieferung." *ZNW* 57 (1966), 1–22.

Hrurby, Kurt. "La Torah identifiée a la Sagesse et l'activité du 'Sage' dans la tradition rabbinique." *BVChr* 76 (1967), 65–78.

Jaeger, H. "The Patristic Conception of Wisdom in the Light of Biblical and Rabbinical Research." In *Studia Patristica*, IV. TU 79, pp. 90–106. Berlin, 1961.

Jervell, Jacob. *Imago Dei. Gen 1:26ff. im Spätjudentum, in der Gnosis, und in den paulinischen Briefen.* FRL 76. Göttingen, 1960.

Kerchensteiner, J. *Platon und der Orient.* Stuttgart, 1945.

Knox, Wilfred Lawrence. "The Divine Wisdom." *JTS* 38 (1937), 230–237.

Kohler, Kaufman. "Wisdom." *JEnc* 12:537–538.

Kroll, J. *Die christliche Hymnodik bis zu Klemens von Alexandreia.* Darmstadt, 1956.

Kümmel, Werner Beorg. "Jesus und der jüdische Traditionsgedanke." *ZNW* 33 (1934), 105–130.

Lambert, W. G. *Babylonian Wisdom Literature.* Oxford, 1960.

Laporte, Jean. *La Doctrine Eucharistique chez Philon d'Alexandrie.* Paris, 1972.

Larcher, Chrysostome. *Études sur le Livre de la Sagesse.* Études bibliques. Paris, 1969.

Lebram, Jurgen Christian. "Die Theologie der spälten Chokma und häretisches Judentum." *ZAW* 77 (1965), 202–211.

Leisegang, H. "Sophia." In Pauly-Wissowa, *Realencyclopädie der classischen altertumswissenchaft,* 3, 2nd series (1929), 1019–1039.

Lewy, Hans. *Sobria Ebrietas.* BZNW, no. 9. Giessen, 1929.

Liebermann, Saul. "Ben-Sira à la lumière du Yerouchalmi." *REJ* 97 (1934), 50–57.

Lührmann, Dieter. *Das Offenbarungsverständis bei Paulus und in paulinischen Gemeinden.* WMANT 16. Neukirchen-Vluyn, 1965.

———. *Die Redaktion der Logienquelle.* WMANT 33. Neukirchen-Vluyn, 1969.

Mack, B. L. *Logos und Sophia. Untersuchungen zur Weisheitstheologie im Hellenistischen Judentum.* SUNT, no. 10. Göttingen, 1973.

Mack, Burton L. "Wisdom Myth and Mytho-logy." *Interpr* 24 (1970), 47–60.

Malingrey, Anne Marie. *'Philosophia': Étude d'un groupe de mots dans la littérature grecque des Présocratiques au IVe siècle apres J.-C.* Paris, 1961.

Marböck, Johann. *Weisheit im Wandel.* Bonn, 1971.

Marcus, Ralph. "On Biblical Hypostases of Wisdom." *HUCA* 23 (1950–51), 157–171.

Martin, R. P. *Carmen Christi. Philippians 2:5–11 in Recent Interpretation and in the Setting of Early Christian Worship.* SNTS Monograph Series, no. 4. London, 1967.

Norden, E. *Agnostos Theos.* Stuttgart, 1956.

Osten-Sacken, Peter von der. *Die Apokalyptik in ihrem Verhältnis zu Prophetie und Weisheit.* Munich, 1969.

Pascher, J. Η ΒΑΣΙΛΙΚΗ ΟΔΟΣ. *Der Königsweg zu Wiedergeburt und Vergottung bei Philon von Alexandreia.* SGKA, no. 17. Paderborn, 1931.

Pearson, Birger. The Πνευματικός-Ψυχικός *Terminology in 1 Corinthians: A Study in the Theology of the Corinthian Opponents of Paul and Its Relation to Gnosticism,* SBL Dissertation Series, no. 12. Missoula, Mont., 1973.

Pepin, J. *Theologie cosmique et theologie chrétienne.* Paris, 1964.

Perrin, Norman, "Wisdom and Apocalyptic in the Message of Jesus." *SBL Proc.* 2 (1972), 543–572.

Peterson, Erik. "1 Korinther 1,18f. und die Thematik des jüdischen Busstages." In his *Frühkirche, Judentum und Gnosis,* pp. 43–50. Rome, 1959.

Philippe, M. D. "La sagesse selon Aristote." *Nova et Vetera* 20 (1945), 325–374.

Pire, Georges. *Stoicisme et pedagogie de Zénon à Marc-Aurele, de Sénèque a Montaigne et à J. -J. Rousseau.* Liège, 1958.

Pohlenz, Max. *Antikes führrertum. Cicero de officiis und das Lebensideal des Panaitios.* Amsterdam, 1967.

Rabbow, Paul. *Seelenführung: Methodik der Exerzitien in der Antike.* Munich, 1954.

Reese, James M. *Hellenistic Influences on the Book of Wisdom and Its Consequences.* AB no. 41. Rome, 1970.

Reitzenstein, R. *Die hellenistischen Mysterienreligionen.* Leipzig, 1900.

Rieth, Otto. "Über das telos der Stoiker." *Hermes* 69 (1934), 13–45.

_____. "Die Hodayot-Formel in Gebet und Hymnus des Frühchristentums." In *Apophoreta: Festschrift für Ernst Haenchen.* BZNW, no. 30. Berlin, 1964.

Robinson, James McKonkey. " 'Logoi Sophon': On the *Gattung* of Q." In James M. Robinson and Helmut Koester, *Trajectories Through Early Christianity*, pp. 71–113. Philadelphia, 1971.

Robinson, James McKonkey, and Koester, Helmut. *Trajectories through Early Christianity*. Philadelphia, 1971.

Röster, Dietrich. *Gesetz und Geschichte; Untersuchungen zur Theologie der jüdischen Apokalyptik und der pharisäischen Orthodoxie.* WMANT 3. Neukirchen-Vluyn, 1960.

Rylaarsdam, J. C. *Revelation in Jewish Wisdom Literature.* Chicago, 1946.

Sanders, Jack T. *The New Testament Christological Hymns.* SNTS Monograph Series, no. 15. Cambridge, Eng., 1971.

Schechter, Solomon. *Aspects of Rabbinic Theology: Major Concepts of the Talmud.* New York, 1961

Schille, G. *Frühchristliche Hymnen.* Berlin, 1962.

_____. "Kerygma und Sophia." In *Die Zeit der Kirche*, pp. 206–232. Freiburg, 1958.

Schmid, Hans Heinrich. *Weisen und Geschichte der Weisheit.* BZAW, no. 101. Berlin, 1966.

Schmithals, W. *Gnosticism in Corinth,* trans. J. Steely. Nashville, 1971.

Schoedel, William. " 'Topological' Theology and Some Monistic Tendencies in Gnosticism." In *Essays on the Nag Hammadi Texts in Honour of Alexander Böhlig.* Nag Hammadi Studies, no. 3. Leiden, 1972.

Scholem, G. G. *Major Trends in Jewish Mysticism.* Rev. ed. New York, 1961.

Schottruff, Luise. *Der Glaubende und die feindliche Welt. Beobachtungen zum gnostischen Dualismus und seiner Bedeutung für Paulus und das Johannesevangelium.* WMANT 37. Neukirchen-Vluyn, 1970.

Schulz, Siegfried. *Q: Die Spruchquelle der Evangelisten.* Zurich, 1972.

Schwarzbaum, H. "Talmudic Midrashic Affinities of Some Aesopic Fables." *Laographia* 22 (1965), 446–483.

Scroggs, Robin. "Paul: ΣΟΦΟΣ and ΠΝΕΥΜΑΤΙΚΟΣ." *NTS* 14 (1967–68), 33–55.

Snell, Bruno. *Leben und Meinungen der Sieben Weisen.* Munich, 1938.

Spoerri, S. "Gnome," *Der Kleine Pauly,* vol. II, pp. 822–829. Stuttgart, 1968.

Staerk, Willy. "Die sieben Säulen der Welt und des Hauses der Weisheit." *ZNW* 35 (1936), 232–261.

Steck, O. H. *Israel und das gewaltsame Geschick der Propheten: Untersuchungen zur Uberlieferung des deuteronomistischen Geschichtsbildes im Alten Testament, Spätjudentum und Urchristentum.* WMANT 23. Neukirchen-Vluyn, 1967.

Stein, S. "Symposia Literature and the Pesach Haggadah." *Journal of Jewish Studies* 8 (1957), 13–44.

Suggs, M. Jack. *Wisdom, Christology, and Law in Matthew's Gospel.* Cambridge, Mass., 1970.

Thyen, Hartwig. *Der Stil der jüdisch-hellenistischen Homilie.* FRL 65. Göttingen, 1955.

Tiede, David Lenz. *The Charismatic Figure As Miracle Worker.* SBL Dissertation Series, no. 1. Missoula, Mont., 1972.

Urbach, Ephraim Elimelich. *Class Status and Leadership in the World of the Palestinian Sages,* trans. I. Abrahams. Israel Academy of Sciences and Humanities Proceedings, vol. 2, no. 4. Jerusalem, 1966.

_____. "Sages." *EncJ* 14:636–655.

_____. *The Sages: Their Concepts and Beliefs.* Jerusalem, 1969.

Urbach, Ephraim Elimelech, *et al.,* eds. *Studies in Mysticism and Religion.* Festschrift G. G. Scholem. Jerusalem, 1967.

Völker, Walther. *Fortschritt und Vollendung bei Philo von Alexandrien.* TU 49, 1. Leipzig, 1938.

_____. "Die Verwertung der Weisheits-Literatur bei den christlichen Alexandrinern." *ZKG* 64 (1952), 1–33.

Wagner, Walter H., "A Father's Fate: Attitudes Toward and Interpretations of Clement of Alexandria." *Journal of Religious History* 7 (1971), 209–231.

Walcot, P. *Hesiod and the Near East.* Cardiff, 1966.

Wallach, L. "Alexander the Great and the Indian Gymnosophists in the Hebrew Tradition." *Proceedings of the American Academy for Jewish Research* 11 (1941), 47–83.

Weaver, M. J. "'Pneuma' in Philo of Alexandria." Ph.D. diss., University of Notre Dame, 1973.

Wechsler (Weksler), Tobiah. *Tsefundt bi-mesorat Visra'el.* Jerusalem, 1968.

Wengst, K. *Christologische Formeln und Lieder des Urchristentums.* SUNT, no. 7. Gütersloh, 1972.

Wilckens, Ulrich. "Kreuz und Weisheit." *Kerygma und Dogma* 3 (1957), 27–108.

———. *"Sophia." TDNT* VII (1971), 465–76; 496–528.

———. *Weisheit und Torheit.* BHTh, no. 26. Tübingen, 1959.

Wilken, Robert L. "Toward a Social Interpretation of Early Christian Apologetics." *Church History* 39 (1970), 437–458.

Wolfson, H. A. *Philo: Foundations of Religious Philosophy in Judaism, Christianity and Islam.* 2 vols., 4th ed. Cambridge, Mass., 1968.

Wuellner, Wilhelm. "Haggadic-Homily Genre in 1 Corinthians 1–3." *JBL* 89 (1970), 199–204.

Subject Index

Alexander the Great, 76f, 93n55

Alexandria, wisdom (school) in, xvi, xix, 197

Alexandrian Christianity, xvi, xix, 171, 197, 199n53

Apatheia, 124, 126f

Apocalyptic and wisdom. *See* Wisdom: and apocalyptic

Apocalypticism, 2, 5, 8, 12f, 14, 48, 49, 56, 59, 170

Apologists, Christian, 143, 156–158, 160f

Apuleius, 47

Athenagoras, 157f, 161, 164, 167n21

Christianity as a philosophical school, 160f, 168n33. *See also* Philosophy: in early Christianity

Christological hymns and Judaism, 24

Christology of Q, 6, 9f, 12–15 (Robinson *passim*)

Cicero, 68, 70, 72, 90n35, 91n40, 98n95, 100n103, 167n25

Clement of Alexandria, xiv, 144, 164, 168n41, 170, 175, 194, 197n10

Corinth, 9. *See also* Corinthian Christianity

Corinthian Christianity, Pearson *passim. See also* Paul: opponents of

Cosmic reconciliation, 24

Cross, 14, 37, 46, 48, 50, 52, 57, 62n23, 65n51

Demonic powers. *See* "Rulers of this age"

Diatribe, 72f, 183f

Diogenes Laertius, 75, 77, 79, 84, 97n89, 98n95

Dreams, 77

Dualism, 23, 32, 49

Ecclesiasticus and the *Sentences of Sextus,* 147, 182. *See also* *Sentences of Sextus:* and the biblical wisdom books

Ephesus, 44, 59

Epictetus, 167n26, 188f, 198n18

Epicurean(ism), 71, 73, 81f, 83, 94nn66, 95n75

Epicurus, 72, 78, 84, 90n35, 98n95, 167n26

Evil, 80f, 109, 137n18

Exemplarism in Philo, 116, 126

Fate, 36

211

experience, 2, 176, 180f; and
folly, 49f, 111f; and *Heilsgeschichte,* 3–5; hypostatization of, 27f, 74, 166n14,
169, 196; and knowledge,
106ff, 120; as knowledge of
things divine and human and
their causes, 106, 116, 126;
myth of, 27f; personified, 1,
27f, 110, 169; and philosophy, 144, 158ff, 173, 189;
as preexistent, 11, 26f, 32,
80, 114–119; and revelatory
speech, 173, 189; and Spirit,
105, 114, 119–121, 139n43;
summons of, 1f, 177f; and
Torah, 48, 71; and Torah,
identified in Judaism, 11,
62n20, 70, 82; withdrawal or
rejection of, 11, 12–14, 27f;
worldly wisdom and Torah
distinguished, 71
Wisdom books, biblical: Christian commentaries on, xv f;
and Philo, 104–106, Laporte
passim; and *Sentences of
Sextus,* 147–149. *See also
Teachings of Silvanus:* and
Jewish wisdom; and Wisdom
of Solomon
Wisdom exhortations: and appeal to reason, 181f, 189;
intensification of (prophetic
character of), 182f
Wisdom material: collections of,
1, 76ff; literary genres of, 8,
13f, 16n23, Fischel *passim,*
193 (Schoedel *passim*)

Wisdom sayings: in Christian
monasticism, xviii, 170, 195,
196; in Q, 8, 10, 13 (Robinson *passim*). *See also* Gnomes
Wisdom sayings, form of: declaratory (classical Jewish), 147,
180f; exhortatory (*Teachings
of Silvanus*), 180f; parallelism, 147, 186f
Wisdom schools, 2, 58. *See also*
Jewish wisdom schools; Pauline school
Wisdom symbolism: as bride or
wife, 27, 110, 122; as harlot,
110, 111; as hostess, 110,
111; as mother, 27, 105, 110,
115, 118, 122; as nurse, 115
Wisdom symbolism in Philo:
wisdom as bride, 105, 122;
Exodus symbolism, 127ff,
136n8; wisdom as daughter
of God, 105, 116ff; wisdom
as Eden, 114, 125f; high
priest symbolism, 129f,
141n67; wisdom as hostess,
111; wisdom as law, 105,
114, 122ff; liturgical symbolism, 127–131, 136n8; wis-
dom as mother, 115, 118,
122; wisdom as nurse, 115;
patriarchs as symbols of the
three ways to perfection,
123f, *cf.* 140n64; wisdom as
rock, 128; wisdom as tabernacle, 114, 121f; wisdom as
water, 128f, 141n67
Wise man. *See* Sage

Modern Author Index

215